WHAT PEOPLE ̶ ̶
MARK VIRKLER, CH ̶ ̶
AND *OVERFLOW OF THE SPIRIT*

I have had the privilege of working with Mark Virkler for over thirty-five years. Not only has his teaching on *Hearing God's Voice* impacted millions, but it has dramatically impacted my own life, as well as my wife Carol's life. In this new book, *Overflow of the Spirit*, Mark and his daughter Charity give a biblical impartation of what it means to be filled with the Holy Spirit, live out of the overflow, and do life from that filled up place. You are no longer on your own trying to live this Christian life, but walking in communion with God the Holy Spirit.

—*John Arnott*
Founder, Catch the Fire Church
Overseer, Partners in Harvest Network of Churches

It's one thing to receive gifts from the Lord. It's quite another to learn how to release what we've been given for the purpose and time God had in mind. Mark and Charity have joined together to invoke their gifts in the form of a book. As you open this book, prepare to read about what you've been missing. You may find it necessary to spend some time in prayers of repentance for allowing your gifts to lay dormant. Don't let "a time such as this" pass you by. Read this book and be prepared to overflow. Then help someone else release their gifts.

—*Dr. Steve Greene*
Publisher and Executive Vice President, Charisma Media Group

We are honored to once again endorse a life-giving resource authored by Mark and Charity. The reality of a close love relationship with the Lord Jesus shines through the pages as they present the vital truth that the constant infilling and overflow of the Holy Spirit is available, accessible, and possible on a full-time basis.

They communicate with such ease that flows from the richness of an in-depth study of the Word and ways of God, and a passion for walking out a lifestyle led by the Holy Spirit. With clear explanation, step-by-step guidance, story, and testimony, Mark and Charity open the door for us to live fully gifted, maturing in the Holy Spirit.

Thank you, Mark and Charity, for sharing your revelations and experiences in order for us to hear the voice of God more clearly, get to know Him more dearly, and express His fullness in our every sphere of influence!

—*Sharon and Trevor Baker*
Revival Fires, Dudley, England

Most believers don't know how to release all the gifts of the Spirit resident in them. Finally, *the* how-to book has arrived!

—*Sid Roth*
Host, *It's Supernatural!*

It would appear that Mark Virkler has captured the systemic insight into the Holy Spirit's working in a follower of Jesus. If you thought the *expression* gifts that are listed in 1 Corinthians 12 were the final landing place for the Holy Spirit to move in you…well, buckle up and hold on! Mark and his daughter Charity have given amazing insight into God's ability in allowing us to manifest the Spirit purposely and intentionally in our lives…beyond what we thought was the period at the end of the sentence. *Overflow of the Spirit* is an awakening, a delightful recipe for the hungry heart for God!

—*Fred Antonelli, Ph.D.*
President, Elim Bible Institute and College

Mark Virkler and his daughter Charity Virkler Kayembe have written this book to serve as a tool that will facilitate spiritual growth in the life of a believer. They've drawn from their personal experiences and have summarized what has worked well in their ministry as teachers and disciple-makers. These have been refined and rewritten here as a "how-to" manual in order to produce authentic fruit in the life of anyone who is seeking to realize a more intimate relationship with God the Father, Son, and Holy Spirit.

As one who is committed to be a disciple and a disciple-maker, I highly recommend this book as a useful tool and methodology for mentoring a new believer who wants to grow in spiritual gifts and graces. It will provide a structured platform that will enable the believer to hear God's voice, to be guided by the Holy Spirit, and to live a life of faith that is pleasing to the Lord.

—*Rev. John R. Miller, Ph.D.*
Professor, Regent University

Mark and Charity have done it again! They have taken a complex topic and made it simple. The mystery of being connected with the Holy Spirit isn't supposed to be a mystery, but an easy thing. Mark and Charity lead us step by step through the various aspects of how to live by the Spirit. The Bible truths, personal stories, and practical action exercises take each reader on the journey of living in the *Overflow of the Spirit*. Well done!

—*Steve Long*
Senior Leader, Catch the Fire Church, Toronto
Author, *The Faith Zone* and *My Healing Belongs to Me*

In *Overflow of the Spirit*, Mark Virkler and Charity Virkler Kayembe weave together Scriptures, journaling with God, and the power of testimony in a relatable manner to provide examples of how to live and walk by the Spirit. They provide practical and easy steps for how to pursue an intimate relationship with God and release the gifts of the Spirit in your life today!

—*James W. Goll*
Founder, God Encounters Ministries

I have read many books on the gifts of the Spirit and this is certainly one of the best. Mark Virkler and Charity Virkler Kayembe offer fresh biblical truths to encourage and enhance every believer. The seventy references for who the Holy Spirit is and what He does in and for the believer are tremendous. I received a fresh, supernatural education and awareness of the gifts. The action exercises and testimonies are fantastic. My faith was increased by the process of revelation-based learning.

—*Rev. Ronald V. Burgio, D.Min*
Senior Pastor, Love Joy Church
Author, *Living in the Spirit of Revival*

Dr. Mark Virkler and his daughter, Charity Virkler Kayembe, have written another *must have* book for your Spirit-filled library! More than just another book, this is a practical how-to manual when it comes to operating in the gifts of the Spirit. And they do believe that you *can* operate in all of the gifts of the Spirit!

I love the Virkler family books because they are always on-point, directing us to Jesus, while activating our spirits to engage with God's heavenly realities through the present-day ministry of the Holy Spirit. I highly recommend you get a copy for yourself, and a few additional copies for those you love. This book will equip you and do exactly what the title says, causing you to release God's goodness everywhere you go, through the *Overflow of the Spirit*.

—*Joshua Mills*
Founder, International Glory Ministries, Palm Springs, CA
Author, *Moving in Glory Realms* and *Power Portals*

I love how God raises up writers who make seemingly complicated issues simple to understand, yet powerful when applied. Mark Virkler has produced over fifty-five books that do this well, but this one on the *Overflow of the Spirit* is made for us in times like these. It will refresh and renew my generation while calling forth a focused passion to influence our world and culture in the emerging generation. I highly recommend it!

—*Dr. Joseph Umidi*
Executive Vice President, Regent University
Founder, Lifeforming Leadership Coaching

OVERFLOW

OF THE

Spirit

HOW TO RELEASE HIS
GIFTS IN EVERY
AREA OF YOUR LIFE

MARK VIRKLER *and*
CHARITY VIRKLER KAYEMBE

WHITAKER
HOUSE

Boldface type in the Scripture quotations indicates the authors' emphasis.

OVERFLOW OF THE SPIRIT
How to Release His Gifts in Every Area of Your Life

Mark Virkler
Communion with God Ministries
3792 Broadway St.
Cheektowaga, NY 14227
www.CWGMinistries.org
cwg@cwgministries.org

Charity Kayembe
Glory Waves Ministries
www.GloryWaves.org
info@glorywaves.org

ISBN: 978-1-64123-491-7
eBook ISBN: 978-1-64123-492-4
Printed in the United States of America
© 2020 by Mark Virkler and Charity Virkler Kayembe

Whitaker House
1030 Hunt Valley Circle
New Kensington, PA 15068
www.whitakerhouse.com

Library of Congress Cataloging-in-Publication Data (Pending)

1 2 3 4 5 6 7 8 9 10 11 ⨆ 27 26 25 24 23 22 21 20

THIS BOOK IS DEDICATED TO OUR FRIENDS:

Brian McLaughlin, for taking the Holy Spirit's miracle-working love and power into the public school, demonstrating the Father's heart for his students.

Marcia Upson, for taking the Holy Spirit's voice and wisdom into the marketplace, impacting the business world for the glory of God.

Cheryl McKay Price, for taking the Holy Spirit's anointing and creativity into Hollywood, proving God is the best Storyteller of all.

Finally, this book is dedicated to every child of God who is manifesting the Holy Spirit's grace and glory in the area of culture to which the Father has called them. May every sphere of society be transformed as sons and daughters of the King release His presence, gifts, and anointing into their world.

You are truly reigning in life!

CONTENTS

FOREWORD

When I was asked to do the foreword, it was an easy decision because of Mark's writing and ministry. I was first introduced to his materials in the early 1990s, which equipped us to train many in the lifestyle of hearing God's voice. For those of you who don't know Mark, he has authored more than fifty-five books in the areas of hearing God's voice and Spirit-anointed living. His most popular books are *4 Keys to Hearing God's Voice* and *Counseled by God*. Mark is an avid student of the Scriptures and gifted teacher. He has established more than 250 church-centered Bible schools around the world. For more than thirty years, Mark has traveled extensively on six continents to conduct workshops on spiritual healing and developing intimacy with God.

Overflow of the Spirit is timely and much-appreciated work. Though there have been hundreds of books published over the years about the gifts of the Spirit, Mark takes a unique track combining theological perspective with fresh insight into the supernatural realm of the gifts of the Spirit. It is more than another book on the Holy Spirit; it is a textbook for the ages, perfectly designed for Bible colleges and seminaries, but written for all to examine and experience.

One of the distinguishing features is how each chapter ends with compelling stories of people who experienced the baptism of the Holy Spirit. Mark believes in the power of a story. He is a lover of stories and believes that they are powerful means of communication, revelation, and insight. Our lives are our stories, and they resonate with others who have encountered God. Mark's reasoning for including these personal testimonies is summed up with these words: "Stories allow the Holy Spirit to speak directly to each of us individually, where we are right now, in a way that systematic theology cannot."

Overflow of the Spirit offers much more than the one amazing gift of speaking in tongues. It opens the door to an entire lifestyle of intimacy with the Holy Spirit; once this lifestyle is fully embraced, it will release the heavens and the provisions of God for your life.

Since the baptism in the Holy Spirit involves increased intimacy with the Holy Spirit, Mark shares keys to journaling throughout this book, showing a unique way to use two-way journaling. Hundreds of chapters of Scripture model this practice, including Psalms, the prophets, and even the book of Revelation. Two-way journaling opens you up to a deeper, more intimate relationship with the Lord than you may have ever experienced.

This book is all about experiencing God's life within and sharing the overflow with those around us. Both the church and the world desperately need to see this again. The overflow of the Spirit will cause the supernatural growth of the kingdom as people are healed, delivered, and set free.

—*Bill Johnson*
Bethel Church, Redding, CA
Author of *The Way of Life* and *Born for Significance*

ACKNOWLEDGMENTS

Special thanks to Pastor Bill Johnson, Senior Leader of Bethel Church in Redding, and one of our generation's heroes of the faith. We are honored with his foreword to this book as he truly models the outworking of this message in his life, his church, and his school of ministry. We are grateful to partner with him in sharing the truth that every believer can flow in every gift of the Spirit in their everyday life.

Thank you for leading by example and demonstrating what a life overflowing with the Spirit looks like. Bless you!

We also want to acknowledge the wonderful publishing family at Whitaker House and especially appreciate Christine Whitaker and Don Milam for their important contributions to this project.

We appreciate our editor, Peg Fallon, who gave many thoughtful suggestions to help make this book the best it can be. It is also a pleasure working with our publicist, Karen Campbell, as well as Judy McDonough.

Releasing a book is always a team effort and we are so grateful for the anointed group of kingdom professionals God has surrounded us with. We appreciate your exceptional gifts, valuable support, and spirit of excellence in this endeavor. Thank you very much!

INTRODUCTION – LIFE IS A STORY

Mark Virkler

This book has taken many years to complete. Because I am a how-to guy, I have received many requests for a book on how to move in the gifts of the Holy Spirit, and I wanted to be as thorough and practical as possible. I began preparing to write the way I always do: with comprehensive biblical research, asking the Lord for revelation, and seeking counsel from spiritual leaders whom I respect. That's where I got stuck.

The baptism in the Holy Spirit is the gateway into the supernatural realm of the gifts of the Spirit. Jesus promised, "You will receive power when the Holy Spirit has come upon you" (Acts 1:8), the power of the Holy Spirit manifesting Himself through you into the world. Therefore, it seemed logical to me to start with a good, clear definition of what baptism in the Spirit is, when you receive it, and how to receive it. Since speaking in tongues is the easiest of the gifts to receive and often comes immediately with the baptism, they have become almost synonymous in our thinking, so I decided I would also tie them together.

That seems like a fairly simple task, right? Unfortunately, I discovered that there is absolutely no agreement in the Spirit-filled community about what the baptism is or when you receive it. One leader told me the baptism in the Holy Spirit is a growth in intimacy with God. Another said it was tears. Another said we all receive the baptism in the Spirit at the point of salvation. Another equated the baptism with the filling of the Holy Spirit. Although there may be a level of truth in each of these responses, none of them satisfied me. I struggled because none of these definitions described how I received the baptism in the Holy Spirit, or what I felt fit its biblical meaning.

Frustrated, I realized that my desire for precise, clear-cut definitions wouldn't work here. Life just wouldn't fit into my desired little boxes. I recognized that this was a place where narrative theology (discourse about God in the setting of story) needed to be added to my cherished systematic theology (a collection and summary of the teachings of all biblical passages on a given subject). So I sent out a request to my readers for their stories of how they received the baptism in the Spirit and began speaking in tongues.

WHY TELL A STORY?

My story is so similar to the accounts I received that I have included several of their testimonies throughout this book. We learn a lot about God through the stories in the Bible. Stories are a powerful means of communication, revelation, and insight. Our lives are our stories, and they resonate with others who have encountered God. Stories allow the Holy Spirit to speak directly to each of us individually, where we are right now, in a way that systematic theology cannot.

Enjoy these stories. Take the time to allow the Holy Spirit to speak to you through them, teaching and encouraging you in your pursuit of Him. Do all the exercises in each chapter; they will draw you into *your own life's story* as you interact ever more intentionally with the Holy Spirit, releasing all the ways He wants to manifest Himself. (See 1 Corinthians 12:7–11.)

MY STORY OF RECEIVING THE BAPTISM IN THE HOLY SPIRIT

Growing up in an ultra-fundamentalist church, I was taught that the gifts of the Spirit were not for today. I actually scorned those who spoke in tongues, seeing them as deceived baby Christians. In college, I met a generous, loving woman who invited my wife Patti and me into her home. She fed us marvelous dinners while she shared stories of healings and miracles her family members received when she prayed for them.

Those stories were the catalyst to my change. This woman was obviously a very mature believer and did not appear to be deceived to me, so I decided to go back and explore my systematic theology that said that the ninefold manifestation of the Spirit (see 1 Corinthians 12:7–11) was not available today.

> SPEAKING IN TONGUES WAS A WAY BIBLICAL BELIEVERS GLORIFIED GOD AND SPOKE MYSTERIES TO HIM, WHICH BUILT UP THEIR SPIRITS.

I changed my mind after much study and research, drawing largely upon the teachings of Derek Prince.[1] I realized that speaking in tongues was a way biblical believers glorified God and spoke mysteries to Him, which built up their spirits. (See 1 Corinthians 14:2, 4.) In addition, Paul, a very mature apostle, said he was *glad* he spoke in tongues more than anyone else! (See 1 Corinthians 14:18.) So speaking in tongues is not just for baby Christians or those who have been deceived. Interesting how a *story* was able to confront and ultimately change my theology. Never underestimate the power of your testimony.

Now I earnestly desired the Holy Spirit. Patti and I set aside a day of fasting, then drove to Ithaca, New York, to attend a service and have some mature Christians pray for us to receive the baptism in the Holy Spirit and the gift of speaking in tongues. Well,

---

1. See www.derekprince.org; www.whitakerhouse.com/book-authors/derek-prince.

Patti received and I didn't. Talk about frustrating. So back home we went. A few weeks later, I was too sick to attend the church where I served as a youth pastor, so I was sitting home, alone in the living room rocking chair, pondering Acts 2:4 where it says *they spoke* as the Holy Spirit gave them utterance. That made me think, *Maybe I need to actually do the speaking rather than just letting my tongue hang loose in my wide-open mouth!*

So I tried speaking, articulating syllables that I was not controlling with my mind. Whatever came, I spoke. Obviously this was very easy and childlike, and even though syllables were spoken, I doubted. It took me two weeks before I hesitantly shared with Patti that I thought I might be speaking in tongues. At that time in my life, I was a mighty man of doubt and unbelief.

About a year later, I was leading a home group and at the close of the evening, we cast some demons out of an individual. We were celebrating with worshipful prayer and praise, and I spoke in tongues briefly during that prayer celebration. On the way home, a young girl who had spent time in Brazil informed me that I had said in Portuguese, "Hurray! Long live Jesus!"

> WHEN YOU SPEAK IN TONGUES, YOUR SPIRIT COMMUNICATES DIRECTLY TO GOD, BYPASSING THE BOTTLENECK OF YOUR MIND.

Wow! I was dumbfounded. God saw fit to confirm very objectively that these syllables I was speaking were actually a language (see Acts 2:8; 1 Corinthians 13:1) and it was my spirit communicating directly to God, bypassing the bottleneck of my mind. Thank You, Lord, for this wonderful confirmation! In truth, by this time, I had already gotten over my doubt about tongues since I found my entire Christian life come alive with a new vitality as I spoke in tongues regularly. However, a nice confirmation is always appreciated.

MY REFLECTIONS ON THE STORIES OF OTHER BELIEVERS

Rather than fuss over the theology of exactly when and how one is baptized in the Holy Spirit, or the precise evidence of receiving it, I pondered the testimonies I received, along with my own story, to see what principles we could discover. Here are my observations:

+ **It took time.** About 75 percent of them did not receive the gift of tongues when they first desired it or received prayer for it.

+ **At home alone.** About 75 percent received the gift of tongues while at home alone.

+ **Lack of knowledge.** About 50 percent said they could have spoken in tongues much sooner had someone explained clearly to them how this miracle occurs.

+ **Fear and doubt.** About 50 percent specifically mentioned they had to battle with fear or doubt and that caused them to resist the baptism and tongues for a period of time.

+ **Emotions.** About 50 percent specifically mentioned that they experienced intense emotion when baptized in the Holy Spirit; this may mean that the other 50 percent did not.

+ **Needing deliverance.** One-quarter specifically mentioned that deliverance opened up the Holy Spirit's flood.

+ **Impact.** The baptism in the Holy Spirit brought new things to people's lives. Here are some of their statements:

  » "I could hear God so much clearer than before."

  » "I experienced an intimate relationship with Jesus."

  » "I had a passion to read and study the Bible and pursue righteousness."

  » "Scriptures I had read countless times before suddenly became alive."

  » "I started getting urges to preach these revelations."

> » "I felt ten pounds lighter within *minutes*."
> » "I couldn't stand under the weight of His glory and went down on my knees."
> » "I was filled with warm liquid Love."
> » "I received the gifts of interpretation of tongues and prophecy."

Many of these were similar to my experience. It took time, as I pursued it for months. When I did speak in tongues, it was when I was home alone. If someone had taught me more clearly, I could have spoken in tongues much sooner. Speaking in tongues was so simple that I battled with doubt for months. The baptism did not come with an emotional rush, but the Bible came alive to me as I realized I *could* live and experience huge sections of Scripture that I had been told were no longer available to me today.

MINISTERING THE BAPTISM IN THE HOLY SPIRIT WAS CENTRAL TO JESUS'S MISSION

When all four of the Gospel writers introduced Jesus, they declared what He came to do: *"He will baptize in the Holy Spirit"* (Matthew 3:11; Mark 1:8; Luke 3:16; see John 1:33). This is truly amazing! This is not a peripheral issue. Being baptized in the Holy Spirit is a key experience. It's something important that we *need*. We can't be ho-hum or passive about it. Jesus came to make this experience available to us.

> BEING BAPTIZED IN THE HOLY SPIRIT IS A KEY EXPERIENCE. WE CAN'T BE HO-HUM OR PASSIVE ABOUT IT.

FIVE VITAL INGREDIENTS

As I pondered the testimonies of how people received the Holy Spirit, I came to some conclusions. I suggest that the following five ingredients open one to receive the baptism in the Holy Spirit and the manifestation of speaking in tongues.

1. **Believe** it is available; according to your faith be it unto you. (See Hebrews 11:6; Matthew 9:29.)

2. **Earnestly desire** it; get passionate and go after it. (See 1 Corinthians 14:1.)

3. **Ask** the Lord for it; we have not because we ask not. (See John 16:24; James 4:2.)

4. **Love;** be of one accord because love is the carrier wave of the Spirit. (See Acts 2:1–4.)

5. **Yield** your tongue from self-control to Spirit-control. (See Acts 2:4.)

SPIRITUAL INTIMACY

Since the baptism in the Holy Spirit involves increased intimacy with the Holy Spirit, I am going to demonstrate this intimacy by sharing journaling throughout this book. I will also teach you how to do two-way journaling yourself. Hundreds of chapters of Scripture model this practice; it is found in the Psalms, the prophets, and the book of Revelation, for example. I believe journaling should be a standard part of our lives.

Two-way journaling is an invaluable initial step toward moving in the gifts of the Spirit. First, it is a powerful tool for learning to recognize the voice of the Spirit within you, giving you the opportunity to gain confidence in your ability to do so. But even more importantly, two-way journaling opens you up to a deeper, more intimate relationship with the Lord than you may have ever experienced. He pours His love into you, affirming His compassion for you in a mighty way. You respond to His love with greater love toward Him. He opens your eyes to His deep love for others and the Spirit grows that love in you as you become more like Him through your times together.

It is no coincidence that Paul talks about love in the middle of his teaching on the gifts of the Spirit. (See 1 Corinthians 13.) Love—both for God and for others—is the only legitimate and solid foundation for moving in the gifts. Two-way journaling has been the single most effective tool I have found for increasing that love in me.

Here is a sample of the journaling of one of our students, where she asked the Lord about the overflow of the Spirit in these last days.

The Latter Outpouring:
Journaling from Stephanie Wylkynsone

Lord, what does the latter outpouring of the Holy Spirit look like?

"The latter outpouring of the Holy Spirit is when all of my people are in one accord, moving and working together to bring in the end-time harvest. Yes, there will be demonstrations of my Spirit and power. I want the people to come to me and drink. Then out of them will flow rivers of living water. I long to fill my people up. All they have to do is ask. I'm ready to fill them up to overflowing so it comes out of them, spilling onto others. When my people start doing this, it will impact the world. Imagine if all believers were filled with the Holy Spirit, not just a few. Imagine what an impact that would make around the world. That's what is going to happen. I want all of my people filled with the Holy Spirit, not just a few.

"I plan to use you in this latter outpouring. I am already getting you prepared. You are filled with the Holy Spirit. You hear my voice. You hunger and thirst for me. You are seeking to follow me. I reveal myself to you. We are working out your salvation together. I will use you alongside others. This is not an individual effort. This is done in the unity of the body of Christ, all acting in one accord. I show and lead the way."

A DAY OF LIVING IN THE OVERFLOW OF THE SPIRIT

In Genesis, God sets the pattern that evening and morning is the way a day is structured. (See Genesis 1:13.) Our day begins in the evening as we meditate on God upon our beds. (See Psalm 4:4.) We fall asleep asking for revelation. When we awaken, we record any dreams, asking the Spirit for help in interpreting them. We tune to flow and God pours out wisdom, love, creativity, healing, and direction. Bible meditation is often a part of these morning devotions.

As you turn to your daily activities, you see Jesus at your side. (See Acts 2:25.) You ask for His input on everything, and then tune to the river of the Spirit within, which bubbles with flowing ideas, flowing images, and flowing emotions. This is God's revelation to you. When you see Jesus, He is smiling. You stay relaxed and smiling so His flow is not obstructed by any striving of your own flesh. The day is amazing because of Jesus's constant input, which provides anointing, creativity, healing, faith, hope, and love. The Holy Spirit manifests Himself through you to everyone you meet in any way they need His touch. You live in celebration of His greatness toward you. He reminds you that you already have the victory in Him.

Experiencing the *Overflow of the Spirit* is fun! Let's get started.

How I Received the Baptism in the Holy Spirit
by Margaret Cornell

I had been seeking God for a number of months and one night, Jesus appeared to me in my bedroom. Recognizing that He was truly the Son of God, I fell at His feet and surrendered my life to Him. The next day, I knew something radical had happened in my life; I felt full of love, joy, and peace. I didn't know it but I had been born again.

Just after that, our vicar had planned a church mission. I had an earnest conversation with a visiting priest that caused me to think seriously about the condition of the church. It was certainly not alive. My recent experience of meeting Jesus affected the way I looked at things. I think I realized that other people just haven't experienced anything remotely like it and didn't really have much faith in God.

Sometime later, I was in a church meeting and I was having a casual conversation with a young woman sitting next to me about the mission. I said, "David says if we don't like our church the way it is, we should get together and pray about it," to which she replied, "Oh, yes, let's."

I was very reluctant to do this as I had only just got the hang of praying by myself. However, not wishing to appear chicken, I said to her, "Okay, let's meet after next Sunday's evensong."

We went to my house as arranged. "We are just going upstairs to pray," I told my husband, who was in the sitting room.

We sat in my bedroom. It felt very awkward as I'd never done this before. I had fortified myself with the Anglican prayer book and I had also gotten a book of prayers out of the public library, so I began by reading a prayer.

Then this young woman began to pray quite naturally and fluently. I thought, *Oh, crumbs, she knows a lot more about this than I do!* Then she prayed what turned out to be quite a significant prayer for me.

She said, "Lord, fill us with your Spirit."

Suddenly a blanket of something terribly powerful and wonderful fell upon me and I couldn't say another word. Thinking about her words, I thought to myself, *This must be the Holy Spirit.* I was so profoundly touched by God that I really couldn't say anything else, which quickly ended our meeting. She must have been puzzled by my silence because she said to me, "Are you okay?" I said yes I was, but I really couldn't explain that in one way I was okay, but in another way, I wasn't. Something very profound that I did not understand had just happened to me.

A few days later, I was happily sweeping my kitchen floor, singing and praising God, when suddenly, I began to sing in a language that I didn't know. I was really surprised but not alarmed because it felt wonderful.

My husband was raised a Baptist and really knew the Bible, so I went to him. He was sitting and reading the newspaper. I asked him if there was anywhere in the Bible where people just suddenly start to speak in a language they didn't know. Without looking up from his paper, he said matter-of-factly, "Yes, Acts chapter 2."

I ran upstairs, looked up the Scripture in my Bible, and discovered what happened to the disciples in the upper room on the day of Pentecost. I was astounded; I thought, *I've had a Bible experience.* I was speaking in tongues.

1

LIVING BY THE SPIRIT IS THE CHRISTIAN LIFESTYLE

If we live by the Spirit, let us also walk by the Spirit.
—Galatians 5:25

NOT YOUR AVERAGE ALTAR CALL

Peter's altar call at the conclusion of the very first sermon in the church age was, "*Repent, and each of you be baptized in the name of Jesus Christ for the forgiveness of your sins; and you will receive the gift of the Holy Spirit*" (Act 2:38). Really? Shouldn't Peter have said, "…and you will receive eternal life"? *That's* what we say in our altar calls. Heaven is the enticement we offer to new believers, not the Holy Spirit. Maybe Peter got it wrong. Or maybe we do. Maybe receiving the Holy Spirit is *central* to our new lives as Christians.

THE APOSTLES' CREED ON THE HOLY SPIRIT

Reading the Apostles' Creed, you notice that it describes what the Father and Son did, with a brief mention that Jesus "was conceived by the Holy Spirit." Otherwise, the creed only says: "I believe in the Holy Spirit."[2] Wow! There is no mention that the

---

2. Apostles' Creed, Christian Reformed Church (www.crcna.org/welcome/beliefs/creeds/apostles-creed).

Holy Spirit actually does anything. This reminds me of my salvation experience. There was no mention that the Holy Spirit was now going to be the active moving force in my life, and that I should focus intentionally on His indwelling presence and release Him because He would now *be* my life.

The New Testament is full of references to Who the Holy Spirit is and what He does in and for the believer. Below is a list of just seventy of those things. Take the time to meditate on them and get excited about the One Who lives within you!

THE SPIRIT AND SALVATION

1. Being a Christian means I have the Spirit in me. (See Romans 8:9.)

2. I must be born of the Spirit to enter the kingdom of God. (See John 3:5.)

3. The Spirit is a river that flows from my innermost being. (See John 7:37–39.)

4. I am the temple of God, and the Spirit of God dwells in me. (See 1 Corinthians 3:16.)

5. By joining my life to the Lord, I become one Spirit with Him. (See 1 Corinthians 6:17.)

6. The Spirit baptizes me into the body of Christ. (See 1 Corinthians 12:13.)

7. I am sealed with the Holy Spirit of promise. (See Ephesians 1:13.)

8. The Spirit has adopted me into the family of God. (See Romans 8:15.)

9. I am saved by the washing of regeneration and renewing by the Holy Spirit. (See Titus 3:5.)

THE SPIRIT WITHIN IS THE POWER I NOW RELY UPON

10. It is the Spirit who gives life; the flesh profits nothing; the words (*rhema*) that I have spoken to you are spirit and are life. (See John 6:63.)

11. The Spirit is the sanctifier working within me. (See 1 Peter 1:2.)

12. The energy of God's Spirit works within, energizing me. (See Philippians 2:13.)

13. If by the Spirit I am putting to death the deeds of the body, I will live. (See Romans 8:13.)

14. I fight with the sword of the Spirit, which is the words (*rhema*) Jesus is speaking to me. (See Ephesians 6:17.)

MY LIFESTYLE IN THE SPIRIT

15. I live and walk by the Spirit. (See Galatians 5:25.)

16. I worship in the Spirit of God. (See Philippians 3:3.)

17. I am led by the Spirit of God, which means I am a child of God. (See Romans 8:14.)

18. The natural mind does not comprehend the wisdom of the Spirit. (See 1 Corinthians 2:14.)

19. I sow to the Spirit, and from the Spirit I will reap eternal life. (See Galatians 6:8.)

20. The kingdom of God is righteousness, peace, and joy in the Holy Spirit. (See Romans 14:17.)

21. I am sanctified by my faith in the truth by the Spirit. (See 2 Thessalonians 2:13.)

22. God's glory rests upon me through the Spirit. (See 1 Peter 4:14.)

23. Christ abides in me through the Spirit He has given me. (See 1 John 3:24; 4:13.)

I HUNGER FOR THE LEADING OF THE SPIRIT

24. I am thirsty to hear from the Spirit. (See Revelation 22:17.)

25. Jesus baptizes me with the Holy Spirit and fire. (See Matthew 3:11; Mark 1:8; Luke 3:16; John 1:33.)

26. I am led by the Spirit. (See Matthew 4:1.)

27. I seek knowledge from the Spirit who lives within me. (See 1 Peter 1:11.)

28. I live under the influence of the Holy Spirit. (See Ephesians 5:18.)

29. I never insult the Spirit. (See Hebrews 10:29.)

30. I make sure to never quench the Spirit so I stay engaged in honoring and loving everyone, and I rejoice, pray, and speak *only* life-giving words. I honor prophecy. (See 1 Thessalonians 5:12–19.)

31. I rejoice in the Holy Spirit when experiencing tribulation. (See 1 Thessalonians 1:6.)

32. Since I am led by the Spirit, I am not under the law. (See Galatians 5:18.)

33. I am released from the law, and serve God in a newness of the Spirit. (See Romans 7:6.)

34. Setting my mind on the Spirit allows me to experience peace and life. (See Romans 8:5–6.)

35. My conscience is moved upon by the Holy Spirit. (See Romans 9:1.)

36. When I pray in tongues, in the Spirit, I am speaking mysteries, which builds me up. (See 1 Corinthians 14:2, 4, 14.)

37. I build myself up in faith by praying in the Holy Spirit. (See Jude 1:20.)

38. It is through revelation of the Spirit that I am strengthened with power through His Spirit in the inner man, which allows Christ to dwell in my heart through faith; and being rooted and grounded in love, I comprehend the breadth, length, height, and depth of the love of Christ, which exceeds knowledge, and I get filled up to all the fullness of God. (See Ephesians 3:16–19.)

39. In a church service, I pray with the Spirit and I pray with the mind also; I sing with the Spirit and I sing with the mind also. This way, the ungifted can say amen. (See 1 Corinthians 14:1.)

40. I tune to the Spirit and I receive wisdom, revelation, prophecy, God's voice, and His vision. (See Revelation 1:9–11.)

41. I have an ear to hear what the Spirit is saying. (See Revelation 3:22.)

42. Since I received the Spirit by hearing and faith, I continue to walk in the Spirit by hearing and believing. (See Galatians 3:2–5.)

43. I pray continuously for a spirit of wisdom and revelation in the knowledge of God and I receive it. (See Ephesians 1:17.)

44. I ask the Holy Spirit to guard the treasure God has implanted in me. (2 Timothy 1:14.)

45. I allow the Spirit to carry me away and show me things. (See Revelation 21:10.)

46. The Holy Spirit moves upon me and I prophesy. (See 2 Peter 1:21.)

I AM EMPOWERED AND ANOINTED BY THE SPIRIT IN EVERY AREA OF MY LIFE

47. The Spirit gives me access to the Father. (See Ephesians 2:18.)

48. The Spirit grants me intimate communion with my heavenly Father. (See Galatians 4:6.)

49. The Spirit helps me pray properly. (See Romans 8:26.)

50. I receive the thoughts of God through the Spirit. (See 1 Corinthians 2:10–12.)

51. The Spirit lets me see the things of God in the spirit world, and I become a reflection of that which I gaze upon. (See 1 Corinthians 3:18.)

52. The Spirit builds me together with other believers into a temple of the Lord. (See Ephesians 2:21–22.)

53. The Spirit guides and forms my prayers. (See Ephesians 6:18.)

54. The energy of the Spirit opens doors for me. (See 1 Corinthians 16:9.)

55. I receive power when the Holy Spirit comes upon me; and I tell others what I am seeing. (See Acts 1:8.)

56. I have the ninefold manifestation of the Holy Spirit. (See 1 Corinthians 12:7–10.)

   » Speaking gifts: tongues, interpretation of tongues, prophecy

   » Revelation gifts: word of knowledge, word of wisdom, discerning of spirits

   » Power gifts: faith, healing, miracles

57. I have the ninefold fruit of the Holy Spirit: love, joy, peace, patience, kindness, goodness, faithfulness, gentleness, and self-control. (See Galatians 5:22–23.)

58. God anointed Jesus, and me as one of Jesus's disciples, with the Holy Spirit and with power, and I go about doing good and healing all who are oppressed by the devil. (See Acts 10:38.)

59. My message and preaching are not in words of wisdom, but in the demonstration of the Spirit, so that people's faith is not dependent on my wisdom, but on the power of God. (See 1 Corinthians 2:4–5.)

60. I cast out demons by the Spirit of God. (See Matthew 12:28.)

61. I make disciples of all the nations, baptizing them in the name of the Father, Son, and Holy Spirit. (See Matthew 28:19.)

62. The law of the Spirit of life sets me free from the law of sin and death. (See Romans 8:2.)

63. Because I walk by the Spirit, I do not carry out the desire of the flesh. (See Galatians 5:16.)

64. I abound in hope because of the power of the Holy Spirit. (See Romans 15:13.)

65. I am made aware of things around me by the Spirit. (See Mark 2:8.)

66. The Spirit of truth guides me into all the truth, discloses what is to come, and brings things to my remembrance. (See John 16:13, 14:26.)

67. The Spirit gives me dreams and visions. (See Acts 2:17.)

68. The Spirit commissions and sends me into ministry. (See Acts 13:2–4.)

69. The Spirit guides my decision-making. (See Acts 15:28.)

70. The Spirit stops me from going in wrong directions. (See Acts 16:6–7.)

After reviewing the above list of things the Spirit accomplishes for us, I believe we can agree with Jesus: *"It is the Spirit who gives life; the flesh profits nothing; the words that I have spoken to you are spirit and are life"* (John 6:63). I think we can also agree that the overflow of the Holy Spirit offers us much more than the one amazing gift of speaking in tongues. It opens the door to an entire lifestyle of intimacy with the Holy Spirit; once this lifestyle is mastered, it releases the heavens and the provisions of God to your life.

> ONCE THE ENTIRE LIFESTYLE OF INTIMACY WITH THE HOLY SPIRIT IS MASTERED, IT RELEASES THE HEAVENS AND THE PROVISIONS OF GOD TO YOUR LIFE.

Let's make it our focus to live and walk in the overflow of the Spirit!

ACTION EXERCISE

Go back through the list of the Holy Spirit's activities and take note of the ones you have been *aware* of in your life. Put an "A" next to each of these. Then ask yourself, "Which works of the Holy Spirit do I want to see *more* of?" Put an "M" next to each of these. Spend time specifically asking the Lord to manifest in your life in these ways, and watch for Him to do so!

VARIETY VERSUS PRINCIPLES

We know that God is free to do anything He wants, and uses a variety of ways to get our attention, break into our lives, and make us aware of how to walk and live by His Spirit. (See Galatians 5:25.) It is useless to try to put God in a box or place limitations on how He will work.

However, that doesn't mean there are not some general principles we can explore that can help us move forward more quickly and easily. We can seek these patterns in Scripture and follow the paths others have walked in. In this manner, we can arrive at our destinations faster than if we walk without Scriptural guidance. (See 1 Corinthians 10:11.)

I HAD A DREAM BEFORE WRITING THIS BOOK

In this dream, I was not prepared to teach. I was still getting things ready for class, which was already beginning.

After awakening from the dream, I went to my laptop and recorded the above summary of the dream and asked, "Lord, what am I not prepared for?"

God's Interpretation in My Journal

You are not prepared to teach and explain how to experience the full release of My Spirit. It comes with full and complete yieldedness.

When you yield from self-control and self-dependence to Spirit-control and Spirit-dependence, you are filled, complete, empowered, and *ready* to face the challenges which are before you. That is what the disciples did on Pentecost and again in Acts chapter 4. That is what I did continuously. I did nothing of My own initiative. (See John 5:19–20, 30.) I put no confidence in the flesh. (See Philippians 3:3.)

Being fully yielded to and trusting in the work and power of My Spirit enables you to be filled, baptized, and empowered by the Holy Spirit. It is a step of yieldedness and a step of faith. You yield in faith to the river that flows within, which fills, and which overflows to fill the entire space that you are in, thus resting upon you. That is what the baptism or the empowering of the Holy Spirit gives to you. That is how it is experienced.

You ask for Him, yield to Him, believe in Him, and release Him in each and every way that He manifests Himself. This manifestation includes the fruit and the gifts of the Spirit and much more. (See Galatians 5:22–25; 1 Corinthians 12:7–11.)

This is My word to you this day. This is the heart of your book, and the heart of the message of walking and living by the Spirit. The end result of one who is indwelt, filled and baptized by the Holy Spirit, is that they live in meekness, entrusting themselves to the One Who lives within and Who guides and directs their every action. Behold I have spoken. Behold it is to be done."

My response was, "Thank You for revealing this to me. I receive this."

A FOUNDATIONAL DOCTRINE

It is not hard to choose to abandon self-effort if you see self-effort as a dead work.

> *Therefore leaving the elementary teaching about the Christ, let us press on to maturity, not laying again a foundation of* **repentance from dead works** *and of faith toward God.*
> (Hebrews 6:1)

A live work is motivated and empowered by the Holy Spirit. A dead work is anything motivated and empowered by myself. Jesus did nothing of His own initiative, but only what He heard and saw His Father doing. He demonstrated the pattern lifestyle we are to live. (See Romans 8:29.)

The Lord has burned into my consciousness this revelation: "*It is the* **Spirit who gives life**; *the* **flesh profits nothing**; *the words* [rhemas or "spoken words"] *that I have spoken to you are spirit and are life*" (John 6:63).

God's plan in the garden of Eden was that man would take strolls and share and communicate with Him. Satan's alternative was that man could know truth on his own. (See Genesis 2.) This puts *self* and my *mind* in the center of life rather than communing with my heavenly Father. So I need to choose: do I think things through on my own, or do I ask the Holy Spirit to anoint and guide my reasoning so that I have the mind of Christ? (See 1 Corinthians 2:16.) Do I focus on my self-effort or do I ask the Spirit to empower me with supernatural abilities?

> OUR GOAL IS TO TRAIN YOU TO GO BACK TO GOD'S ORIGINAL INTENT OF LIVING OUT OF COMMUNION WITH HIM, RATHER THAN THE LIE THAT YOU CAN LIVE SEPARATE FROM HIM.

Every moment of every day, I am making this decision. The goal of this book is to train you to go back to God's original intent of living out of communion with Him, rather than the lie that you can live separate from Him. Then the Holy Spirit will manifest Himself through you in every way that He wants to meet your needs and the needs of others.

Speaking to me through journaling, Jesus said, "We are walking together, so close. No one can separate us. You turn away but I take your hand and draw you back to Me. I hold you in My arms. That is how you receive My strength—it flows from Me to you. You ask what you should do; it is what *We* should do."

GOD'S FOUNDATIONAL DOCTRINES FOCUS ON THE RELEASE OF THE HOLY SPIRIT

Scripture states what God considers the *foundational doctrines* of our spiritual life. They are very different from what man considers essential. I studied doctrine (theology) in Bible college, and we never covered the six that God calls foundational. Truly unfortunate.

> *Therefore, leaving the discussion of the elementary principles of Christ, let us go on to perfection, not laying again the **foundation of** repentance from dead works and of faith toward God, of the doctrine of baptisms, of laying on of hands, of resurrection of the dead, and of eternal judgment. And this we will do if God permits.*   (Hebrews 6:1–3 NKJV)

1. **Repentance from dead works.** A dead work is anything that begins, continues, and ends with self-effort rather than with God's wisdom and power available through the Holy Spirit. My goal is to learn to live as Jesus did, doing only what the Spirit directs. (See John 5:19–20, 30.)

2. **Faith toward God.** I choose to *believe* that the river of the Spirit flows within me. (See John 7:37–39.) I live by His Spirit. (See Galatians 5:25.) I honor His flow within.

3. **Doctrine of baptisms.** I am baptized in water, in the Holy Spirit, in fire, and by the Holy Spirit into the body of Christ. (See Acts 2:1–38; 1 Corinthians 12:13.)

4. **Laying on of hands.** Like Jesus, I release healing and blessing by the Spirit when I lay hands on people. (See Mark 6:5; 16:18.)

5. **Resurrection of the dead.** I am conscious that I was crucified with Christ. Christ now lives out through me. (See Galatians 2:20.) I choose to reckon myself dead to sin and alive to God through the power of the Spirit. (See Romans 6:11.)

6. **Eternal judgment.** I release judging people and situations to God. (See John 8:15; James 4:12.) I choose instead to live like Jesus, who was moved by compassion and healed. (See Matthew 14:14.)

In summarizing these six doctrines, I suggest that what God considers foundational is that we learn how to walk and live by the Spirit. Obviously there is much more that can be said about each of these, but the above statements are their core meanings. I recommend *The Spirit-Filled Believer's Handbook* by Derek Prince for a full treatment of the foundational doctrines of Hebrews 6:1–2.

ACTION EXERCISE

Make a list of the points from this chapter that speak to you.

_____

_____

_____

_____

_____

Meditate/ponder over a minimum of five verses from this chapter and be ready to share insights with friends or with a small group that is studying this book together.

What are your reflections on the verse *"The flesh profits nothing; the words* [rhemas] *that I have spoken to you are spirit and are life"* (John 6:63)?

_____

_____

_____

_____

_____

How I Received the Baptism in the Holy Spirit
by Susan Caley

I had been a Christian for about six years and was feeling that my heart toward Jesus had grown cold, my prayer life was practically nonexistent, and my walk with the Lord was superficial; I kept thinking that there must be more than this. I kept sending up prayers to God, asking Him to fill me with the Holy Spirit. At the same time, I was scared as I didn't know what would happen. The Toronto blessing happened and God poured out His Spirit on certain places in England where I live. I met in my home with a youth worker. She prayed for me and the Holy Spirit filled me.

This filling happened in stages. I was filled more powerfully in my quiet times, then at a conference at Holy Trinity Brompton, God's power went down into my head and through my body; I felt drunk! I was so hungry for more of Jesus. I felt like I'd woken up. I was given a new joy in God, a new love for Jesus that has never left. My prayer life was transformed. I received pictures and Bible verses, and I heard the Lord speak to me within. I had a deep desire to encourage other Christians and still have. This has gone on for twenty years.

At a Christian conference, a lady on a prayer team asked if she could pray for me. As she prayed, I heard an inner voice that I seemed to know was God the Father. He said, "I want you to join in partnership with Me, to pray for what's on My heart." This urging or inner nudging became so insistent that I just said to God one day, "Father, will You show me what's on Your heart?" Immediately a picture came into my mind of a statue of Jesus standing with

His arms open over a city. Then the Holy Spirit interceded through me with groans and sighs. I had never experienced this before but I felt like I was in the school of the Spirit. I then prayed for revival in that place.

Since then, for the last fifteen years, I ask the Father who or what is on His heart. Sometimes I see in my mind the name of a country or a people group, like the aborigines or a people group in China. Sometimes I see in my mind the actual people; the Dalai Lama is on God's heart, which surprised me. Sometimes I feel God's pain in my heart for those whom He leads me to pray for. Sometimes the country will be in the news after I've prayed for it. Something that I will never forget is Rwanda and the massacre between the Hutu and Tutsi tribes. The Spirit caused me to do physical actions of wrestling.

I had never thought much about speaking in tongues, but at the Holy Trinity Brompton Conference, the minister said, "If anyone would like to speak in tongues, come forward to be prayed for." I was hungry for everything God wanted to give me so I went forward, the lady prayed for me to be given that gift, and told me to open my mouth in faith and see what happens. I must admit, I felt embarrassed, but I wasn't going to miss what God had for me. I went for it and I started speaking in words I didn't understand.

When I talk to God in tongues, He draws near. I also sang in tongues, which sounded beautiful. The notes seem to come from my heart. As I sang, it felt like I was being refreshed too. The most precious thing that happened as a result of being filled with the Spirit is an intimate relationship with Jesus.

A friend who was ill called me and I immediately felt the Lord's presence. All through our conversation, I kept getting pictures and encouragements to the effect that this illness was not going to be a part of her life story that God has planned for her life. After I got off the phone, to my surprise, the Holy Spirit's power and God's presence flowed into my heart and at the same time, the Holy Spirit's power and presence flowed outwards from within my heart. This went on for a long time. I asked the Lord what happens next and heard Him say within me, "The only way is up."

I had been feeling dry and was crying out to God for a fresh filling of His Spirit. Now I have a freedom when I pray for people and a new freedom and intimacy with God the Father and Jesus, a hunger to press in for more of Jesus and I want God's plan for my life wherever He wants to take me. I want to go with Him. Interestingly, a few months ago during a prayer time, Jesus said, "Welcome the Holy Spirit," so I started to do that before I pray and the Holy Spirit's presence is more evident in my prayer times. I feel He is my friend and helper and I want to be more sensitive to Him.

I would say to any believer that the Lord has more for you. Don't settle for little; keep asking the Lord for more. Press in with boldness. I believe God is the same yesterday, today, and forever. I want to do the things Jesus did, and I believe we are meant to. The Lord keeps bringing Isaiah 61 into my mind. Our God is an awesome God!

2

THE FOUNDATION: INTIMACY WITH GOD

In order to live out of the Father's initiative, we first need to develop the ability to recognize His voice within us. We must be able to discern when the Spirit is speaking secrets to us, showing images of what He wants to do, or impressing us with His desire to heal or release other miracles.

Without the confidence that we are sensing His leading and initiative, we will waver in doubt, never stepping out to be the vessel of God's grace that He wants us to be.

Two-way journaling is the most effective tool we have to develop that confidence. Those who follow its principles find it is foundational to their growth in moving in the Spirit's gifts. Two-way journaling is simply recording your conversations with the Lord—your words to Him and His words back to you.

> TWO-WAY JOURNALING IS SIMPLY RECORDING YOUR CONVERSATIONS WITH THE LORD—YOUR WORDS TO HIM AND HIS WORDS BACK TO YOU.

Because you are writing what you believe God is saying, it is essentially personal revelation: prophecy, words of wisdom, and words of knowledge. Journaling gives you the chance to practice discerning the Spirit's moving within you and receive confirmation that you are hearing clearly, while at the same time building a deeper, more intimate relationship with the Lord. That's powerful! The four keys to hearing God's voice will help you begin to live more fully out of the Father's initiative every day.

THE LORD SHOWED ME HOW TO EASILY HEAR HIS VOICE DAILY

Rachel, our foster daughter, had once again broken the house rules and I needed to confront her on her disobedience and irresponsibility. I was irritated with her and concerned for Patti, who bore the brunt of Rachel's actions. But I had recently been learning to hear God's voice more clearly, so I thought I should try to see if I could hear anything from Him about the situation before I talked with Rachel. Maybe He could give me a way to get her to abide by our family rules and be more responsible. So I went to my office and reviewed what the Lord had been teaching me from Habakkuk 2:1–2: "*I will stand on my guard post and station myself on the rampart; and I will keep watch to see what He will speak to me.… Then the* LORD *answered me and said, 'Record the vision.'*"

> THE FIRST KEY TO HEARING GOD'S VOICE IS TO GO TO A QUIET PLACE
> AND STILL OUR OWN THOUGHTS AND EMOTIONS.

Habakkuk said, "*I will stand on my guard post.*" The first key to hearing God's voice is to go to a quiet place and still our own thoughts and emotions. Psalm 46:10 encourages us to be still, let go, cease striving, and know that He is God. We are called to "*be still before the* LORD *and wait patiently for him*" (Psalm 37:7 NIV). There is a deep inner knowing in our spirits that each of us can experience when we quiet our flesh and our minds. Practicing the art of biblical meditation helps silence the outer noise and distractions clamoring for our attention.

I didn't have a guard post, but I did have an office, so I went there to quiet my temper and my mind. Loving God through a quiet worship song is a very effective way to become still. In 2 Kings 3:15, Elisha needed a word from the Lord, so he said, *"Bring me a minstrel,"* and as the minstrel played, the Lord spoke. I have found that playing a worship song on my autoharp is the quickest way for me to come to stillness. I need to choose my song carefully; I arrive at stillness not with boisterous songs of praise, but rather with gentle songs that express my love and worship. And it isn't enough just to sing the song into the cosmos; I come into the Lord's presence most quickly and easily when I use my godly imagination to see the truth that He is right beside me and I sing my songs to Him personally.

The prophet said, *"I will keep watch to see"* (Habbakuk 2:1). To receive the pure word of God, it is very important that my heart be properly focused as I become still, because my focus is the source of the intuitive flow. If I fix my eyes upon Jesus (see Hebrews 12:2), the intuitive flow comes from Jesus. But if I fix my gaze upon some desire of my heart, the intuitive flow comes out of that desire. To have a pure flow, I must become still and carefully fix my eyes upon Jesus. Quietly worshiping the King and receiving out of the stillness that follows quite easily accomplishes this.

THE SECOND KEY TO HEARING GOD'S VOICE IS TO FIX THE EYES OF YOUR HEART ON JESUS AS YOU PRAY, SEEING IN THE SPIRIT THE DREAMS AND VISIONS OF ALMIGHTY GOD.

The second key to hearing God's voice is to fix the eyes of your heart on Jesus as you pray, seeing in the Spirit the dreams and visions of Almighty God. Habakkuk was actually looking for vision as he prayed. He opened the eyes of his heart, and looked into the spirit world to see what God wanted to show him.

God has always spoken through dreams and visions, and He specifically said that they would come to those upon whom the Holy Spirit is poured out. (See Acts 2:1–4, 17.)

Being a logical, rational person, observable facts that could be verified by my physical senses were the foundations of my life, including my spiritual life. I had never thought of opening the eyes of my heart and looking for vision. However, I have come to believe that this is exactly what God wants me to do. He gave me eyes in my heart to see in the spirit the vision and movement of Almighty God. There is an active spirit world all around us, full of angels, demons, the Holy Spirit, the omnipresent Father, and His omnipresent Son, Jesus. The only reasons for me not to see this reality are unbelief or lack of knowledge.

In his sermon in Acts 2:25, Peter refers to King David's statement "*I saw the* Lord *always in my presence; for He is at my right hand, so that I will not be shaken.*" The original psalm makes it clear that this was a decision of David's, not a constant supernatural visitation: "*I have set* [placed] *the* Lord *continually before me; because He is at my right hand, I will not be shaken*" (Psalm 16:8). Because David *knew* that the Lord was always with him, he determined in his spirit to *see* that truth with the eyes of his heart as he went through life, knowing that this would keep his faith strong.

In order to *see*, we must *look*. Daniel saw a vision in his mind and said, "*I was looking*" (Daniel 7:2); multiple times, he said, "*I kept looking*" (see, for example, Daniel 7:4). As I pray, I look for Jesus, and I watch as He speaks to me, doing and saying the things that are on His heart. Many Christians will find that if they will only look, they will see. Jesus is Emmanuel, God with us. (See Matthew 1:23.) It is as simple as that. You can see Christ present with you because Christ *is* present with you. In fact, the vision may come so easily that you will be tempted to reject it, thinking that it is just you. But if you persist in recording these visions, your doubt will soon be overcome by faith as you recognize that the content of them could only be birthed in Almighty God.

YOU CAN SEE CHRIST PRESENT WITH YOU BECAUSE CHRIST IS PRESENT WITH YOU.

Jesus demonstrated the ability of living out of constant contact with God, declaring that He did nothing on His own initiative, but only what He saw the Father doing, and heard the Father saying. (See John 5:19–20, 30.) What an incredible way to live!

Is it possible for us to live out of divine initiative as Jesus did? Yes! We must simply fix our eyes upon Jesus. The veil has been torn, giving access into the immediate presence of God, and He calls us to draw near. (See Luke 23:45; Hebrews 10:19–22.) *"I pray that the eyes of your heart may be enlightened"* (Ephesians 1:18).

When I had quieted my heart enough that I was able to picture Jesus without the distractions of my own ideas and plans, I was able to *"keep watch to see what He will speak to me"* (Habakkuk 2:1). I wrote down my question: "Lord, what should I do about Rachel?"

Immediately the thought came to me, "She is insecure." That certainly wasn't *my* thought! Her behavior looked like rebellion to me, not insecurity.

But like Habakkuk, I was coming to know the sound of God speaking to me. Elijah described it as *"a still small voice"* (1 Kings 19:12 NKJV). I had previously listened for an inner audible voice, and God does speak that way at times. However, I have found that usually, God's voice comes as spontaneous thoughts, visions, feelings, or impressions.

For example, have you ever been driving down the road and had a thought come to you to pray for a certain person? Didn't you believe it was God telling you to pray? What did God's voice sound like? Was it an audible voice, or was it a spontaneous thought that dropped into your mind?

Experience indicates that we perceive spirit-level communication as spontaneous thoughts, impressions, and visions, and Scripture confirms this in many ways. For example, one definition of *paga*, a Hebrew word for intercession, is "a chance encounter or an accidental intersecting." When God lays people on our hearts, He does it through *paga*, a chance encounter thought that pops up in our minds.

> ## THE THIRD KEY TO HEARING GOD'S VOICE IS RECOGNIZING THAT GOD'S VOICE IN YOUR HEART OFTEN SOUNDS LIKE A FLOW OF SPONTANEOUS THOUGHTS.

The third key to hearing God's voice is recognizing that God's voice in your heart often sounds like a flow of spontaneous thoughts. Therefore, when I want to hear from God, I quiet my mind so that these can come through.

Finally, God told Habakkuk to record the vision. (See Habakkuk 2:2.) This was not an isolated command. The Scriptures record many examples of individuals' prayers and God's replies, such as the Psalms, many of the prophets, and Revelation. I have found that obeying this final principle amplified my confidence in my ability to hear God's voice so that I could finally make living out of His initiatives a way of life. The fourth key, two-way journaling or the writing out of your prayers and God's answers, brings great freedom in hearing God's voice.

I have found two-way journaling to be a fabulous catalyst for clearly discerning God's inner, spontaneous flow, because as I journal, I am able to write in faith for long periods of time, simply believing it is God. I know that what I believe I have received from God must be tested. However, testing involves doubt and doubt blocks divine communication, so I do not want to test while I am trying to receive. (See James 1:5–8.) With journaling, I can receive in faith, knowing that when the flow has ended, I can test and examine it carefully.

> THE FOURTH KEY, TWO-WAY JOURNALING OR THE WRITING OUT OF YOUR PRAYERS AND GOD'S ANSWERS, BRINGS GREAT FREEDOM IN HEARING GOD'S VOICE.

So I wrote down what I believed God had said: "She is insecure."

But the Lord wasn't done. I continued to write the spontaneous thoughts that came to me: "Love her unconditionally. She is flesh of your flesh and bone of your bone."

My mind immediately objected: Rachel is not flesh of my flesh. She is not related to me at all—she is a foster child, just living in my home temporarily. It was definitely time to test this "word from the Lord"!

There are three possible sources of thoughts in our minds: ourselves, Satan, and the Holy Spirit. It was obvious that the words in my journal did not come from my own mind because I certainly didn't see Rachel as insecure *or* flesh of my flesh. And I sincerely doubted that Satan would encourage me to love anyone unconditionally!

Okay, it was starting to look like I might have actually received counsel from the Lord. It was consistent with the names and character of God as revealed in Scripture, and contrary to the names and character of the enemy. So that meant that I was hearing from the Lord, and He wanted me to see the situation in a different light. Rachel *was* my daughter—part of my family not by blood but by the hand of God Himself. The chaos of her birth home had created deep insecurity about her worthiness to be loved by anyone, including me *and* God. Only the unconditional love of the Lord expressed through an imperfect human would reach her heart.

But there was still one more test I needed to perform before I would have absolute confidence that this was truly God's word to me: I needed confirmation from someone else whose spiritual discernment I trusted. So I went to my wife and shared what I had received. I knew if I could get her validation, especially since she was the one most wronged in the situation, then I could say, at least to myself, "Thus sayeth the Lord."

Needless to say, Patti immediately and without question confirmed that the Lord had spoken to me. My entire planned lecture to my foster daughter was forgotten. I returned to my office anxious to hear more. As the Lord planted a new, supernatural love for Rachel within me, He showed me what to say and how to say it to not only address the current issue of household responsibility, but the deeper issues of love, acceptance, and worthiness.

Rachel and her brother remained as part of our family for another two years, giving us many opportunities to demonstrate and teach about the Father's love, planting spiritual seeds in thirsty soil. We weren't perfect and we didn't solve all of her issues, but because I had learned to listen to the Lord, we were able to avoid creating more brokenness and separation.

> THE FOUR SIMPLE KEYS FROM HABAKKUK HAVE BEEN USED BY PEOPLE OF ALL AGES TO BREAK THROUGH INTO INTIMATE, TWO-WAY CONVERSATIONS WITH THEIR LOVING FATHER.

The four simple keys that the Lord showed me from Habakkuk have been used by people of all ages from every continent, culture, and denomination, to break through into intimate, two-way conversations with their loving Father and dearest Friend. Omitting any one of the keys will prevent you from receiving all He wants to say to you. The order of the keys is not important, just that you *use them all.* Embracing all four, by faith, can change your life. Simply quiet yourself down, tune to spontaneity, look for vision, and journal. He is waiting to meet you there.

You will be amazed when you journal! Doubt may hinder you at first, but throw it off, reminding yourself that it is a biblical concept, and that God is present, speaking to His children. Relax. When we cease our labors and enter His rest, God is free to flow. (See Hebrews 4:10.)

WISDOM FOR BEGINNING JOURNALERS

Two-way journaling—God and you conversing on paper—is essentially personal prophecy. Prophecy is best restricted to edification, exhortation, and comfort. (See 1 Corinthians 14:3.) Predictive guidance is *outside* these three categories and is to be avoided as the future is in flux (see Ezekiel 33:13–16), and one can suffer shipwrecked faith (1 Timothy 1:19) if a prediction does not come true (see Jonah 3:4, 10).

SUMMARIZING HABAKKUK'S FOUR KEYS TO HEARING GOD'S VOICE

4 keys exemplified in Habakkuk 2:1–2	Succinctly Stated
"I will stand on my guard post" (verse 1)	Quiet yourself down by…
"And I will keep watch to see" (verse 1)	Fixing your eyes on Jesus.
"What He will speak to me" (verse 1)	Tune to flow/spontaneity, then…
The Lord said, *"Record the vision"* (verse 2)	Write down the flow of thoughts and images.

+ Key 1: Quiet yourself so you can hear God's voice.

+ Key 2: Look for vision as you pray. Fix your eyes upon Jesus.

+ Key 3: Recognize God's voice as spontaneous, flowing thoughts that light upon your mind.

+ Key 4: Write down the flow of thoughts and images that come to you.

Here are four words that summarize the four keys: *stillness, vision, spontaneity,* and *journaling.* You can also put it this way: *hearing God's voice is as simple as quieting yourself down, fixing your eyes on Jesus, tuning to spontaneity, and writing.* More information can be found in the book *4 Keys to Hearing God's Voice.*[3]

These keys are an incredibly effective tool for learning to discern the movement of the Spirit within you. Use them daily to deepen your personal relationship with the Lord. Begin living out of His initiative, obeying and responding to His voice. When the time is right, He will begin to lead you to use the same keys to manifest His gifts more publicly as He wills. But don't be in a hurry; enjoy the times of fellowship with the Father and Jesus. Seek Him first and the gifts will follow.

> SATAN HAS AN ARSENAL OF LIES TO KEEP US FROM HEARING
> GOD'S VOICE, BUILDING A LOVE RELATIONSHIP WITH THE LORD, AND
> MANIFESTING HIS LOVE TO THE WORLD.

SATAN AND HIS ARSENAL OF LIES

Satan will use any lie to make sure you don't hear God's voice. Satan's passion is that we do not return to God's original intent as displayed in the garden of Eden. Adam and Eve walked in

---

3. Mark and Patti Virkler, *4 Keys to Hearing God's Voice* (Shippensburg, PA: Destiny Image, 2010).

the garden in the cool of the day and had fellowship with God, depending on Him for everything.

Satan has an arsenal of lies to keep us from hearing God's voice, building a love relationship with the Lord, and manifesting His love to the world. Below are his most common ones, and I have believed most of them at one point or another in my life.

Repent of Satan's Lies	Affirm God's Truths
Dispensationalism: God no longer speaks in this dispensation.	*"'And it shall be in the last days,' God says, 'that I **will** pour forth of My Spirit…; and your sons and your daughters **shall prophesy**"* (Acts 2:17).
Demythologization: The Bible's supernatural accounts are myths.	*"A natural man does not accept the things of the Spirit of God, for they are foolishness to him"* (1 Corinthians 2:14).
It is so hard to hear: You must earn the right to hear God's voice. When you are good enough and try hard enough, you can get a word from God. It is not enough to simply be a believing Christian. If you want to hear His voice, you need to fast forty days and then do this…. (The list is endless.)	*"My sheep hear My voice"* (John 10:27). *"Did you receive the Spirit by the works of the Law, or by hearing with faith?…Having begun by the Spirit, are you now being perfected by the flesh?…Does He who provides you with the Spirit and works miracles among you, do it by the works of the Law, or by **hearing with faith?**"* (Galatians 3:2–5).

Repent of Satan's Lies	Affirm God's Truths
It can't be that easy: Once you discover His voice is as simple as spontaneous, flowing thoughts, Satan tries to convince you these are only your thoughts and not God's voice.	*"Truly I say to you, unless you are converted and become like children, you will not enter the kingdom of heaven"* (Matthew 18:3).
My sins are too big: God could never forgive me for what I have done. I can't even forgive myself.	*"He made Him who knew no sin to be sin on our behalf, so that we might become the righteousness of God in Him"* (2 Corinthians 5:21).

If you believe any of these lies, take a moment now to repent. Then speak God's truth as your own belief. Do it now!

FIVE WAYS TO BE SURE YOU'RE HEARING FROM GOD

Get in the habit of applying these tests to what you receive in your two-way journaling so that when you begin to move in the gifts, you will continue to naturally apply them to what you are receiving for others.

1. TEST THE ORIGIN (SEE 1 JOHN 4:1)

Thoughts from our own minds are progressive, with one thought leading to the next, however tangentially. Thoughts from the spirit world are spontaneous. The Hebrew word for true prophecy is *naba*, which literally means to bubble up. False prophecy is *ziyd* meaning to boil up. True words from the Lord will bubble up from our innermost being; we don't need to cook them up ourselves.

2. COMPARE IT TO BIBLICAL PRINCIPLES

God will never say something to you personally that is contrary to His universal revelation as expressed in the Scriptures. If the Bible clearly states that something is a sin, no amount of journaling can make it right. However, much of what you journal about will not be specifically addressed in the Bible, so an understanding of biblical principles is also needed.

3. COMPARE IT TO THE NAMES AND CHARACTER OF GOD AS REVEALED IN THE BIBLE

Anything God says to you will be in harmony with His essential nature. Journaling will help you get to *know* God personally, but knowing what the Bible says *about* Him will help you discern what words are from Him. Make sure the tenor of your journaling lines up with the character of God as described in the names of the Father, Son, and Holy Spirit.

4. TEST THE FRUIT (SEE MATTHEW 7:15–20)

What effect does what you are hearing have on your soul and your spirit? Words from the Lord will quicken your faith and increase your love, peace, and joy. They will stimulate a sense of humility within you as you become more aware of Who God is and who you are. On the other hand, any words you receive that cause you to fear or doubt, bring you into confusion or anxiety, or stroke your ego—especially if you hear something that is "just for you alone; no one else is worthy"—must be immediately rebuked and rejected as lies of the enemy.

5. SHARE IT WITH YOUR SPIRITUAL COUNSELORS (SEE PROVERBS 11:14)

We who are Christian are members of one Body! *"A cord of three strands is not quickly torn apart"* (Ecclesiastes 4:12). God's intention has always been for us to grow together. Nothing will increase your faith in your ability to hear from God like having it

confirmed by two or three other people! Share it with your spouse,
your parents, your friends, your elders, or your group leader. Even
your grown children can be your sounding board. They don't need
to be perfect or super-spiritual; they just need to love you, be committed to being available to you, have a solid biblical orientation,
and most importantly, they must also willingly and easily receive
counsel. Avoid the authoritarian who insists that because of their
standing in the church or with God, they no longer need to listen
to others. Find two or three people and let them confirm that you
are hearing from God!

> LIVING OUT OF GOD'S INITIATIVE INVOLVES STEPPING OUT
> IN FAITH THAT YOU ARE RECEIVING AND RECOGNIZING THE FLOW OF
> THE SPIRIT WITHIN YOU.

EMBRACING FAITH IN FLOW

As you can see, living out of God's initiative involves stepping
out in faith that you are receiving and recognizing the flow of the
river of the Spirit within you. When you journal, you tune to that
flow and write in faith that what you are receiving is from the Lord.
You will find that living and walking by the Spirit—from responding to His leading from within you, to receiving the baptism in the
Holy Spirit, to manifesting the gifts of the Spirit—involves the
combining of the same two foundational principles: the principle
of faith and the principle of flow.

1. THE PRINCIPLE OF FAITH

> But without **faith** it is impossible to please Him, for he who
> comes to God must believe that He is, and that He is a
> rewarder of those who diligently seek Him.
>
> (Hebrews 11:6 NKJV)

2. THE PRINCIPLE OF FLOW

[Jesus said,] *"He who believes in Me, as the Scripture said, 'From his innermost being will **flow** rivers of living water.'" But this He spoke of the Spirit, whom those who believed in Him were to receive.* (John 7:38–39)

3. THE "FAITH IN FLOW" PRINCIPLE

The gifts of the Holy Spirit operate through the one who, *in faith, yields* his outer faculties to the control of *the river of God that flows within.* In faith, yield your faculties to the flow.

EXPLORING THE PRINCIPLE OF FAITH

Hebrews 11:6 says it is impossible to please God unless I choose to believe that He is and that He will reward me when I diligently seek Him. God is pleased when I believe He is with me and loves, guides, protects, delivers, and interacts with me.

> GOD IS PLEASED WHEN I BELIEVE HE IS WITH ME AND LOVES, GUIDES, PROTECTS, DELIVERS, AND INTERACTS WITH ME.

For many years, I did not give God this pleasure of believing in Him because my embrace of dispensationalism and rational theology had removed God's immediacy from my life. Now, finally, I can bring Him pleasure by believing that He is and that He will reward me as I seek Him.

The Bible says that faith comes by hearing and hearing a word (*rhema*) from Christ. (See Romans 10:17.) This means that faith is born in your heart *when God speaks* into your heart by revelation knowledge. The result of this revelation, in the context of the baptism and gifts of Holy Spirit, is that I *know* with confidence and certainty that I *should* manifest the Holy Spirit and His gifts, that I *can* receive them, and that I *will* receive them when I ask.

RECEIVING FAITH FOR THE BAPTISM IN THE HOLY SPIRIT

Pray for God to pour revelation into your heart. Ask Him to give you spiritual understanding of the Scriptures that deal with the baptism of the Holy Spirit and speaking in tongues. Prayerfully meditate on them. Ask Him to impart the gift of faith for the baptism of the Holy Spirit and speaking in tongues into your heart. Then step out of the boat in faith, believing God will meet you with a divine miracle.

EXPLORING THE PRINCIPLE OF FLOW

In John 7:38, Jesus describes the Holy Spirit as a river that *flows* within. I had never learned about or honored the flow within me until God taught me that *flow* or *spontaneity*, as I have come to call it, is the way we sense the river of God within us, and is one of the four keys that I needed to learn in order to clearly hear His voice. Journaling is writing down the *flow* of spontaneous thoughts that come to me as I focus my attention on Him.

When I speak in tongues, I do not consciously guide the formation of the syllables. I tune to *flow*, and speak syllables that are not consciously formed by my mind. Spontaneously, according to the dictates of the flow of the Holy Spirit within me, sounds just pour out of my mouth. I speak in simple childlike faith. A spiritual conviction grows that this flow of words is coming from the river of the Holy Spirit within me.

Since the educational system taught me to scorn flow and trust the logical development of my thoughts instead, I had a hard time honoring, believing in, and operating in the gift of tongues during those first months. By God's grace, I gradually came to the point where I believed that flow is the Holy Spirit within me. If you were like me, I encourage you to pray as I did:

I repent of my belief that flow is nothing and that it is to be disdained and set aside. I turn from that belief and I confess the truths of God's Word that the river of God *flows* within me and that when I fix my eyes on Jesus and tune to flow, the stream of sounds, thoughts, and images I receive is coming from the indwelling Spirit of God. The words that I speak are being formed by the Spirit. I honor flow, for it is the river of the Spirit of God within my heart.

Make this your prayer and your confession, speaking it aloud from your heart. Let it set you free from the god of rationalism that has controlled the western world for over five hundred years.

OWNING THE REVELATION OF FAITH IN FLOW

Unfortunately, I was not able to state or fully understand this principle of *faith in flow* at the time I first used it for speaking in tongues in 1975. It would take twenty-three more years before I would be able to put it down on paper and grasp its universal application to the operation of the other gifts of the Holy Spirit.

This same principle of faith in flow is used to intentionally manifest all the gifts of the Holy Spirit in one's life. The manifestation of the Spirit occurs naturally when we yield and tune in to the flow:

- The *mind* yielded to the flow of the Holy Spirit results in anointed reasoning, words of wisdom, and words of knowledge.

- The *mouth* yielded to the flow of the Holy Spirit results in tongues, interpretation, prophecy, and persuasiveness of speech.

- The *heart* yielded to the flow of the Holy Spirit results in hearing God's voice, distinguishing of spirits, faith, peace, and unrest.

- The *hands* yielded to the flow of the Holy Spirit results in miracles and healing as His power flows to those whom you touch.

* The *eyes* yielded to the flow of the Holy Spirit results in dreams, visions, and divine perspective.

PRESS IN TOWARD THE GIFTS OF THE SPIRIT

Take a few minutes to ponder what has been said, for you *can* press in and learn to intentionally operate the gifts of the Holy Spirit if you will but yield your outer faculties to the river of God within you. Once the Lord gives you revelation concerning this, you will begin operating in the supernatural.

Don't put it off. Stop, ponder, meditate, and receive this revelation. Your life will go on whether you operate in this revelation or not. But if you receive it and live in it, you will release a supernatural manifestation of the power of the Holy Spirit in the world today. If you don't, you will be a manifestation of yourself. The world needs you, but it needs Christ much more.

ACTION EXERCISE

What new ideas have you received from this chapter?

_____

_____

_____

_____

_____

Use some soft music like Communion With God Ministries' visionary meditation "A Stroll Along the Sea of Galilee."[4] Visualize yourself walking with Jesus. Then spend four or five minutes writing a paragraph to tell the Lord some of the reasons why you love Him so much.

_____

_____

_____

_____

_____

Now fix your eyes on Jesus. Picture yourself as a happy, smiling child; you're in a fun, comfortable setting with Jesus. Now write another paragraph from flow, which will be Jesus telling you how much He loves you.

_____

_____

_____

_____

_____

Submit this second paragraph to a spiritual friend and ask them if they feel it is God speaking. Communion With God Ministries also has some skilled journalers who would be happy to help you.[5]

Make two-way journaling a standard part of your devotional time. Begin living out of the initiatives of heaven.

4. cwgministries.org/galilee
5. cwgministries.org/SkilledJournalers

How I Received the Baptism in the Holy Spirit
by Betsey Jean

In the 1980s, I was a baby Christian in a rural, religious, mainline church with no teaching on the Holy Spirit. They were traumatized when several of us began to raise our hands in worship in the back row, so we were invited to do that elsewhere! Then I read *Something More* by Catherine Marshall ... and I wanted something more.

When I got invited to a Full Gospel Business Men's Fellowship meeting, I was all excited to get prayed for to receive tongues, but didn't know to open my mouth. I went home downcast thinking, *Well, I didn't get it.* The next morning, I sat in my chair bummed about it, but said, "I'm gonna praise God anyway." I began to sing ... and out came a beautiful language! But within minutes, along came the enemy in my ear: "That wasn't tongues, that was Hebrew you've been reading in the Bible." Then, "That wasn't tongues, it was Spanish" (I'm fluent in Spanish). Finally, the enemy said, "That wasn't tongues, it was baby talk!" Shot down with no ammo, I closed my mouth and believed that lie for about six weeks.

Then, supernaturally God moved to restore! I went upstairs to rest in the early evening and had fallen into a deep sleep when the phone rang. Disoriented, I rushed downstairs to answer it, but no one was there. Then all of a sudden, out came those tongues again, and I told the sucker, "There, devil, those are tongues and you're never gonna fool me again!"

Unfortunately, his next tactic worked for more years than I want to admit. I got the gift, but not the *why*—I'm a left-brainer, all logic—so with no understanding, I didn't value this precious gift, or use it too often. My loss: a miracle in my mouth, a hotline to heaven, but lightly esteemed. Thank God, in His mercy and forgiveness, He doesn't give up as easily on us!

3

SEEING MYSELF CLEARLY

DO I SEE MYSELF CORRECTLY?

It seems so obvious. I am a self-contained unit. I make up my own mind, set my own will, and accomplish by my strength. God gave me a brain; I'm supposed to use it, right? Well, maybe not. Paul was quite passionate that there was another Person living Himself out through him:

> I have been crucified with Christ; and it is no longer I who live, but Christ lives in me.   (Galatians 2:20)

Self-help books teach self-actualization: become all you can be! All of my secular education and much of my religious education taught that this was an appropriate view of reality. I was told, "Don't bother God with the things you can handle on your own."

It sounds like it could be right … but I am quite convinced it is wrong.

GOD SAYS I AM A VESSEL WHOM HE DESIRES TO FILL

Yes, God says we are *vessels*. This totally contradicts my past belief that I am a self-contained unit. However, if I want my life to work well, I *must* adopt God's views of reality. *My* images are distorted.

God calls me a *vessel* designed to be filled by His Spirit:

We have this treasure in earthen vessels. (2 Corinthians 4:7)

God calls me a *temple* designed to house His Spirit:

Your body is a temple of the Holy Spirit who is in you.
(1 Corinthians 6:19)

The main purpose of a vessel is to contain something, such as a liquid. We contain the Holy Spirit, Who is a river flowing from our innermost being.

> *Jesus stood and cried out, saying, "If anyone is thirsty, let him come to Me and drink. He who believes in Me, as the Scripture said, 'From his innermost being will flow rivers of* **living water.'"** **But this He spoke of the Spirit,** *whom those who believed in Him were to receive; for the Spirit was not yet given, because Jesus was not yet glorified.* (John 7:37–39)

- Salvation is the indwelling of the Spirit as I yield my heart to Him.
- Sanctification is ongoing fillings of the Spirit as I yield additional areas to Him.
- Baptism in the Spirit is the overflow and empowering of the Holy Spirit where He now rests upon me, filling the atmosphere around me or the room I am in. (See Acts 2:1–4.)

Living by the Spirit means intentionally staying tuned to the flow within, which is the Spirit, the living water that flows from the throne of God. (See Jeremiah 2:13; Revelation 22:1.) Let's explore these concepts more deeply.

SALVATION: WHEN THE HOLY SPIRIT DWELLS IN ME

*He abides with you and will be **in** you.*   (John 14:17)

*Unless one is **born of…the Spirit** he cannot enter into the kingdom of God.*   (John 3:5)

*The **Spirit of God dwells in you.** But if anyone does not have the Spirit of Christ, he does not belong to Him. If **Christ is in you**, though the body is dead because of sin, yet the **spirit is alive** because of righteousness.*   (Romans 8:9–10)

When I repented of my sins and asked Jesus to be my Lord and Savior, the Holy Spirit entered me and took up residence *in* me. This was a joy-filled and completely life-transforming day for me. I was fifteen years old. I felt peace flood my being, and excitement about a new life ahead with Jesus in charge rather than me in charge.

> JESUS'S PROVISION OF SALVATION TO ALL MANKIND BECAME AVAILABLE AS A RESULT OF HIS DEATH AND RESURRECTION.

Jesus's provision of salvation to all mankind became available as a result of His death and resurrection. Within days of Jesus's resurrection, He appeared to the disciples behind closed doors and breathed upon them, saying, *"Receive the Holy Spirit"* (John 20:22). Obviously, they did receive the Holy Spirit, for Jesus now had the authority to release the Spirit into the hearts of all who choose to follow Him. (See John 7:39.)

So at the point of salvation, we are *indwelt* by the Holy Spirit.

SANCTIFICATION: WHEN THE HOLY SPIRIT FILLS ME

As we yield more to God, He is able to fill more.

*If anyone cleanses himself from these things, he will be a **vessel
for honor, sanctified,** useful to the Master, prepared for every
good work.* (2 Timothy 2:21)

As a Christian, I certainly want to be sanctified and useful
to my Master, the Lord Jesus Christ. So how does sanctification
occur? It is accomplished not through the grunting of self-effort,
but by drawing on the power of the indwelling Spirit.

*If **by the Spirit** you are putting to death the deeds of the body,
you will live.* (Romans 8:13)

THE PROCESS OF SANCTIFICATION IS A WORKING OF THE HOLY SPIRIT WITHIN ME.

The process of sanctification is a working of the Holy Spirit
within me. That's a relief because I certainly don't have the power
in my flesh to overcome its sinful tendencies. So instead of battling
them on my own, I see Jesus, who is at my right hand (see Acts
2:25); I thank Him for my new heart and new spirit, and ask Him
to cut out the evil tendencies within me. I invite the Holy Spirit
within to overrule self, the flesh, and demons. I smile and relax as
He does the work that I am unable to accomplish on my own. I
feel an inner peace, an inner strengthening, and an inner miracle
of transformation being performed by the Spirit within. This happens because I set my mind on the Spirit doing the work, not on
my flesh doing the work.

*The mind set on the flesh is death, but the **mind set on the
Spirit** is life and peace.* (Romans 8:6)

*Now may the God of peace Himself **sanctify you entirely;**
and may your spirit and soul and body be preserved complete,
without blame at the coming of our Lord Jesus Christ.*
(1 Thessalonians 5:23)

As I am being sanctified by the Spirit, the Spirit is *filling* me repeatedly as I am learning to yield more fully to His ever-presence. The disciples were filled with the Spirit at Pentecost (Acts 2:1–4), and they were *filled again* in Acts 4:31. So I stay hungry for fillings and even more fillings of the Holy Spirit. Just like I refill a glass with water, so the Holy Spirit can and does refill me. The tense and mood of the Greek in Ephesians 5:18 could be accurately translated as "be being filled with the Holy Spirit"—an ongoing, continuous process.

I learn to yield additional areas of my life to the Spirit and as I do, He fills each area, and I more fully express the fruit of the Spirit. (See Galatians 5:22–23.) What a marvelous life! (See Romans 8:5–11.)

Here are New Testament references to being *filled* with the Spirit:

+ Luke 1:15, 41; 4:1

+ Acts 4:8; 6:3; 9:17; 13:9, 52

+ Ephesians 5:18

I strongly encourage you to look them up and pray over them, asking God for revelation.

"FILL MY CUP, LORD"

An old hymn entitled "Fill My Cup, Lord"[6] is about the Lord filling us up and quenching our thirsty souls. A cup or glass that holds water is a vessel. If my cup has a chunk of heavy wood in it, I can fill it up, but the water sure isn't filling every square inch. If I remove the wood, the vessel can become fuller.

The same is true in my life. If sinful habits are removed, I become *"a vessel for honor, sanctified, useful to the Master, prepared for every good work"* (2 Timothy 2:21). If I stop using self-effort

---

6. Richard Blanchard, "Fill My Cup, Lord" (Word Music, LLC, 1988).

and instead rely on the Spirit to do the work, I am ready for the overflow. (See Titus 3:5.)

HOLY SPIRIT BAPTISM: WHEN THE SPIRIT RESTS ON ME

*You will receive **power** when the Holy Spirit has come **upon** you.*   (Acts 1:8)

*There appeared to them tongues as of fire distributing themselves, and they **rested on** each one of them.*   (Acts 2:3)

This group of disciples in the upper room *had already received the Spirit* in John 20:22. They were already indwelt with the Holy Spirit. However, now they were being filled to overflowing, and so they had all three works of the Holy Spirit manifest within them. The Spirit was *in* them, He was *filling* them, and He was resting *upon* them. Wow! What an amazing way to live: indwelt, filled, and anointed as the Spirit rests upon you.

BAPTIZED

*I baptized you with water; but He will **baptize you with the Holy Spirit**.*   (Mark 1:8)

The Greek word baptize is *baptizō*, which means "to dip repeatedly," "to immerse," or "to overwhelm." So when I am baptized in the Holy Spirit, *I am immersed in Him*, overwhelmed by Him.

> WHEN I AM BAPTIZED IN THE HOLY SPIRIT, I AM IMMERSED IN HIM, OVERWHELMED BY HIM.

WHEN THE SPIRIT RESTS UPON YOU

Amazing things happen when the Spirit rests upon a person:

THE INCARNATION

> *The Holy Spirit will come* **upon** *you, and the power of the Most High will overshadow you; and for that reason the holy Child shall be called the Son of God.*   (Luke 1:35)

ANOINTING TO PREACH AND RELEASE CAPTIVES

> *The Spirit of the Lord is* **upon** *Me, because He anointed Me to preach the gospel to the poor. He has sent Me to proclaim release to the captives, and recovery of sight to the blind, to set free those who are oppressed, to proclaim the favorable year of the Lord.*   (Luke 4:18–19)

CASTING OUT DEMONS

> *If I cast out demons by the Spirit of God, then the kingdom of God has come* **upon** *you.*   (Matthew 12:28)

SPEAKING IN TONGUES

> *While Peter was still speaking these words, the Holy Spirit fell* **upon** *all those who were listening to the message. All the circumcised believers who came with Peter were amazed, because the gift of the Holy Spirit had been poured out on the Gentiles also. For they were hearing them speaking with tongues and exalting God.*   (Acts 10:44–46)

PROPHESYING

> *And when Paul had laid his hands upon them, the Holy Spirit came* **on** *them, and they began speaking with tongues and prophesying.*   (Acts 19:6)

DO YOU EARNESTLY DESIRE MORE OF THE SPIRIT?

Is this not what we hunger for? "Spirit, rest upon me. Move with power and cause the kingdom to come upon those whom I touch." Our heart's cry is, "More, Holy Spirit." This results in continual fillings and overflow so that the atmosphere of heaven surrounds us and whoever comes into our presence is touched by God. Even Peter's shadow brought healing!

*At the hands of the apostles **many signs and wonders were taking place** among the people; and they were all with **one accord** ... multitudes of men and women, were **constantly added** to their number, to such an extent that they even carried the sick out into the streets and laid them on cots and pallets, so that when Peter came by at least **his shadow** might fall on any one of them. Also the people from the cities in the vicinity of Jerusalem were coming together, bringing people who were sick or afflicted with unclean spirits, and **they were all being healed.*** (Acts 5:12, 14–16)

This is what the church is intended to look like! We are to be on the streets, filled to overflowing with the anointing of the Holy Spirit, carrying the atmosphere of heaven with us, and releasing it to those we touch. The Bible says:

Whatever city you enter and they receive you ... heal those in it who are sick, and say to them, "The kingdom of God has come near to you." (Luke 10:8–9)

But if I cast out demons by the finger of God, then the kingdom of God has come upon you. (Luke 11:20)

THE CHURCH AND THE WORLD DESPERATELY NEED TO SEE THE OVERFLOW OF THE HOLY SPIRIT.

The church and the world desperately need to see this again. The overflow of the Spirit will cause the supernatural growth of the kingdom as people are healed, delivered, and set free.

JESUS LIVED BY THE SPIRIT

*Jesus was also baptized, and while He was praying, heaven was opened, and the **Holy Spirit** descended upon Him in bodily form like a dove, and a voice came out of heaven, "You are My beloved Son, in You I am well-pleased."*
(Luke 3:21–22) (See also Matthew 3:16–17; Mark 1:9–11.)

*Jesus, full of the **Holy Spirit**, returned from the Jordan and was led around by the **Spirit** in the wilderness for forty days, being tempted by the devil. … And Jesus returned to Galilee in the power of the **Spirit**.*
(Luke 4:1–2, 14) (See also Mark 1:12.)

*You know of Jesus of Nazareth, how God anointed Him with the **Holy Spirit** and with power, and how He went about doing good and healing all who were oppressed by the devil, for God was with Him.*   (Acts 10:38)

*I can do nothing on My own initiative. As I hear, I judge; and My judgment is just, because I do not seek My own will, but the will of **Him who sent Me**.*
(John 5:30) (See also John 8:28, 42; 12:49; 14:10.)

Since Jesus is my perfect example, I choose to live by the Spirit. I have the Holy Spirit within me, guiding me.

When He, the Spirit of truth, comes, He will guide you into all the truth; for He will not speak on His own initiative, but whatever He hears, He will speak; and He will disclose to you what is to come.   (John 16:13)

OBTAINING THE SPIRIT'S GUIDANCE

The Spirit's guidance is not difficult to obtain. I simply see Jesus at my right side (see Psalm 16:8), ask Him for His input, tune to flowing thoughts, images, and emotions, and honor that the flow that is coming is His divine initiative (the faith in flow principle). The alternative is to picture myself as alone—that is, not with Jesus beside me or in me—and tune to my mental abilities in an effort to try to figure things out. So let me ask you: is it any harder to live out of divine initiative than it is to live the wrong way? Does it take more time? Which way makes more sense? Which way honors Christ?

> SINCE THE HOLY SPIRIT IS ALWAYS WITH US,
> NOT SEEING THIS REALITY IS NOT SEEING TRUTH.

Wrong images cause me to go backward. Since the Holy Spirit is always with us (see John 14:16), not seeing this reality is not seeing truth. Seeing lies simply messes up our life.

[They] *walked in the counsels and in the **imagination of their evil heart**, and **went backward**, and not forward.*
(Jeremiah 7:24 KJV)

Let's remain passionate to hold images of biblical truth in our minds!

REASONING TOGETHER WITH GOD

What happens when I live out of my own reasoning? Several times in the Gospels, Jesus is rebuking someone for reasoning without divine perspective. (See Matthew 16:5–12; Mark 2:5–12; 8:15–18.) Consider Isaiah 55:9: *"For as the heavens are higher than the earth, so are My ways higher than your ways and My thoughts than your thoughts."* Our thoughts are totally different than the Lord's. We must gain God's perspective for our reasoning to be fruitful.

In the Bible, God commands the prophet Isaiah to reason *with* Him, not alone. It's also clear that imagery is a big part of reasoning together with God.

> "Come now, and let us **reason together**," *says the* LORD, *"though your sins are as scarlet, they will be as white as snow; though they are red like crimson, they will be like wool."*
>
> (Isaiah 1:18)

ANOINTED REASON

Luke let God use his mind and his reasoning capacity. Luke's gospel is an example of reasoning together with God. (See Luke 1:1–3; 2 Timothy 3:16–17.) So whenever I reason, I always picture Jesus with me, ask for His input, and let flow guide my reasoning process.

OUR INHERITANCE

God is omnipresent, so He can give His full attention to everyone at the same time. His passion for companionship is revealed in the fact that after creating mankind, He chose to stroll together with them in the garden of Eden in the cool of the day. He desired daily fellowship.

> GOD IS OMNIPRESENT, SO HE CAN GIVE HIS FULL ATTENTION TO EVERYONE ALL AT THE SAME TIME, AND HE DESIRES DAILY FELLOWSHIP.

Jesus was in *constant* contact with His Father. (See John 5:19–20, 30.) Jesus died to restore the experience of Eden to mankind. We are now restored to daily communion with God. Living out of the Father's initiative is our heritage; living in the overflow of the Spirit is our joy.

ACTION EXERCISE

List anything you have learned from this chapter that strikes your heart.

_____

_____

_____

_____

_____

How many of the three works of the Holy Spirit have you experienced?

_____

_____

_____

_____

_____

Meditate on at least five verses from this chapter that are speaking to you. Be prepared to share the revelations you receive with others.

How I Received the Baptism in the Holy Spirit
by Marlene Santefort

I am a denominational girl who has wanted all God has for me. So when I heard of the baptism of the Holy Spirit, watched others who enjoyed this blessing, and saw it in the Bible, I set a day to seek God for this empowering gift. I spent the day reading the Word. Then I decided to ask God for this experience. I was home alone. The Holy Spirit came and filled me up from the bottom of my being to the top with warm liquid love. Then I had a vision of the Bible from beginning to the end. It all flowed together like I had never understood before. I couldn't say how long the vision lasted, but when it finished, I could understand the Bible in a whole new way. It was the history of God and His dealing with His people throughout time. I was very glad and grateful and really knew the love of God for me like never before, one on one. The Bible then came alive to me and became a personal letter to me. I did not manifest tongues or the other gifts at that time.

Later on, at one point at a prayer meeting, I felt my tongue moving in my mouth and went into the washroom to watch it! I didn't know God was trying to give me tongues and I only needed to cooperate by giving it air and sound. I didn't tell anyone and so it stopped. But a year or so later, the tongues came painstakingly slow with only one word. Hallelujah!

One day some time later, my son told me he was going to get married. When he left, I dropped to my knees to pray and my prayer language released and flowed fully and freely. It still does. If I spend enough time praying in tongues, I find it changes to different languages, I can laugh or, more often, cry without being connected to why but trusting the Holy Spirit to give me the prayers He wants prayed through me. And when I pray through, my prayer tends to change to singing in tongues. At times, God the Holy Spirit gives an interpretation, a prophecy, or words of knowledge in a meeting setting. I also found many times as I go into travailing prayer for increased salvations before a meeting I am leading, the number of people who get saved in that meeting is greatly increased.

4

THE OVERFLOW OF THE SPIRIT

JESUS'S BAPTISM IN THE HOLY SPIRIT

*The heavens were opened, and he saw the Spirit of God descending as a dove and **lighting on Him**, and behold, a voice out of the heavens said, "This is My beloved Son, in whom I am well-pleased."* (Matthew 3:16–17)

When the Spirit rested upon Jesus, He heard His Father's voice and was then led by the Holy Spirit into the wilderness to be tempted by the devil. (See Luke 4:1–2.) Jesus overcame the three temptations and returned *"in the power of the Spirit"* (Luke 4:14).

THREE TEMPTATIONS

JESUS OVERCAME THE DESIRES OF THE FLESH

And the tempter came and said to Him, "If You are the Son of God, command that these stones become bread." But He answered and said, "It is written, 'Man shall not live on bread alone, but on every word that proceeds out of the mouth of God.'" (Matthew 4:3–4)

JESUS OVERCAME THE GLAMOUR OF THE WORLD

The devil said to Him, "I will give You all this domain and its glory; for it has been handed over to me, and I give it to whomever I wish. Therefore if You worship before me, it shall all be Yours." Jesus answered him, "It is written, 'You shall worship the Lord your God and serve Him only.'"   (Luke 4:6–8)

JESUS OVERCAME THE DEVIL'S ACCUSATION ABOUT HIS IDENTITY

"If You are the Son of God, throw Yourself down from here; for it is written: 'He will command His angels concerning You to guard You,' and, 'On their hands they will bear You up, so that You will not strike Your foot against a stone.'" And Jesus answered and said to him, "It is said, 'You shall not put the Lord your God to the test.'"   (Luke 4:9–12)

The result of overcoming is receiving the Spirit's power. Jesus was led into the wilderness *full* of the Spirit (see Luke 4:1), but He returned from the wilderness in the *power* of the Spirit (see Luke 4:14), with *authority* (see Luke 4:32) and doing *miracles* (see Luke 4:33–35).

Since I choose to be like Jesus, I will follow His example. I will honor and follow God's leading. I will accept the refining process as God leads me into the wilderness to overcome temptation. I will overcome the glamour of the world, the temptations of my flesh, and Satan's accusation concerning my identity and authority in Christ.

Practically speaking, this means I look into the spiritual realm and honor the flowing images I see. I listen with the ears of my heart and honor the flowing thoughts that light upon me. I feel the emotions deep within, and honor the flow or inner awareness of peace that guides and leads me. (See Philippians 4:7.) I understand that I need to go through a purifying process so I am prepared to be invested with power from Almighty God.

THE BELIEVERS BAPTIZED AT PENTECOST

Let's look at the account of the first group to be baptized in the Holy Spirit.

> *And when the day of Pentecost was fully come, they were all with one accord in one place. And suddenly there came a sound from heaven as of a rushing mighty wind, and it filled all the house where they were sitting. And there appeared unto them cloven tongues like as of fire, and it sat upon each of them. And they were all filled with the Holy Ghost, and began to speak with other tongues, as the Spirit gave them utterance.*
>
> (Acts 2:1–4 KJV)

WHAT CAN WE LEARN FROM THIS STORY?

+ They were obeying Jesus's instructions. (See Acts 1:4–5.)

+ They were in prayer. (See Acts 1:14.)

+ They were with one accord; there was unity.

+ The Holy Spirit came with a sound.

+ The Spirit filled them and the entire room where they were sitting.

+ Tongues of fire were seen resting on each of them.

+ They spoke in tongues and preached with power, and three thousand people were baptized. (See Acts 2:41.)

Some people have suggested that the reason they spoke in tongues was so the gospel could be spread in all the languages of those present for the Jewish Feast of Weeks, which we now celebrate as Pentecost. (See Acts 2:8–11.) However, that is not the case, for when the salvation message was preached, Peter addressed the crowd in *one* language. (See Acts 2:14–36.)

THE VALUE OF SPEAKING IN TONGUES

If tongues was not used to preach the gospel, then what is the value of speaking in tongues?

SPEAKING IN TONGUES IS A WAY FOR OUR SPIRITS TO WORSHIP GOD FREELY, UNHINDERED BY THE LIMITATIONS OF OUR MINDS.

Speaking in tongues is a way for our spirits to worship God freely, unhindered by the limitations of our minds. Our spirits tell of His mighty deeds.

*We hear them in our own tongues speaking of the **mighty deeds of God.*** (Acts 2:11)

When I speak in tongues, my spirit is speaking mysteries to God, and this builds me up.

For one who speaks in a tongue does not speak to men but to God; for no one understands, but in his spirit he speaks mysteries. … One who speaks in a tongue edifies himself.
(1 Corinthians 14:2, 4)

Dr. Carl Peterson, a psychiatrist, conducted research on the relationship between the brain and glossolalia or speaking in tongues. He reported:

A very significant percentage of the central nervous system is directly and indirectly activated in the process of extended verbal and musical prayer over a period of time. This results in a significant release of brain hormones which, in turn, increases the body's general immunity. It is further enhanced through joyful laughter.[7]

---

7. James Bramlett, *The Power: What It Is, How to Get It—Now! How to Release It* (Maitland, FL: Xulon Press, 2003), 40–41.

A 2010 study in the *American Journal of Human Biology* found that being filled with the Holy Spirit and speaking in tongues led to a decrease in cortisol, the fight or flight hormone.[8]

In another study involving nearly 1,000 clergy members of a British evangelical group, researchers found that the 80 percent who practiced glossolalia had greater emotional stability and less neuroticism.[9]

WE GET TO JOIN THE HOLY SPIRIT PARTY

The apostles at Pentecost were so under the influence of the Holy Spirit, they were accused of drunkenness. (See Acts 2:13.) Similarly, we are encouraged:

> Do not get drunk with wine, for that is dissipation, but **be filled with the Spirit**, speaking to one another in psalms and hymns and spiritual songs, singing and **making melody** with your heart to the Lord; **always giving thanks** for all things in the name of our Lord Jesus Christ to God, even the Father.
> (Ephesians 5:18–20)

Sure sounds like a party lifestyle: singing, making melody, always thankful. No wonder people at revivalist services cry, "More, Lord!" in their passion for more of the Holy Spirit.

FIVE HEART POSTURES TO PREPARE US TO RECEIVE

Throughout this book, we are sharing testimonies of how people received the baptism in the Holy Spirit. Most of the people say that Holy Spirit baptism was harder than it needed to be, and had they been taught better, they could have received it much earlier.

---

8. Christopher Dana Lynn et al., "Salivary Alpha-Amylase and Cortisol Among Pentecostals on a Worship and Nonworship Day," *American Journal of Human Biology*, Sept. 28, 2010 (www.ncbi.nlm.nih.gov/pmc/articles/PMC3609410).
9. Leslie J. Francis and Mandy Robbins, "Personality and Glossolalia: A Study Among Male Evangelical Clergy," *Pastoral Psychology*, May 2003 (link.springer.com/article/10.1023/A:1023618715407).

Below is a summary of the five heart attitudes that we need to make this simple and easy. Let's explore them.

1. BELIEVE

We must believe that speaking in tongues and the other manifestations of the Spirit are for today, are valuable, and are available to us.

> He who comes to God **must believe** that He is and that He is a rewarder of those who seek him.   (Hebrews 11:6)

> Does He who provides you with the Spirit and works miracles among you, do it by the works of the Law, or by **hearing with faith?**   (Galatians 3:5)

> But having the same spirit of faith, according to what is written, "I believed, therefore I spoke," **we also believe,** therefore we also speak.   (2 Corinthians 4:13)

2. DESIRE

Earnest desire for spiritual gifts is placed within us by the Holy Spirit. We need to honor and act on this inner passion. God's Spirit rides on the wave of intense emotion and, in this case, the emotion is earnest desire. We must *earnestly desire* the manifestation of speaking in tongues, knowing it is a gift from God that allows our spirit to speak mysteries directly to God, edifying or building us up. (See 1 Corinthians 14:2, 4.) *"If I pray in a tongue, my spirit prays, but my mind is unfruitful"* (1 Corinthians 14:14).

3. ASK

We need to ask in faith for the baptism in the Holy Spirit and gift of speaking in tongues. We have not because we ask not. (See John 16:24; James 4:2.)

4. BE OF ONE ACCORD

The greatest commandment is to *love* God, others, and self. In Acts 2:1, the apostles were of one mind, one accord, and one passion. The Bible teaches that faith is energized by love. (See Galatians 5:6.) Love is the switch that turns on Spirit power. Jesus said, "*Whenever you **stand praying, forgive,** if you have anything against anyone*" (Mark 11:25). The clear implication is that anger, unforgiveness, bitterness, and judgment cut off the flow of God's power, thus hindering my prayer from releasing results. Jesus, moved by compassion, healed. (See Matthew 14:14.)

Spirit power flows where there is love and compassion. I need to love God, myself, and others. God said to me, "My anointing does not flow on the waves of anger or hatred. My anointing flows on the carrier wave of love. What you love, you will have an anointing for." Psalm 133 says unity releases God's anointing.

5. YIELD

The Spirit fills that which I yield to Him. Jesus had the Spirit *without measure.* (See John 3:34.) Jesus said:

> I do **nothing on My own initiative**, but I speak these things as the Father taught Me. And He who sent Me is with Me; He has **not left Me alone**, for I **always do** the things that are pleasing to Him.   (John 8:28–29)

Doing anything on my own initiative is self-reliance, self-dependence, and a dead work. The *first* foundation doctrine that I must learn if I want a Spirit-anointed lifestyle is that I must *stop doing dead works.* (See Hebrews 6:1–2.) As I die to self-initiated behavior, self-dependence, and trusting in my own abilities, the anointing of the Spirit flows. The flesh accomplishes *nothing.* (See John 6:63.) "*We are the true circumcision, **who worship in the Spirit of God** and glory in Christ Jesus and **put no confidence in the flesh***" (Philippians 3:3). I come alive to the revelation that "*in Him we live* *and move and exist"* (Acts 17:28). I learn to sense, trust, and live by the Spirit. (See Galatians 5:25.)

ROADBLOCKS TO BAPTISM IN THE HOLY SPIRIT

Below are the traits necessary to receive the baptism, in contrast to the roadblocks that hinder us from receiving.

Requirement	Thoughts that must be taken captive. (See 2 Corinthians 10:3–5)
Believe	I don't believe this is for me or that the sounds I'm making are actually tongues.
Desire	The Spirit would be nice to have, but I'm not going to get unduly fanatical about it.
Ask	If God wants to give it to me, He will, but I'm not going to pursue it.
Love	Discord, anger, and judgment toward self, others, and God for perceived wrongs.
Yield	I'm afraid to give up self-control and self-effort and trust Spirit flow. (See John 7:37–39.)

YIELDING SELF-CONTROL TO SPIRIT CONTROL

When we yield to the Holy Spirit, the anointing can flow. When I yield any outer faculty to the flow of the indwelling Spirit of God, that faculty, at that moment in time, becomes a manifestation of the Holy Spirit.

WHEN I YIELD MY...

+ *Vocal cords*, I begin speaking in tongues, uttering syllables from the Spirit.

+ *Lips*, I manifest interpretation of tongues and prophecy.

+ *Mind*, I experience words of wisdom and words of knowledge.

- *Heart,* I experience faith, discerning of spirits, and gifts of healings.
- *Hands,* I experience miracles as the power of God flows through them.
- *Eyes,* I see in the spirit world, visions and dreams, and share what I see.
- *Flesh,* the law of the Spirit of life breaks the power of sin in my life. (See Romans 8:2.)
- *Emotions,* I experience kingdom emotions of love, joy, peace, compassion, thankfulness, and gratitude.

"*Yield yourselves unto God*" (Romans 6:13 KJV). *Thayer's* Greek definition of this word "yield" (Strong's #G3936) is "to present, to place a person or thing at one's disposal." Jesus *yielded His will* to the Father's; as a result, He was able to release God's judgments.

> I can do nothing on My own initiative. As I hear, I judge; and **My judgment is just**, because **I do not seek My own will**, but the will of Him who sent Me. (John 5:30)

> WHEN WE YIELD OURSELVES TO GOD,
> WE BECOME HIS INSTRUMENTS WHOM HE USES WITH KINGDOM
> ANOINTING, RELEASING HEAVEN TO EARTH.

When we yield ourselves to God, we become His instruments whom He uses with kingdom anointing, releasing heaven to earth.

YIELDING TO SPEAK IN TONGUES

If I want to speak in tongues, I need to yield my tongue from my mind's control to the Spirit's control. This means *I speak*, but do not consciously form the syllables. Rather, I tune to flow, with my eyes fixed on Jesus, and speak, honoring the sounds that emerge as coming from the river of the Spirit, which flows from the throne, to my belly, and then out through my lips. (See Ezekiel 47:1–12; John 7:37–39; Revelation 22:1–2.) We want our being, our vessel, to be filled to overflowing by the Holy Spirit.

Let's return to our earlier illustration of a cup that contains a heavy block of wood. It cannot hold a lot of water like that. In order to really fill up the cup properly and completely, we need to remove the block of wood.

That block of wood is the stumbling block that Satan put in our lives when he tempted Adam and Eve in the garden. His temptation was, *"You will be like God, knowing good and evil"* (Genesis 3:5). Satan was suggesting that rather than spending time in fellowship with God daily, allowing Him to share His wisdom, insight, love, and knowledge, they could choose to trust *self* to arrive at truth through their own mental reasoning. By stepping from divine initiative (God revealing) to self-initiative (man deciding), they stepped from supernatural empowerment to self-effort. They stepped from God to man, from glory to disarray, from power to weakness. So self-effort and man's logic became their prisons, walling them off from Spirit power.

In the baptism of the Holy Spirit, we are stepping back into God's original design. We are once again entrusting ourselves to Spirit flow and heavenly wisdom!

> ### IN THE BAPTISM OF THE HOLY SPIRIT, WE ARE STEPPING BACK INTO GOD'S ORIGINAL DESIGN, ENTRUSTING OURSELVES TO SPIRIT FLOW AND HEAVENLY WISDOM.

Jesus, the second Adam (see 1 Corinthians 15:45), reversed what the first Adam had done. Jesus renounced Satan's lie of self-effort (humanism) and of the value of man's unanointed reason (rationalism) as two false gods that He was unwilling to serve.

Jesus said, *"I do nothing on My own initiative"* (John 8:28; see also John 5:19, 30; 8:42; 10:18; 12:49; 14:10). That's *seven times*

Jesus repeats that He doesn't do things on His own initiative, but at the behest of His Father! It makes me think He is really trying to make a point concerning how we are to live.

My schools, colleges, and churches taught me to rely on my own initiative, use my mind, and determine what I am going to say and do. You know, it is going to be pretty hard for the Spirit to give me the gift of tongues if I will not release control of my tongue from my mind to the Spirit Who is flowing out from my innermost being.

HAVING FAITH IN FLOW

No one ever suggested to me that I should have faith in flow. The flow, of course, is the river within. (See John 7:37–39.) Faith is what enables me to receive things from God. (See Hebrews 11:6.) So I must yield self-control of my tongue, my mind, my strength, my everything, to Spirit-control of my tongue, my mind, my strength, and my everything. As I do, I discover that I begin manifesting the ninefold manifestation of the Spirit. I break free from the lie of Satan, who said I can't trust in God being good. (See Genesis 3:3–5.)

God's wise, compassionate words of counsel release me from the strongholds of fear, doubt, and unbelief that I have built up in my mind. I have a new mind, a mind that believes more in the presence and power of the Spirit and in the goodness of God than it believes in self-effort and mental control. I have taken a big step of faith. I have chosen to step out on the water and believe the Spirit will hold me up.

We are going to talk a lot more about doing this as we go along, so let's just settle it now. If you want to be baptized in the Holy Spirit and speak in tongues, you need to believe God is here and present. He loves you and He wants you to receive the baptism in the Spirit and the manifestation of speaking in tongues. You decide that you earnestly want this and are passionate to have it. Be willing to set aside your self-control, reason, and logic to receive the power, wisdom, and revelation of Almighty God.

> BE WILLING TO SET ASIDE YOUR SELF-CONTROL, REASON, AND LOGIC TO RECEIVE THE POWER, WISDOM, AND REVELATION OF ALMIGHTY GOD.

If you are ready, go for it now. Receive the baptism in the Spirit by believing, asking, earnestly desiring, loving, and yielding yourself, especially your tongue. Walk out on the water; speak without forming the syllables with your conscious mind, and trust that the Spirit is forming them into a language. He is!

SOME THINGS THAT ASSIST IN RECEIVING THE SPIRIT

+ Have someone pray and lay hands on you.
+ Be in an atmosphere of praise and worship.
+ Lift up your eyes to the heavens, and see Jesus seated on the throne with multitudes of angels worshipping before Him. Enter in and worship along with this heavenly host.

When my native language runs out of words and my spirit wants to say more, I just let syllables flow and continue speaking. I am no longer consciously controlling the sounds. I am simply speaking any flowing syllables, trusting that they are coming from the river within, the Holy Spirit. I believe the flow I experience within is the river flowing. I see the river flowing. I tune to the river within. I speak words that come from flow.

AM I SUPPOSED TO EXPERIENCE STRONG EMOTIONS?

Those wired for strong emotions and prepared to freely express them will probably have a strong emotional response. Those who are not so wired or not free to express emotions may notice little occurring emotionally. It makes no difference. Step forward in faith. Speak, believe, and receive.

THE THEOLOGY OF HOW A MIRACLE OCCURS

A miracle occurs when I do my part and God does His part. When Peter walked on the water, Peter did the walking, and the Spirit kept his feet on top of the water. If Peter had not walked, there would have been no miracle. As applied to speaking in tongues, *I speak* but I trust the *Spirit forms the syllables*, so I don't control the formation of the sounds with my conscious mind.

+ **My part:** *And they were all filled with the Holy Spirit and began to speak with other tongues …*

+ **The Spirit's part:** *as the Spirit was giving them utterance.* (See Acts 2:4.)

Obviously for the miracle of speaking in tongues to occur, I need to *believe* it is possible and valuable, and have enough *emotional intensity* to break through the *hardwired* responses of self-dependence and self-reliance. I then *yield* by simply speaking syllables that flow unpremeditated. (See John 7:37–39.) As I do this, I have stepped into *a new level of faith, obedience, and release* of the Holy Spirit.

Our tongue, our most unruly member (see James 3:6, 8), is now under Spirit control. Rather than quenching the Spirit with negative speech, my tongue is now glorifying God.

> *Rejoice always; pray without ceasing; in everything give thanks.… **Do not quench the Spirit;** do not despise prophetic utterances.* (1 Thessalonians 5:16–20)

In Acts, prophecy and tongues flowed together when the Spirit came upon people.

When Paul had laid his hands upon them, the Holy Spirit came on them, and they began speaking with tongues and prophesying. (Act 19:6)

HOW DO I KNOW IF I AM BAPTIZED IN THE HOLY SPIRIT?

As you may recall, I mentioned that Patti and I set aside a day of fasting, and drove a few hours to a Spirit-filled church that was willing to pray for us to receive it. They prayed, we believed, Patti spoke in tongues … and I felt nothing and did not receive the gift of tongues. I had no idea why I hadn't received. I believed, I asked, I fasted, I had hands laid on me, yet nothing happened as far as I could discern.

A week or two later, I was sitting in my living room rocker, meditating on Acts 2:4 and wondering why I had not received the gift of tongues. The Lord showed me that the *disciples spoke* and the *Spirit gave the utterance* (i.e. the syllables). I thought, *You mean I have to do the speaking and just not form the syllables myself?* So I tried that with great timidity. Sure enough, I began uttering sounds that my mind wasn't controlling. But was it tongues? I didn't know. There were no overwhelming emotions, probably because I was anti-emotion at that time in my life. (I had cut emotions off as being soulish.) Over the next weeks and months, a newness of spiritual life flowed within me as I continued to speak in tongues and doubt was replaced by faith.

So when was I baptized in the Holy Spirit? Was it when I prayed, asking and believing, and had hands laid on me, or was it a week later alone in my living room rocker?

Some may say, "You received it when you asked for it." The Bible says in 1 John 5:14–15 that we have what we ask for, as long as we are asking according to God's will. We know it is Jesus's mission to baptize us in the Holy Spirit as all four Gospels clearly state that Jesus came to baptize us in the Holy Spirit! (See Matthew

3:11; Mark 1:8; Luke 3:16; John 1:33.) Therefore, when we ask, don't we receive the baptism even if we don't sense or feel anything or speak in tongues?

> CHRISTIANITY IS A HEART AND SPIRIT ENCOUNTER WITH JESUS CHRIST THROUGH THE HOLY SPIRIT, WHICH RESULTS IN PERSONAL TRANSFORMATION.

I agree that when we ask in faith, according to His will, we receive. However, I also believe Christianity is more than a cogitative lineal system of rules. It is a heart and spirit encounter with Jesus Christ through the Holy Spirit, which results in personal transformation. So if I am not changed then I am not comfortable to simply relegate Christianity to a set of mechanical laws. I expect transformation!

WHEN DID I RECEIVE THE HOLY SPIRIT BAPTISM?

I'm still not sure when I received the baptism in the Holy Spirit—and I wonder if I *need* to know the answer. It strikes me that the more important question is, "Am I continuously pressing in for more of the release of the Holy Spirit through my life? Am I learning to yield, believe, and step out on the water, trusting His power will hold me up?"

I believe we need to believe, ask in faith, earnestly desire, experience love, and yield. I think the point I yielded was when I chose to articulate syllables that I no longer controlled with my mind, but trusted they were being formed and guided by the flow of the Holy Spirit within me. That yielding was a step of faith, obedience, and trusting that as I walked out on the water, speaking sounds I did not control with my mind, they would not be baby talk but would be a language given by the Holy Spirit. My faith was rewarded. I was worshipping God in the language of His choosing.

Journaling: Asking the Lord

Lord, when did I actually receive the baptism in the Holy Spirit?

Mark, you receive My Spirit when you ask for it. This occurs at salvation, at the baptism in the Holy Spirit and at any filling. You ask, you yield, you receive. Receiving is always *jurisdictional*, and *becomes operational as you yield, in faith*, believing that all that I am is now inside you, filling you and clothing you.

As you put on Christ, in faith, you operationally experience My provisions and blessings. Faith is the key that opens up the door to the operation of the gifts (manifestation) of the Spirit. Faith and knowledge work together. As you know what is available to you, you choose to *believe* it and step forward in faith acting on your newfound knowledge. *Now* it is *yours*! It is yours as you ask in faith believing, and step out in faith receiving.

So yes, all receive theoretically when they ask, but it is the *unpacking* of it, or the acting upon it in faith, that benefits you and sets you free, releasing the captives. For yes, you were held captive by your mind. Now, by praying with the Spirit (see 1 Corinthians 14:15), you are free to worship in spirit and truth. Your heart and spirit worship, unhindered by the confines of your mind. (See 1 Corinthians 14:1–4.) So indeed you have been released from captivity and entered into a new freedom in the Spirit.

So ask, believe, yield, receive, and step forth in faith, manifesting that which I have said is *yours*, and your joy will be made complete!

Lord, is this like salvation? I receive oh-so-much at salvation, but understand oh-so-little, so the outworkings of salvation trickle out little by little as I go along, understand more, and step out in faith to experience more.

Yes, Mark, it is exactly the same. All is available immediately, but it takes a lifetime to work it all out.

DID YOU UNPACK YOUR CHRISTMAS GIFTS LAST YEAR?

Let's say you are given this amazing sixty-inch flat-screen TV for Christmas. You are so excited, you tell everybody about it. They ask how you like it. You tell them you have not yet unpacked it. Then the question becomes, how valuable is that gift to you before you decide to unpack and learn to use it? How much does it benefit you while it is still in the box? How much do you really appreciate it?

The same is true with receiving the gift of the Holy Spirit. We received it when we asked for it. However, if we never unwrapped it and began releasing the Spirit's manifestation into our lives, exactly how valuable is it to us? Since Christianity is more than a theory or a theology, let's get stuff unpacked and begin enjoying all of the manifestations of the Holy Spirit.

I Didn't Know I Had to Speak by Diana Meyers

I was so hungry for more of God, I started going to a tent revival where they were praying for people to receive the manifestation. I was excited but also a little apprehensive, but I went up and they prayed for me. Nothing happened, so they kept praying for me but no one told me I had to speak. I was a baby Christian so I had no idea I was supposed to speak. I went home discouraged. I asked God to show me why I didn't receive and a few days later, I was invited to a church service where people were baptized in the Spirit. So I went and was told that when I heard a syllable in my mind, to speak it. I did, and I received. It wasn't difficult and it has been wonderful to speak in tongues. So as you hear syllables, speak each one and you will receive supernaturally.

GIVE YOUR MIND A JOB

I don't want you to struggle with doubt when you begin speaking in tongues like I did. I want you to confidently step out in faith that the Spirit is guiding the sounds you are making. So let me share a secret that has helped countless seekers shorten the awkward phase as they began speaking in tongues: give your mind something to do that *facilitates* the process, rather than sitting *in judgment* of it.

> GIVE YOUR MIND SOMETHING TO DO THAT FACILITATES THE PROCESS OF SPEAKING IN TONGUES, RATHER THAN SITTING IN JUDGMENT OF IT.

I tell my mind, "You *do not need to judge each syllable* to try to determine if it is a language or not"—not that my mind even has the ability to perform such a function! "Instead, I want you to picture the throne room as John did in Revelation 4, and see the multitude worshipping before God's throne, and then picture yourself entering in with them to worship the King of Kings."

By doing that, my mind is now *facilitating* worship in tongues, and the flow of tongues expands more quickly and easily. Try this for several days and see where it takes you. Start by worshipping in your native language; partway through, while your eyes are fixed on the throne room scene, and your heart is bursting with joy, gratitude, and love for Jesus, switch over to speaking syllables that are not controlled by your mind, but simply flowing.

Are you ready? Go for it!

ACTION EXERCISE

Jot down any new insights from this chapter.

_____

_____

_____

_____

_____

Review and memorize the five ingredients necessary to receive the baptism and filling of the Spirit (believe, earnestly desire, ask, love, yield).

Have you received the baptism in the Holy Spirit? Have you believed, earnestly desired, asked, and then stepped out in faith to operate any of the ninefold manifestation of the Spirit? Do you want to now? Are you ready to? Take the time now to pray and ask for the baptism in the Holy Spirit and the gift of speaking in tongues. Get into a quiet place. Using your *sanctified imagination*, picture the worship going on in heaven's throne room. You may want to first read Revelation 4. Join in with all of the heavenly hosts and worship in English for a bit. Feel your heart fill with *love and gratitude* for all Jesus has done for you. With your eyes fixed on Jesus in the throne room, picture yourself as *a child* with a *big smile* on your face and continue worshipping Him, speaking aloud. Stop forming the syllables with your mind, and let any sound that comes just tumble out. *Don't judge it.* Have faith in flow. *Keep your eyes on Jesus*, feel gratitude and speak whatever is coming. You will be speaking in tongues. If you don't speak, you don't receive, *so speak!*

Do this daily for a couple of weeks and see where it takes you. I believe you will be thrilled and impressed. It is just this easy. *Do not make it hard.* It must be easy enough for children to do, so remain childlike, and keep picturing yourself as a child.

It is also appropriate to have someone lay hands on you and pray for you to receive the baptism in the Holy Spirit and the gift of tongues.

How I Received the Baptism in the Holy Spirit
by Michelle Simons

I became a Christian in the 1980s when people in our area (Ottawa, Ontario) were just beginning to talk more seriously about the Holy Spirit. My mother, who had a Catholic background, and I, age sixteen, were attending a small Anglican church. One of the landmark books that everyone was reading was *The Holy Spirt and You* by Dennis and Rita Bennett.

My mother very much wanted to receive the gift of tongues. She prayed about it quite a lot. She had laying on of hands for the gift as well. One morning, she woke up and her tongue felt funny. She felt that something was up. On another day, the same thing happened. When she did her morning devotions, she would often light a candle. On this day, she was unable to blow out the candle when she had finished praying. Sensing it was the Lord asking her to continue, she kept on praying and it was then that she began to speak in tongues.

Meanwhile, I had my own but very different journey. I picked up the book *The Holy Spirit and You*, which had been left on the coffee table, opened it randomly and read a page. I thought, *That's interesting*, and put it down. Later on when I was praying in my room, I thought, *I should try that*. I began to speak in tongues immediately and have ever since.

I have often chuckled at the difference in my own and my mother's story that happened around the same time. One story is filled with heartfelt intercession, numb tongues, and candles not blowing out. The other story is a simple childlike assumption and a thought of, *I should try that.* I love the gifts that God gives and I love the variety of ways that He gives them.

5

BACK TO EDEN:
RESTORING GOD'S SUPER TO OUR NATURAL

by Charity Kayembe

You will receive power when the Holy Spirit has come upon you; and you shall be My witnesses. (Acts 1:8)

Even though we haven't actually been there, I think we all agree the garden of Eden was a pretty awesome place to live. Everything about it was good, amazing and glory-filled in every way.

Adam and Eve experienced what it felt like to live fearless, shameless, sinless, fully loved, and freely loving. Of course, the best part by far was the intimate communion and unbroken fellowship they had with God. They lived naturally to the supernatural realm, doing life together with their heavenly Father.

In Eden, Adam and Eve had supernatural eyesight. They were created in God's image and He is Spirit. (See John 4:24.) So as spirit beings, they interacted with God easily, walking and talking with Him in the cool of the day. They also effortlessly engaged other spirit beings, such as in that long-ranging conversation with the devil, who is a fallen angel. (See Genesis 3:1–5.)

That is why I find it so interesting that they were tempted by the words *"your eyes will be opened"* (Genesis 3:5) when you eat the forbidden fruit. From what we read in Scripture, their eyes were already wide open! They are interacting with spiritual beings in the spirit realm—angels and God Himself—so their eyes were *already* open to see and hear in the supernatural realm, naturally and easily.

When they sinned, the Bible says, *"The eyes of both of them were opened"* (Genesis 3:7), but what were they opened to? What they saw, which they had not been aware of before, was their humanity, their nakedness, and their physical bodies.

> AS SOON AS ADAM AND EVE'S EYES WERE OPENED TO THE NATURAL WORLD, IT WAS AS IF THEY WERE SIMULTANEOUSLY CLOSED TO THE SPIRITUAL WORLD.

As soon as their eyes were opened to the natural world, it was as if they were simultaneously closed to the spiritual world. They didn't talk with angels, fallen or otherwise, and they didn't enjoy fellowshipping with God in the garden anymore either. They had been effortlessly living in a world where the spiritual and physical coexisted beautifully and perfectly, but all of a sudden, the supernatural dimension became closed off to them.

THE SECOND ADAM

Thankfully, the story doesn't end there! We can fast forward through the timeline of history and find the one other person in Scripture who had a similar long-ranging conversation with the devil, just like Eve had: Jesus Christ.

We all know about Jesus's temptation in the wilderness. His whole back and forth conversation with the devil was basically a repeat of the temptation in the garden of Eden. But how could Jesus see Satan so well? Nobody had seen into the spiritual world like that since Adam and Eve cut themselves off from the super-natural realm by choosing self and sin over the Spirit.

To find our answer, we must look at what happened right before Jesus's interaction with the devil. What happened that sensitized Him to the spiritual dimension? What made it possible for Jesus to see into the supernatural world?

He was baptized in the Holy Spirit.

This is a powerful revelation that sets a precedent and example for us to follow. Whatever happened to Jesus when the Holy Spirit baptized Him is what we, too, can expect to happen in our own lives when the Holy Spirit baptizes us. Let's explore Scripture to discover the exciting potentials and prophetic takeaways for us.

> *Immediately coming up out of the water,* [Jesus] *saw the heavens opening, and the Spirit like a dove descending upon Him; and a voice came out of the heavens: "You are My beloved Son, in You I am well-pleased." Immediately the Spirit impelled Him to go out into the wilderness.*　　　(Mark 1:10–12)

Three specific things happened when the Holy Spirit baptized Jesus. First, He saw the heavens open and the Spirit descending. This is actually the first record we have in Scripture of Jesus seeing anything from heaven. Second, Jesus heard a voice come from heaven. This is the first record we have in Scripture of Jesus hearing from heaven. Third, because Jesus is seeing into heaven and hearing from heaven, it is very easy for Him to now be led by heaven. That is, He was immediately led by the Spirit to go to the wilderness. Again, this is the first time we have a record anywhere in Scripture of Jesus being led by the Spirit to do anything.

HOLY SPIRIT BAPTISM EMPOWERED JESUS TO BE ABLE TO SEE INTO
HEAVEN, HEAR FROM HEAVEN, AND THUS BE LED BY HEAVEN,
LIVING AND WALKING BY THE SPIRIT.

Holy Spirit baptism empowered Jesus to be able to see into heaven, hear from heaven, and be led by heaven, living and walking by the Spirit. This is relevant and revolutionary to us because those same three empowerments are available to us when we are baptized by the Holy Spirit.

Jesus is our example and we are expected to model His ministry and do even greater works. If we have any chance of seeing that happen, we would do well to model His preparation for ministry too. And what happened before Jesus ever performed His first miracle? What was Jesus waiting for before He ever preached His first sermon? He was waiting to be baptized in the Holy Spirit.

We know everything hinged on that epic moment of anointing and equipping because Jesus emptied Himself of divine power and walked as a man on earth, demonstrating to us how humanity, anointed by divinity, could live. (See Philippians 2:5–8.) We learn through His experience what Holy Spirit baptism can do for us as well.

SPIRIT REALM SENSITIVITY

As believers in Jesus and anointed by the Holy Spirit, we are able to see and hear in the Spirit. We can now perceive the initiatives of heaven and be led moment by moment by the Holy Spirit's inner guidance. Just like Jesus, we understand that being baptized by the Holy Spirit sensitizes us to the spirit realm all around us. This baptism makes us aware of the spiritual realm that permeates this physical realm.

Sometimes we might be tempted to imagine heaven is a couple billion light-years away, far off in a distant galaxy somewhere. But Jesus said, *"The kingdom of heaven is at hand"* (Matthew 10:7), *"The kingdom of God has come near to you"* (Luke 10:9), and *"Behold, the kingdom of God is within you"* (Luke 17:21 kjv).

I'm not sure how many other ways Jesus could tell us, "It's here! It's now! Live into heaven and live out of it." Just like magnetic fields, radio waves, and Wi-Fi signals, it is invisible. Obviously we know that just because we can't see any of those things doesn't mean they aren't there, surrounding us all the time, literally permeating our atmosphere. And so it is with heaven.

The spiritual realm of the kingdom of God is *right here*, all around us. The supernatural infuses the natural. *"Christ is all and in all"* and *"in Him, all things hold together"* (Colossians 1:17; 3:11). Indeed, we live, move, and exist *in God*, which makes Him pretty close. If we reach out for Him, we will find Him because He is not far from any one of us. (See Acts 17:27–28.)

RECOVERY OF SIGHT

To make this concept more relatable, we can imagine it like night vision goggles, which enable you to see things that would otherwise remain hidden. That is what Holy Spirit baptism did for Jesus. It reversed what happened in Eden, when the eyes of Adam and Eve were closed to the spirit realm. Now through the Holy Spirit, the eyes of Jesus's heart were opened and He could see clearly into the supernatural world.

How do we know for sure that the spirit world was now accessible and visible to Him? Because Jesus then proceeded to have His long back and forth conversation with the devil, who is a spiritual being. (See Matthew 4:1–11.) Afterward, angels ministered to Him. (See also Mark 1:13.)

After Jesus was baptized in the Holy Spirit, He became aware of the heavens opening, His Father's voice, a fallen angel, and faithful angels. It is almost as if a switch was flipped as the eyes of His heart were enlightened and He was now able to see clearly what had been there all along.

Of course, we know that all of this was what He had been waiting for because immediately afterward, He launched His ministry. We're back to the garden of Eden! We're connected to the spiritual dimension of heaven again! And this is exactly what Jesus tells us in the very next verses, essentially saying, "Game on, guys! Seeing and hearing into the supernatural realm? Living and walking by the Spirit? That can only mean one thing: *The kingdom of God is at hand!*" (See Mark 1:15.)

Then for three years, Jesus went around doing good and healing all who were oppressed by the devil because the Father had anointed Him with the Holy Spirit and power. (See Acts 10:38.) Jesus taught, delivered, and performed all manner of signs and wonders because God was with Him.

Now let's fast forward again, this time toward the end of Jesus's life on earth.

LUKE PART TWO

We know that Luke the Physician wrote the gospel of Luke. What is not quite as obvious is that he also wrote the book of Acts. In our canonical record we have Matthew, Mark, Luke, John, and then Acts. However, if we remove the gospel of John, it is easy to see how the last chapter of Luke dovetails seamlessly with the first chapter of Acts. Just look how closely the language mirrors itself.

In Luke 24:47–49, we find Jesus mentioning three specific things:

*That repentance for forgiveness of sins would be proclaimed in His name to all the nations, beginning from **Jerusalem**. You are **witnesses** of these things. And behold, I am sending forth the promise of My Father upon you; but you are to stay in the city until you are clothed with **power** from on high.*

First, Jesus speaks of *Jerusalem*. Then He calls His disciples *witnesses*. Lastly, Jesus lets them know how they can continue to be His witnesses: by waiting until they receive the Father's promise of Holy Spirit baptism, which will clothe them with supernatural power.

We find all three of these concepts clearly stated again in Acts 1:8. Jesus told His disciples:

> *You will receive* **power** *when the Holy Spirit has come upon you; and you shall be My* **witnesses** *both in* **Jerusalem***, and in all Judea and Samaria, and even to the remotest part of the earth.*

Here we see the same three ideas from Luke 24: Jerusalem, Holy Spirit power, and witnessing. This shows the continuous stream of thought and flow of the storyline. We see how important these concepts were to Jesus and Luke and why they both repeated themselves to make sure we didn't miss it.

But I'm getting ahead of myself. First, we need to look at Acts 1:1, which is itself an extraordinary passage. I think all too often, we have overlooked what God is seeking to communicate through this loaded Scripture. To our detriment, we read right past the incredible potential and promise hidden within.

> *In my former book, Theophilus, I wrote about all that Jesus began to do and to teach until the day he was taken up to heaven.*   (Acts 1:1–2 NIV)

Did you catch that? The gospel of Luke was not about *all* of Jesus's ministry; it was simply the *very beginning* of Jesus's ministry. Luke's former book was all that Jesus *began* to do and teach, until He was taken to heaven. The point is clear: Jesus has not stopped being about the Father's business. He is *still* teaching. He is *still* touching lives and bringing freedom. Jesus's ministry didn't end just because He went to heaven. He is still actively engaged in our lives and our world every single day.

> JESUS HAS NOT STOPPED BEING ABOUT THE FATHER'S BUSINESS.
> HE IS STILL TEACHING, TOUCHING LIVES, AND BRINGING FREEDOM.

We know that Jesus only did what He saw the Father doing and He only spoke what He heard the Holy Spirit saying. We want to follow Jesus's example and do nothing on our initiative, but only what we see Jesus Himself doing. Jesus called the disciples with a simple, "Follow Me" and that has not changed. Today His invitation to us is the same. Jesus still says, "Follow Me."

WITNESSING JESUS

But Jesus has gone to heaven. How can we follow Him now? It was easy for Peter and John; they saw Jesus every day. They listened to Him share the parables of the kingdom. They watched Him set the captives free and witnessed His ministry of miracles and healing daily. But what about us? How are we supposed to see Jesus in order to follow Him? How can we be His witnesses today?

Jesus knew we would have this question and provided the answer before we even asked:

> *You will receive power when the Holy Spirit has come upon you; and you shall be My witnesses both in Jerusalem, and in all Judea and Samaria, and even to the remotest part of the earth.*   (Acts 1:8)

Because of the Holy Spirit's baptism, "*you shall be My witnesses.*" Basically, Jesus is saying that because of the Holy Spirit's baptism, you can *continue* to be My witnesses, you can *continue* to watch what I do and hear what I teach, "*both in Jerusalem, and in all Judea and Samaria, and even to the remotest part of the earth.*"

Up until now, the disciples had been observing Jesus in the natural as He lived on earth. Here, Jesus is letting them know that they can continue to observe His life and ministry in the spiritual realm, as He continues His life in heaven.

WHAT WOULD JESUS DO?

It has been popular to ask the question, "What would Jesus do?" While it is good to consider a Christ-like response to situations that arise, the misunderstanding inherent in that question is the unspoken phrase "if He were here." The underlying assumption is that Jesus is *not here*. However, Jesus is God and God is omnipresent. We know that Jesus most certainly *is* here, as He promised He would never leave us or forsake us. (See Hebrews 13:5.)

The confusion comes because Jesus said He was going away and would send another to us. We understand that the Holy Spirit is to be our Comforter and Teacher and He is with us now. Jesus did go away to the grave, but then He came back. He appeared to the disciples and ascended to heaven. And heaven is not far off—it is near, at hand, and in our midst. As a man on earth, Jesus could only live with us; as the Spirit of Christ, He actually lives in us. Jesus is closer to us now than He's ever been!

> WHEN WE RECEIVE THE HOLY SPIRIT'S BAPTISM, HE OPENS THE EYES
> OF OUR HEART TO THE SUPERNATURAL REALM OF HEAVEN,
> AND WE SEE JESUS IS STILL WITH US.

We often mistakenly see it as an even exchange: Jesus left and the Holy Spirit came to take His place. However, a more accurate way to picture it is like a three-for-one special. When we receive the Holy Spirit's baptism, He opens the eyes of our heart to the supernatural realm of heaven, and we see Jesus is still with us. He's right here, at our right hand! (See Acts 2:25.) And Father God is here too! He's not an absent Father. He is the involved, compassionate, doting Father who always has His loving gaze upon us. Jesus, the Holy Spirit, and the Father are always right here with us and we have never been alone.

While it may have seemed that Father God was far off, that Jesus just came and went, and that only the Holy Spirit came to stay, we see a much more empowering reality unfolding. All of them are here. They have always been here with us. They will always continue to be with us. It is only that we have been blinded to their presence. The Holy Spirit's baptism opens our spiritual eyes to the spiritual realm of heaven that has come near us, and the reality of our spiritual Father in whom we actively, presently, live with and exist in.

A BETTER QUESTION

What does this have to do with releasing spiritual gifts? A lot. Let's return to the question, "What would Jesus do?" In the Bible, we learn that Jesus healed every single person who came to Him for help. So we could try to figure it out independently with our own minds based on our own memorized knowledge of Scripture and say, "Jesus would heal."

But that still begs the question, *how* would Jesus heal? How does Jesus want to heal the broken person standing in front of us? Does He want to lay His hands on them? Does He want to cast a demon out of them? Does He want to spit in the ground and smear some mud on them? If we rely only on our memorized biblical knowledge and our best educated guess and ask, "What would Jesus do?" we're stuck. We have no idea what He would do!

Instead, a better question would be, *What IS Jesus doing?* Right now, in heaven, what is He doing? This question allows us to continue to remain dependent on His leading. We continue to simply be His witnesses and follow Him. We continue to listen as

He teaches and observe as He ministers. And just as Jesus only did what He saw the Father do, we too will act only and exclusively on the initiatives of heaven.

As we say what we hear the Father saying, we release words of wisdom and knowledge. As we do what we see Jesus doing, we release healing and miracles. As we speak what we hear the Holy Spirit speaking, we release tongues and the interpretation of tongues. We understand then that observing the spirit realm is the most effective way to release the gifts of the Spirit. And the way we observe and see in the spirit is through Holy Spirit baptism.

SUPERNATURAL SCIENCE

Let's explore some of the fascinating ways quantum physics correlates with Holy Spirit baptism and how to more effectively release His supernatural gifts through our lives and into the world.

In physics, the observer effect is the theory that merely observing some thing or situation changes it. For example, physicists have discovered that an electron exists as a wave of energy until it is observed. Once observed, it collapses into a particle of matter. Observing changes the wave of *invisible potential* into a particle of *visible reality*. The act of observing collapses all possibilities distributed along the wave and it's now manifested and locked into a specific place and time as a single electron or photon, the stuff that makes up matter and light. This phenomenon is called *wave function collapse*.

> WITH THE BAPTISM OF THE HOLY SPIRIT, WE CAN OBSERVE THE GLORY OF HEAVEN AND COLLAPSE THAT POTENTIAL TO RELEASE SPIRITUAL GIFTS AND BLESSINGS ON EARTH.

For our purposes, we can define collapse to mean that we are bringing what is unseen into the seen realm, making what is invisible visible, and moving what exists in the supernatural world into our natural world. In the same way, with the baptism of the Holy Spirit, we are releasing spiritual gifts and blessings into our physical atmosphere, collapsing the glory and bringing heaven to earth.

WORLD OF FAITH

The quantum realm is one of potential, where any possible outcome is available at every moment in time. That's actually how physicists define the quantum dimension.

That sounds familiar! That is the world of faith, where all things are possible for those who believe (see Mark 9:23) and nothing is impossible with God (see Matthew 19:26). We know that God already gave us everything when He gave us Christ. Jesus is our Healer, our Provider, and our Peace. It's all in Him and it's all ours, available right now. We have already been given all things for life. (See 2 Peter 1:3.) We have already been blessed *"with every spiritual blessing in the heavenly places"* (Ephesians 1:3).

It's great we have the blessings in heavenly places, but we want them here in earthly places as well! How do we get that? Through the observer effect. Hebrews 11:3 speaks to this understanding of wave function collapse when it says that *"we understand ... that what is seen was not made out of things which are visible."* What is seen—matter, particles, and this natural world—is made out of what is unseen: waves of potential energy in the invisible spirit realm.

So we see that wave function collapse is a picture in the natural world of what happens when we pray. In the realm of the Spirit, every possibility is available to us in Christ, including healing, provision, and divine perspective. But we want to bring those heavenly resources into our physical dimension. We want these infinite possibilities of blessing in the Spirit to collapse and materialize in our tangible world.

Through our practiced observation and vision, these heavenly waves of glory collapse into a definite manifested miracle, a *particle* of healing or blessing, something that is concrete and available in our localized dimension of time and space. All we need to do is collapse these promised resources and gifts of the kingdom into our everyday lives.

A REAL LIFE EXAMPLE

One of my graduate students is a medical missionary overseas. She had given a little girl all the medicine she had available, yet the child only continued to grow weaker. Having done all she could in the natural, she sent the two-year-old home with her family. And then she prayed.

In a vision, she saw Jesus go to the girl's home, lay His hands upon her, and heal her. She was in the Spirit with Jesus and prayed into that vision, agreeing with what Jesus was doing and speaking life over the little girl.

She became the quantum observer of Jesus and collapsed that visionary wave of potential healing from heaven into the physical world. Her visual agreement with the spirit realm became a bridge for the supernatural blessing to cross and become manifest as a miracle in the natural world.

The next day, she called to check on the girl and confirmed that at the very hour she had been with the Lord and the girl in Spirit, she was healed. She had suddenly awakened, jumped out of bed full of energy, and had been playing with the other children ever since. It was an instantaneous miracle and they were so grateful to have their little girl back!

In this way, we see the observer effect in action and how when we observe something, we change it. My student saw the wave of glory and changed it so it was no longer just a potential reality in heaven, but now it collapsed into a manifested reality on earth. Observation caused transformation.

ANOINTED TO BE OBSERVERS

Let's look again at how Jesus Himself actually called us to be His witnesses or observers. After Jesus died, was buried, resurrected, and then came back to earth, He gave some final instructions to His disciples. Right before He ascended to heaven, He told them to wait for the promise of the Father. We know the very last thing someone tells us right before they leave is often the most important. The last thing Jesus told His apostles was not to leave Jerusalem until they had been baptized with the Holy Spirit, when they would receive power to be His witnesses. (See Acts 1:1–8.)

Normally, we Christians understand witnessing to be something we do with our mouths; yet everyone else knows it is something we do with our eyes. If we witness a crime or accident, we might be asked to appear in court to tell everyone what we observed. First and foremost, in order to be a witness, we must be an observer and a seer.

> JESUS TAUGHT US THAT THE BAPTISM OF THE HOLY SPIRIT OPENS THE EYES OF OUR HEARTS TO THE SUPERNATURAL WORLD THAT IS ALL AROUND US.

Jesus taught us that the baptism of the Holy Spirit opens the eyes of our hearts to the supernatural world that is all around us. It unlocks the spiritual dimension to us, so we have the power to see the spirit realm that permeates and infuses the physical realm. The Holy Spirit anoints us to observe the kingdom of heaven that is so close, it's within us. (See Luke 17:21.)

We know this is how Jesus lived. He said He did nothing on His own, only what He saw the Father do. So for us to model Jesus, we need to be able to see what He and the Father are doing, and hear what the Holy Spirit is saying. Right now, we're real-time witnesses and present-tense observers of the activity of heaven; that's what Jesus was talking about in Acts 1:8.

This is the kind of witness the apostle Paul was. We recall that Paul did not come to faith in Christ until after Jesus had already ascended to heaven. He became a disciple of Jesus and saw the Lord in the same way that we do: through vision with the eyes of our hearts and not in the natural realm with our physical eyes. (See Acts 9:3–8.)

In recounting his dramatic conversion experience, Paul shares the prophetic word Ananias gave him:

> He said, "The God of our fathers has appointed you to know His will and to **see the Righteous One** and to hear an utterance from His mouth. For **you will be a witness** for Him to all men of what you have **seen** and heard." (Acts 22:14–15)

Paul was a seer and an observer of Jesus; he was that kind of witness. We can be that kind of witness of Jesus, too.

THE SECRET

Holy Spirit baptism enables us to fix our eyes on Jesus. (See Hebrews 12:2.) It allows us to set our mind on the Spirit (see Romans 8:5–6) and equips us to look at the eternal things that are unseen (see 2 Corinthians 4:18). We receive power when the Holy Spirit has come upon us to be Jesus's witnesses—seers, lookers, watchers, and observers of Jesus. Jesus wants a witness to His life, the one He's living right now.

Now we understand that when we see the potential God is showing us through our visions by day and our dreams by night, we create a visual agreement. This agreement is a bridge upon which these promises of heaven can cross. However, they remain in a spiritual state of possibility until someone on earth sees what God has made available, until someone observes it.

When we see snapshots of the Spirit, we are able to agree with them, releasing God's blessing into our lives as manifested miracles.

We release the revelation and resources of the kingdom into our world: collapsing the invisible into the visible, collapsing the unseen into the seen, collapsing the glory and bringing heaven to earth.

SCRIPTURAL QUANTUM OBSERVERS

JACOB AND HIS STRIPED FLOCKS

There is a fascinating dream saga in the Old Testament that illustrates these principles. Remember the story of Jacob and his striped and speckled sheep? His father-in-law, Laban, was taking advantage of Jacob and kept changing his wages. An angel came to Jacob in a dream and told him what to do about it. He instructed Jacob that when the strongest, healthiest animals of the flock mated, he should put striped branches by the watering troughs in front of them. (See Genesis 30–31.)

Jacob acted on the revelation from his dream. The surprising result was that when the strong sheep *looked upon* the striped branches, they produced striped offspring. The best of the animals became striped just like the branches they *observed*. Laban had agreed that Jacob could have all the striped sheep for himself so this was how God provided a strong, healthy flock for Jacob's own possession.

The observer effect is at work here even with animals and because of it, Jacob *"became exceedingly prosperous"* (Genesis 30:43). We see then how God has created this as a universal principle. Like the law of sowing and reaping, it works all the time for everyone. Incredibly, the flock collapsed what they observed and created what they were seeing. And if this principle works for sheep, it can certainly work for you too!

ABRAHAM SAW A FAMILY

What about some other biblical stories where seeing and observing proved crucial in releasing God's promises and collapsing them into the world? Consider Abraham, our father of faith. He had no children but God told him to change his focus and provided a new picture for him to meditate on and observe.

> ABRAHAM HAD NO CHILDREN BUT GOD TOLD HIM
> TO CHANGE HIS FOCUS AND PROVIDED A NEW PICTURE FOR HIM TO
> MEDITATE ON AND OBSERVE.

Before changing his name to Abraham (see Genesis 17:5), God told Abram he would be the father of a multitude and gave him an image of his promised future: stars in the sky and sand on the seashore. (See also Genesis 22:17.)

> [God] *took him outside and said, "Now* **look toward the** **heavens**, *and count the stars, if you are able to count them." And He said to him, "So shall your descendants be." Then he believed in the* Lord; *and He reckoned it to him as righteousness.* (Genesis 15:5–6)

That picture created faith in Abraham's heart. He saw what God was seeing, the end from the beginning. (See Isaiah 46:10.) He saw God's promise fulfilled, a son born, and descendants without number. Abraham observed the vision God gave him and collapsed the promised blessing of Isaac into his life.

JOSHUA COLLAPSED JERICHO

Joshua is another excellent example of the observer effect in the life of a biblical hero. Most of us know the story of how the enemy stronghold came crashing down after the Hebrew army marched around it seven times. But something important happened even before they began their march that precipitated the miracle.

The Lord told Joshua, "*See, I have given Jericho into your hand, with its king and the valiant warriors*" (Joshua 6:2).

At that point in time, Jericho, the king, and its warriors had *not* been given into Joshua's hand in the natural realm—but God told him to *see* it. In effect, God told Joshua, "Envision it all in your hands as already done. Observe how I have already given it, in the spiritual realm, into your hands."

Joshua obediently observed the potential and possibility, that image God gave him. And just as quantum scientific principles would predict, he *collapsed* that image into reality! Joshua collapsed greatness, glory, and God's promises when the walls of Jericho literally collapsed and fell down. This is a perfect picture of the observer effect in action, demonstrating how when we observe the Spirit-inspired potentials of heaven, we collapse those prophetic possibilities into actualized realities in our physical world.

JESUS OBSERVED HEAVEN

We also see this example demonstrated in the life of Jesus when He fed the multitudes of men, women, and children. Scripture says thousands were hungry, and there were only a few loaves of bread and some fish. We know that the food was multiplied, but there were critical steps of progression in that miracle that we can learn from and model.

Jesus didn't look at the *need*, or consider anything lacking; He wasn't consumed with this natural world and its version of reality. While the disciples' hearts were troubled because they were looking only at the material realm, Jesus's heart was peaceful and thankful because He was looking at the unseen, heavenly realm.

> *Taking the five loaves and the two fish and **looking up to heaven**, he gave thanks and broke them. Then he gave them to the disciples to distribute to the people.*   (Luke 9:16 NIV)

When Jesus received the loaves of bread and the fish, He first looked into heaven, where there is no lack, no hunger, and no need.

So Jesus saw the truth that abundance and provision were available and there was more than enough.

The second step Jesus took was to thank the Father. Jesus agreed with the vision and was grateful for the provision, even before the provision was manifest.

The third and final step in the progression of this miracle was that Jesus gave the food to the disciples, who passed it out to the multitudes. We see then that the food was not multiplied before He thanked Father for it; it was multiplied afterward. Again, to use quantum scientific terms, Jesus observed the potential provision of heaven, thereby collapsing those resources into this world.

> WHEN WE ENVISION WHAT THE FATHER HAS PROVIDED FOR US,
> OUR HEARTS ARE FILLED WITH KINGDOM EMOTIONS
> OF PEACE AND GRATITUDE.

This is a key principle for us. We can live like Jesus and look to see what the Father has provided for us. When we see that image, our hearts are filled with kingdom emotions of peace and gratitude. We're not stressed out and our hearts aren't troubled because we see the end from the beginning. We see what God sees and we are confident that we already have the requests we have made known to Him. (See 1 John 5:14–15.) We observe God's version of our situation, are grateful for His blessing, collapse that glory into our lives, and bring heaven to earth.

SPIRITUAL PRAYER

Paul tells us that we can pray with our mind *and* our spirit. (See 1 Corinthians 14:14–15.) Our spirit is one with the Holy Spirit. (See 1 Corinthians 6:17.) So we are connecting with the Spirit and allowing Him to pray with and through us. (See Romans 8:26–27.) Wow, talk about supernaturally empowered intercession!

Dr. Steve Greene, executive vice president of Charisma Media, describes these types of Spirit-filled prayers as the Lord's *love language* and explains how praying in the Spirit can bring true intimacy with Him. He writes, "The Holy Spirit brings us a special love language that magnifies our expression of love and ability to communicate with Him."[10] Yes! We want to love God in *His* love language.

Many anointed leaders such as Sid Roth, Mahesh Chavda, and Gloria Copeland testify to praying an hour in the Spirit daily. Bill Johnson shares that he prays in tongues constantly. The apostle Paul thanked God that he prayed in tongues more than everyone around him. (See 1 Corinthians 14:18.)

These heroes of the faith regularly see the gifts of miracles and healing—even resurrections—through their ministries. One important key to unleashing that spiritual power is their faithful preparation and equipping before they ever lay hands on anyone, before they even speak a word of faith. It happens through their lifestyle of consistent *spiritual prayer,* their commitment to always praying in the Spirit.

SACRED SUPERPOWER

We are exhorted to pray in the Spirit at all times, as this kind of prayer gives us a supernatural edge. (See Ephesians 6:18.) It is our sacred superpower. Moreover, we want to combine this spiritual prayer with our spiritual sight. We observe what God is showing us in the spiritual realm while at the same time praying in the Spirit. This supernatural prayer strengthens and supercharges our godly imaginations, energizing our times of meditation with the flow of the Holy Spirit Himself.

---

10. Dr. Steve Greene, "Why You Need to Pray in Tongues More," *Charisma* magazine (www.charismamag.com/spirit/prayer/43592-why-you-need-to-pray-in-tongues-more).

This has become one of my favorite ways to pray with God. After one such time of visionary intercession together, He shared how it works by explaining it to me in this way:

> Thank you for allowing My Spirit to pray through you. The amalgamation of our entangled spirits—Mine in yours and yours in Mine—and what is released through our united *praying in Spirit* is unique. That is, how I am expressed through you, with you, and in you is all distinct to you. My prayers, even by My Spirit through each individual, are unique to each one.
>
> This is one way each one of My children glorifies Me in a way no one else can. It is also a way I can create with each of you in ways no one else can. This is My intention. To co-create with you in visionary prayer as we pray in the Spirit together. Faith is not blind; faith is visionary.
>
> When I pray inside and out through you, that is a profound picture of heaven on earth. You are formed of the earth. My kingdom of heaven is being proclaimed, established, released, and created through My spiritual prayers. And where are those Spirit prayers taking place? In you. In earth. On earth. On earth as it is in heaven.
>
> So you see then how you, one individual, are truly a powerful microcosm of My kingdom. A microcosm of My intention for the world. When you combine that kind of spiritual prayer with practiced observation—focused envisioning and imagination—extraordinary potential and supernatural creative power are released. It's atomic, dynamic, explosive—in a good way! And besides that, it's just something I really enjoy doing together with you....

In Scripture, God speaks to this revelation of united vision and the power of imagination when He says, "*Behold, they are one people ... now nothing which they purpose [have imagined* – KJV] *to do will be impossible for them*" (Genesis 11:6). One of the reasons this principle works so elegantly is because when we see what God sees, we feel what He feels and experience faith and joy. These kingdom emotions displace fear and unbelief, thereby positioning our hearts to become better conduits of the miracles God is seeking to release through us.[11]

BRINGING IT ALL TOGETHER

In summary, we have seen that in the Bible, God often gave His children a glimpse of His perspective. Their practiced observation coupled with faith-filled gratitude, confession, and obedient action collapsed heaven's potential promises and perfect possibilities into their world.

To confess means to *say the same thing as*; specifically, we understand it to mean that we must say the same thing as God. Whatever God's Word says about our health, finances, and relationships is the truth we must speak and declare.

Equally important, though, is for us to also *see* the same thing God sees. God sees the end from the beginning and we must come into alignment and agreement with His vision and version of ourselves. We must observe this sacred reality to collapse its fullness into our hearts and lives.

The baptism of the Holy Spirit empowers us to be witnesses, seers of the spiritual realm and observers of the sacred supernatural world. When we can see what God sees, we will feel what He feels and can thereby pray from a place of peace, hope, and thankfulness.

Through visionary meditation, we create memories of our future. To us, it is future, but when we live to observe the timeless realm of the Spirit, we know that what *will be* is already present in

11. To learn more about kingdom emotions and how to live from God's heart, see: Mark Virkler and Charity Virkler Kayembe, *Unleashing Healing Power Through Spirit-Born Emotions* (Shippensburg, PA: Destiny Image, 2017).

the *eternal now* of God. We can look into the supernatural realm in our meditations with God, observe His perspective of our lives, and collapse His vision and blessing into our situation.

> WHEN WE CAN SEE WHAT GOD SEES, WE WILL FEEL WHAT HE FEELS AND CAN THEREBY PRAY FROM A PLACE OF PEACE, HOPE, AND THANKFULNESS.

Finally, in addition to our practiced observation of the heavenly potentials the Father shows us in the spirit realm, we can *pray in the Spirit* while holding these God-breathed visions in the imagination of our heart. We are seeing what God sees, feeling what He feels, thinking His thoughts, and declaring His truth. Spirit, soul, and body, our triune being, is aligned with the Trinity Himself.

This is the place of miracles, where the manifestation of spiritual gifts and power are released. And it all starts with Holy Spirit baptism. His anointing takes us back to Eden, where we are once again able to hear from heaven. His empowering enables us to once again see in the Spirit. And once our spiritual senses are awakened and our awareness of the supernatural dimension is restored, we happily find that it is possible to live and walk by the Spirit, releasing His life every day, in every area of our lives.

ACTION EXERCISE

Is there an area of your life where you are struggling to see the same thing God sees? Quiet down into your heart and ask the Lord for His point of view on your situation. How does He see your finances? What does He say about your health? What is His perspective on your relationships? Ask the Holy Spirit to give you a picture of His version of the situation.

Repent for imagining anything that doesn't line up with God's will and word for your life. Purpose in your heart by His grace and Spirit's power to look only at His vision of your life, agreeing to only see and imagine what God sees and says. Let His word be the final word!

Infuse your meditation with supernatural power by continually praying in the Spirit.

With your godly imagination, envision what He says as true and see yourself financially prosperous, physically healed, with loving and peaceful relationships. Experience the faith, relief, joy, and thankfulness that come from feeling that your prayer has already been answered. Observe God's vision for your life, and with a grateful heart, collapse His prophetic promises and blessings into your world.

How I Received the Baptism in the Holy Spirit
by Kim Ulmer

I had been spiritually hungry for a while and the teachings and home prayer participation sparked something within me. One night, at the end of the meeting, the Lord laid it upon the pastor's heart to pray for me. They put me in the chair, gathered around me and began to pray in general for me. Suddenly, the Spirit of the Lord poured into me at such a tangible rate that I was gasping just to breathe. The pastor, who happened to be Spirit-filled, began to speak in tongues. It was the first time I had heard tongues, but my spirit recognized it for what it was. Suddenly, I had an unction to prophesy in English. I knew in my spirit, as did the others in the group, that I was interpreting the tongue being spoken, and it was a corporate message for the body of Christ.

That baptism powerfully changed me. Scripture I had read countless times before suddenly became alive and fresh in my heart. Suddenly, I could hear God so much clearer than before; it was like a radio antennae being adjusted within my being. I desired to speak in tongues and exercise the other spiritual gifts as well.

A few weeks later, a Spirit-filled minister visiting from Wales came to our church and prayed for the spiritual gifts to be released. I received in faith and told the Lord, "I want it all, everything that You want to give." Although I didn't have any major unction to speak in tongues, I believed and felt that I was simply to just open my mouth and speak out, trusting in the Spirit. What came out was only a few syllables, and at first, I thought I might have just made it up. But when I repeated the same exact phrase the next day, I became convinced. After that, I began to speak in tongues regularly as well as develop other spiritual gifts.

My personal takeaway is to be awestruck by our amazing God and how He never does the *cookie-cutter* thing. He knows what each of His children need. Just as the Holy Spirit poured out on the Gentiles in Acts 10:44–48 and they spoke in tongues before they were water baptized, my own experience of interpreting a prophetic message in tongues before speaking in tongues just underscores how unique and fascinating our personal relationship with the Lord is.

6

THE NINEFOLD MANIFESTATION

Now concerning spiritual [pneumatikos] ***gifts***, *brethren, I*
do not want you to be unaware.
—1 Corinthians 12:1

What does the Greek word *pneumatikos*, translated "spiritual gifts," actually mean? In the above verse, the word *gifts* is *not* in the Greek. That is why the KJV, NKJV, and NASB, among other translations, put the word *gifts* in italics, a lighter color, or both. So the verse correctly reads, *"Now concerning spirituals…"*

Pneumatikos (*Strong's* G4152) literally means "belonging to the Divine Spirit."

So the meaning of 1 Corinthians 12:1 is, "Now concerning the things which belong to the Spirit."

The nine things in the list that follows are *nine ways the Holy Spirit can and does manifest Himself.* Those who are tuned to the Spirit are considered spiritual since they release this ninefold manifestation.

The ninefold manifestation of the Spirit releases the power, anointing, and wisdom of God into a situation. This results in the *kingdom of God being made manifest.* Jesus said, *"If I cast out demons by the Spirit of God, then the **kingdom of God has come upon you"** (Matthew 12:28). The world today needs to see God's kingdom.

We decree, *"Thy kingdom come"* (Matthew 6:10 KJV) and watch as what we see in the heavenlies is released on earth!

PRECISE DEFINITIONS ARE PRICELESS

I love the precision of my car's GPS system. I can put a specific address into it and it offers me the best, safest, and quickest route to get to my destination.

Anytime I can precisely define a destination or goal, I can go after it. Without a clearly defined goal, I won't know the clearest, simplest route to get there and I probably won't even be aware that I have arrived!

For example, I hungered for ten years wanting to hear God's voice, but had never defined His voice as spontaneous, flowing thoughts. So I was actually hearing God's voice but just not aware I had arrived at my destination because I had no clear definition of what His voice sounds like, nor did I have a clear roadmap to get me there.

Now I have a roadmap that involves quieting my analytical reasoning, picturing Jesus at my right side, tuning to flowing thoughts, and writing them down. I test what I have written with Scripture and with my spiritual advisors. With this clearly described goal and excellent roadmap, I can hear God's voice easily every day. I get to live as Adam did, walking and talking with God in the cool of the day.

Now I can say with certainty, "I am living the verse, *'My sheep hear My voice'"* (John 10:27). I am also able to use biblical terminology to describe my experience. So I can confidently say, "I *heard* His voice," rather than just saying, "I had a thought." I have taken another step forward in my Christian life. I am living one more verse of Scripture.

PRECISE DEFINITIONS APPLIED TO THE NINEFOLD MANIFESTATION OF THE SPIRIT

Let's take the ninefold manifestation of the Spirit and apply the above process of creating a clear roadmap to a precisely defined goal.

> I BELIEVE A SPIRIT-FILLED CHRISTIAN WHO LIVES BY THE SPIRIT IS RELEASING THE NINEFOLD MANIFESTATION OF THE INDWELLING SPIRIT BUT SIMPLY MAY NOT RECOGNIZE THAT FACT.

I believe a Spirit-filled Christian who lives by the Spirit *is* releasing the ninefold manifestation of the indwelling Spirit but simply may not recognize that fact nor do they call their experiences by their 1 Corinthians 12 names.

The following chart provides precise definitions of each manifestation and how we prepare to release the Spirit. Our goal is to give you a clear understanding of how to naturally and normally experience and release the manifestation of the Spirit. Ponder it prayerfully, letting God speak to you. For each of the ninefold manifestation ask, "Lord, when have I experienced this manifestation?"

Notice that for most of them—the exceptions being tongues and interpretation of tongues—other biblical passages refer to the same experience by different names. We have gotten so focused on the list in 1 Corinthians that we limit the manifestation of the Spirit to just those nine things. But I don't believe that was Paul's point in this passage. He wasn't saying that these are the only ways the Spirit shows Himself to us. Instead, they were illustrations of the limitless ways that the One Lord and Spirit might manifest Himself among His people.

Once we see the greatness of the Spirit within us and realize He is constantly equipping us, we become bold world-changers.

DEFINITIONS OF THE NINEFOLD MANIFESTATION		
Precise Definitions of Each Spirit Manifestation	How to Experience This Spirit Manifestation	Other Biblical Names for This Manifestation of the Spirit
Speaking Gifts: *The Spirit communicating freely, edifying, exhorting, and comforting (see 1 Corinthians 14:1–4)* **1. Tongues:** My spirit is speaking a language I didn't learn with my rational mind **2. Interpretation of Tongues:** Interpreting a message given in tongues **3. Prophecy:** God's thoughts for the moment or the future	**I behold Jesus (see Hebrews 12:1–2; Acts 2:25; John 5:19–20, 30); ask for** the Spirit's guidance, tune to the river within, and speak from flow (in my native language or another language). This results in anointed, quickened, impassioned, powerful, authoritative communication. When speaking in tongues, my spirit speaks mysteries to God, glorifies God and this builds me up. (See Acts 2:11; 1 Corinthians 14:1–4.)	Speaking the oracles of God (see Hebrews 5:12); my heart teaching my mouth what to say (this adds persuasiveness to my lips (see Proverbs 16:26); combining spiritual thoughts with spiritual words (see 1 Corinthians 2:13)
Revelation Gifts: *Spirit revealing information and insight on properly utilizing the information* **1. Discerning of Spirits:** Immediate inner awareness of the presence of a spiritual force **2. Word of Wisdom:** A piece of God's wisdom **3. Word of Knowledge:** A piece of God's knowledge	**I behold Jesus (see Hebrews 12:1–2; Acts 2:25; John 5:19–20, 30); ask for** the Spirit's guidance, tune to the river within, and minister from flow. I receive spontaneous, flowing ideas, pictures, emotions and bodily sensations which release to me the knowledge and wisdom of God. This revelation provides insights for effective outcomes.	Mind of Christ (see 1 Corinthians 2:16) Revelation (see 1 Corinthians 14:26); reasoning together with God, anointed reasoning, Spirit-led reasoning, God's thoughts (see Isaiah 1:18; Luke 1:1–3 coupled with 2 Timothy 3:16)

DEFINITIONS OF THE NINEFOLD MANIFESTATION		
Power Gifts: *Spirit's power flowing freely as He deposits faith into one's heart and ministers healing and miracles* **1. Faith:** An instantaneous welling up of faith within me **2. Gifts of Healings:** Wisdom and anointing to provide a specific health remedy **3. Miracles:** An instantaneous release of divine energy producing immediate change	I behold Jesus (see Hebrews 12:1–2; Acts 2:25; John 5:19–20, 30); **ask for** the Spirit's power, tune to the river within and receive spontaneous, flowing energy and faith, which is often accompanied with warmth and tingling in my hands as I lay them on individuals. The result is people being delivered, set free and healed.	A work of power (see 2 Thessalonians 1:11); the kingdom of God coming upon you (see Luke 10:9); casting out demons (see Luke 11:20)

TWO DIFFERENT VOCABULARIES I CAN USE IN DESCRIBING MY EXPERIENCES

If I am a Spirit-filled Christian seeking God continuously, quieting down my independent thoughts, seeing Jesus at my right hand (see Acts 2:25), asking for His input, and tuning to flow, then I *am* releasing the manifestation of the Spirit. He *is* expressing Himself through me. That is what He wants to do and, when I give Him the opportunity, He does it!

> THE SPIRIT WANTS TO EXPRESS HIMSELF THROUGH ME AND WHEN I GIVE HIM THE OPPORTUNITY, HE DOES IT.

There is no need to super-spiritualize the gifts; the Holy Spirit lives in me and will express Himself if I ask Him to.

Rather Than Saying This…	It Is More Biblical to Say This…
I had this great thought.	Lord, thank You for this word of knowledge.
This might be a good solution.	Thank You, Lord, for this word of wisdom.
I sense something is off with this person.	Thank You, Lord, for the discerning of spirits.
I was speaking gibberish.	Thank You, Lord, for the gift of tongues.
I just burst out talking and said…	Thank You, Lord, for this prophecy.
As you were praying in tongues, I had this thought.	Thank You, Lord, for interpretation of tongues.
I felt a wave of faith well up within me.	Thank You, Lord, for the gift of faith.
Here is something you could try to get healed.	Thank You, Lord, for Your gifts of healings.
I felt heat in my hands when I was praying for you.	Thank You, Lord, for the gift of miracles.

*I have been crucified with Christ; and it is no longer I who live, **but Christ lives in me**; and the life which I now live in the flesh I live by faith in the Son of God.*   (Galatians 2:20)

MY AMAZING REALITY IS THAT CHRIST LIVES IN ME

I am always blown away by what God says when I do two-way journaling. He loves me unconditionally, even when I fail by falling into sin. He just washes it away with His blood and is likely to consider it a learning curve mistake that I can grow from.

He believes in me, and tells me how to view and handle each situation I am facing. He believes I have the power and wisdom of the Spirit within me and through the Holy Spirit, I can release the kingdom just as Jesus did. He calls me to peace, belief, love, compassion, and authority. He is at peace with world events. He is convinced that He rules as King of Kings and Lord of Lords.

He calls me to be a world-changer. He wants me to walk on the water, confront the powers that be, minister healing and deliverance, and even raise the dead. I choose to see this as my true reality. I believe it. I speak it. I act on it, lay hands on the sick, and cast out demons. I offer wisdom, counsel, and discernment. As I do, I live in victory and not as a victim. I live as an expression of the Spirit within me.

> WHEN I TUNE TO FLOW, THE RIVER OF GOD RELEASES THE NINEFOLD MANIFESTATION OF THE SPIRIT.

When I tune to flow, the river of God releases the ninefold manifestation of the Spirit. If I am living the lifestyle of intimacy with Jesus, which the Bible calls abiding in Christ (see John 15:1–11) or living by the Spirit (see Galatians 5:25), then the ninefold manifestation of the Holy Spirit is easily, continuously experienced through flowing thoughts, flowing images, flowing emotions, and flowing power. Obviously the flow is from the river of the Holy Spirit within me (see John 7:37–39), which flows from the throne of grace (see Revelation 22).

Flowing thoughts and flowing images provide me with words of wisdom, words of knowledge, tongues, interpretation of tongues, prophecy, and perhaps discerning of spirits. Discernment could also come from peace versus unrest in our spirit.

Flowing energy or power provides me with faith, miracles, and gifts of healings. Gifts of healings could also come through flowing thoughts and images.

Keep it easy! Seeing the operation of the ninefold manifestation of the Holy Spirit this way makes it easy enough for children to release the Spirit.

Lean on the strengths God has built into you. Some see images from the Lord outside their heads and some inside, but that makes no difference. Either way is fine. Some who are extreme feelers will feel discerning of spirits rather than getting a flowing thought or flowing image. That is fine. Since I am a thinker, flowing thoughts are strongest within me. For a visual person, flowing pictures are likely to be strongest within them. And for the feeler, flowing emotions are most likely strongest within them.

> HONOR AND LEAN HEAVILY UPON THE STRENGTHS GOD HAS PUT WITHIN YOU TO RECEIVE HIS GUIDANCE.

I always suggest that you honor and lean more heavily upon the strengths God has put within you. Receive His guidance through those pathways that are strongest within you, whether auditory, visual, or kinesthetic. Jesus was all three: He could hear His Father's voice, see His vision, and be moved by compassion to heal. So I am not going to limit myself to just one of the three. I am going to be like Jesus and press into receiving every way possible.

TAKING THE FASTEST ROUTE

As discussed in chapter two, I believe that two-way journaling using the four keys—quieting yourself down, fixing your eyes on Jesus, tuning to the flow, and writing what you see and hear—is the easiest and fastest way to cultivate an intimate love relationship with Jesus. The eyes, ears, and emotions of your heart are the faculties that allow you to experience flowing thoughts, flowing images, flowing emotions, and flowing power. Hearing God's voice daily and walking daily with Him in the garden was God's original intent, and *is still His intent*. A relationship built on love, intimacy, and faith is what Christian spirituality is all about.

SINCE I AM IN CHRIST, AM I A VICTIM OR A VICTOR?

Jesus was no victim of circumstances. He ministered kingdom authority into each and every situation He encountered. That is different from what I see in much of the church today. I sense the attitude of many is that we as Christians are downtrodden, weak, and unable to stand up to the ever-expanding forces of evil in our world. We tend to believe evil is big and powerful and we are weak and small. We have even found verses that would seem to confirm such a view of reality. The world is getting ever more evil, Satan's kingdom is increasing, and there is nothing we can do about it. Of course, we *help* Satan's kingdom increase by believing for its increase, picturing its increase, and speaking of its increase! I for one sure don't want to help enlarge the kingdom of Satan! I don't think you do either.

When I look at myself, I can see myself and not Christ living my life. (See Galatians 2:20.) If this is the vison I am holding, which of course is a false vision, then yes, I am weak and the forces around me are much more powerful than I. Therefore I will cower in fear. In this case I *see* myself weak. I *believe* I am weak. I *speak* that I am weak and *act* like I am weak. Sure enough, *I am weak.*

I AM JOINED TO CHRIST, A PARTAKER OF THE DIVINE NATURE, COMMISSIONED AND EMPOWERED TO RELEASE GOD'S DOMINION INTO THE WORLD THAT I TOUCH.

But I can change the way I picture myself by seeing that I am joined to Christ (see 1 Corinthians 6:17), a partaker of the divine nature (see 2 Peter 1:4), commissioned and empowered to release God's dominion into the world that I touch (see Mark 16:15–18). If I focus on that image of myself—and believe, speak, and act on that—then I am more than a conqueror! (See Romans 8:37.)

I CHOOSE TO ADOPT A KINGDOM WORLDVIEW

+ **Whose government is ever increasing? God's!** (See Isaiah 9:7.) That means Satan's impact must constantly be decreasing. We simply resist Satan and he flees from us. (See James 4:7.) We command God's kingdom come to earth as it is in heaven, and in doing so, we demolish Satan's kingdom. (See Matthew 6:10.) As we heal the sick and cast out demons, God's kingdom is coming upon us. (See Matthew 12:28.)

+ **Who is defeated? Satan!** (See Ephesians 2:4–7; Colossians 2:15; Hebrews 2:14–15.) So we don't re-empower him by putting misplaced faith in him. We fix our eyes *only* on Jesus and never the antichrist. (See Hebrews 12:1–2.)

+ **Who rules? Almighty God** rules heaven and earth! (See Daniel 4:17.) The heart of the king is in the Lord's hand. (See Proverbs 21:1; Romans 13:1–7.) We pray for those in authority. (See 1 Timothy 2:1–2.)

+ **Who accesses everyone's hearts? God** provides counsel nightly to *all* through our dreams. (See Psalm 16:7; Genesis 41:1.) He speaks into the hearts of everyone nightly, providing wisdom, counsel, protection, and compassion. Do you think that gives God a winning edge? Take the time to learn the biblical art of Christian dream interpretation so you can receive His nightly counsel to you. (*See more in Appendix C, "Dig Deeper with These Links."*)

+ **Who are the New Agers?** People hungering for spiritual reality and not going through our Lord and Savior Jesus Christ to get it. Many of these people could not find spiritual reality in dead churches so they turned to the New Age. I met a man who used to teach Sunday school, but when he incorporated vision into his prayer life and began to teach it to his class, he was removed as a teacher and told to leave the church. Now he is part of the New Age movement because they accept the use of the eyes of one's heart as part of spiritual experience. Providing true supernatural encounters in the Holy Spirit is the church's birthright. The church must not forsake its inheritance by driving hungry people away. *Cults are the unpaid bills of the church.*

+ **What are God's plans toward us?** To prosper us! (See Jeremiah 29:11–12.) And He has promised to work all things out for our good. (See Romans 8:28.)

+ **What are God's exams?** God tests us to see if there is faith in our hearts or if we are still grumblers. (See Deuteronomy 8:2.) *Never* grumble. It is unhealthy in every respect. It is a slap in God's face, saying to Him, "You are not watching out for me, and You are not working all things out for good. You don't really have a good plan for my life. You don't rule."

+ **We pass God's exams by always giving thanks.** We are to give thanks *for* everything (see Ephesians 5:20) and *in* everything (1 Thessalonians 5:18).

+ **We extend mercy, honor, and compassion to *all* people.** Honoring *all* allows us to minister God's grace to all and receive God's grace from all. (See 1 Peter 2:17.) Jesus loved and honored all sinners and everyone was hungry for His touch. Moved by compassion, Jesus healed. (See Matthew 14:14.) Greeting those we meet with respect, a smile, and asking God how we can release His healing grace to each individual is part of the kingdom lifestyle. Loving, touching, healing—that's the example Jesus left us. Honoring and loving displaces the opposite, which is judging and rejecting. We are cautioned not to judge others. (See Matthew 7:1–4; John 8:15; 12:47; Romans 2:16; 14:4, 10, 13; James 4:11–12; 5:9). Satan is the accuser. (See Revelation 12:10.) We are not called to be supporters of Satan's work.

+ **We look for and see the gift in every situation.** We can honor the Baptists for their passion to save the lost and know the Bible. We can honor the Methodists for their passion for holiness and sanctification. We can honor the Pentecostals and Charismatics for their passion for the supernatural power of God. We can honor liturgical churches for their amazing imagery that convinces us once again that "a picture is worth a thousand words." Each group *has a gift* for us to receive if we look for it, and honor it by embracing it. We honor *all* people. (See 1 Peter 2:17.)

> WHEN WE KEEP A KINGDOM WORLDVIEW IN THE FOREFRONT OF OUR THOUGHTS, WE BECOME VESSELS THAT OVERFLOW WITH THE CHARACTER AND POWER OF THE HOLY SPIRIT.

Keeping this kingdom worldview in the forefront of our thoughts will transform every aspect of our lives—our attitude, our health, our relationships, and our words. We will become vessels that overflow with the character and power of the Holy Spirit.

ACTION EXERCISE: TWO-WAY JOURNALING

Lord, am I living in a way that allows You to manifest Yourself through me easily and naturally?

_____

_____

_____

Lord, when have I experienced the ninefold manifestation of the Spirit?

_____

_____

_____

Lord, how do You see this challenging situation that I am currently facing? How do You want me to meet it through the ninefold manifestation of Your Holy Spirit?

_____

_____

_____

Lord, what do You want me to take away from this chapter?

_____

_____

_____

Lord, is there someone to whom You want me to minister by using the ninefold manifestation of the Spirit?

_____

_____

_____

Lord, in what area do You want me to see myself as a victor? Can You show me a vision of what victory looks like for this situation?

_____

_____

_____

Lord, what is Your worldview? Is it different from my worldview?

_____

_____

_____

How I Received the Baptism in the Holy Spirit
by Kelly Haynes

At age twenty, I began actively pursuing the baptism of the Holy Spirit. The experience was happening to my beloved friends as well as many youth group members that I was ministering to at the church I attended at the time but had not happened to me yet. I was really sore about it and began reading every book written about the topic, studied the Scriptures fervently, stood in prayer lines, and talked to my Spirit-filled friends about Him. However, none of those things played a part in the recipe for my receiving the baptism of the Holy Spirit.

One evening, returning home after a Wednesday night church service, I was all alone with the Lord and I began telling Him through tears how sad I was and that I felt so left out and rejected and wondered if there was something wrong with me. As I was talking to Him, I raised my hands to heaven and told Him with an honest and pure heart that I only wanted what He wanted for me—and *bam*!

I could feel His presence throughout my entire being from the top of my head to the tip of my toes. I buzzed, tingled, quivered, trembled, and shook and was filled with overflowing joy and tears and began speaking in tongues immediately praising Him all the while! That was twenty-seven years ago and I am a life forever changed because of walking and talking with the Holy Spirit every day!

I love how personal the Lord is. He didn't want me to follow a recipe or a step-by-step process to receive more of Him; He just wanted my heart to pour out to Him, loving and seeking Him one on one!

7

DO I ONLY GET ONE GIFT OR CAN I HAVE THEM ALL?

MY THESIS

There are three convictions I have come to that I offer for your consideration:

1. The Spirit-baptized believer who has submitted their will to the Lord, who is walking in a close, personal relationship with Jesus and devotes themselves to the Scriptures, *is already* manifesting the Spirit regularly; they simply aren't recognizing it. Just as every follower of Christ *is* hearing His voice but often without distinguishing it from their own thoughts, so those who are walking by the Spirit are expressing Him without being aware of it. (See John 10:27.) *"Christ lives in me"* (Galatians 2:20). *"[I] have the mind of Christ"* (1 Corinthians 2:16). The Holy Spirit has been joined to my spirit. (See 1 Corinthians 6:17.) Unless I suppress Him through sin, doubt, or ignoring Him, He cannot help but be expressed through me. Particularly the revelation gifts (word of wisdom, word of knowledge,

prophecy, discerning of spirits) are flowing within me and will naturally come out.

2. The list in 1 Corinthians 12 is exemplary, not exhaustive. The nine expressions given are only examples of the way the Spirit of God may reveal Himself through His people; they are not the *only* ways He will do so.

3. We can grow in our ability to manifest the Spirit intentionally. By learning to quiet ourselves and listen for the voice of the Spirit within us, we will recognize the initiatives of heaven. As we respond to them, we will display the Spirit in every area of our lives.

WHAT DOES THE WORD "MANIFESTATION" MEAN?

Sometimes these are called gifts, but in 1 Corinthians, they are called manifestation. *"But to each one is given the **manifestation** of the Spirit for the common good"* (1 Corinthians 12:7). The word manifestation in this verse is *singular*, not plural. So it's not nine manifestations; it is a ninefold manifestation, having nine elements or parts.

The Greek word for manifestation is ανερωσις transliterated to *phanerōsis*. The definition is *exhibition, disclosure, coming to light or the way He expresses Himself.* The manifestation of the Spirit is the Spirit disclosing or expressing Himself through us.

> THE MANIFESTATION OF THE SPIRIT IS THE SPIRIT DISCLOSING OR EXPRESSING HIMSELF THROUGH US.

HOW MUCH OF YOU IS MANIFEST?

If you walk into a room, your hands, feet, arms, legs, head, and torso are all manifest or disclosed to those present. They don't just see a foot; they see your entire being.

I believe the same thing is true of the Holy Spirit. Since He indwells, fills, and rests upon you, His ninefold manifestation (and more) shows effortlessly through your being.

JESUS'S EXAMPLE

Since Jesus had laid aside His divine privileges while here on earth (see Philippians 2:5–8), He declared that everything He did was by the Spirit (see John 5:19–20, 30; 8:26, 28–29), which is the same Holy Spirit we have working in us (see John 7:37–39). Note how Jesus manifested the Spirit:

1. Speaking in tongues

Not mentioned one way or the other. However, John does say:

And there are also many other things which Jesus did, which if they were written in detail, I suppose that even the world itself would not contain the books that would be written.

(John 21:25)

2. Interpretation of tongues

See above answer.

3. Prophecy

One of you will betray Me ... he who dipped his hand with Me in the bowl. (Matthew 26:21, 23)

4. Word of knowledge

You have had five husbands, and the one whom you now have is not your husband; this you have said truly. (John 4:18)

5. Word of wisdom

He said to them, "Then render to Caesar the things that are Caesar's; and to God the things that are God's."

(Matthew 22:21)

6. Discerning of spirits

You are of your father the devil. (John 8:44)

Jesus, aware in His spirit that they were reasoning that way within themselves.... (Mark 2:8)

7. Faith

"Rabbi, look, the fig tree which You cursed has withered." And Jesus answered saying to them, "Have faith in God."
(Mark 11:21–22)

8. Healing

He healed them all. (Matthew 12:15)

9. Miracles

And He got up and rebuked the wind and said to the sea, "Hush, be still." And the wind died down and it became perfectly calm. (Mark 4:39)

PAUL DEMONSTRATED THE MANIFESTATION OF THE HOLY SPIRIT

1. Speaking in tongues

I thank God, I speak in tongues more than you all.
(1 Corinthians 14:18)

2. Interpretation of tongues

Therefore let one who speaks in a tongue pray that he may interpret. (1 Corinthians 14:13)

3. Prophecy

There will be no loss of life among you, but only of the ship.
(Acts 27:22)

4. Word of knowledge

A vision appeared to Paul in the night: a man of Macedonia was standing and appealing to him, and saying, "Come over to Macedonia and help us." (Acts 16:9)

This piece of knowledge answered Paul's question, "Where should I go next on my missionary journey?"

5. Word of wisdom

By revelation there was made known to me the mystery…as it has now been revealed…in the Spirit…that the Gentiles are fellow heirs and fellow members of the body, and fellow partakers of the promise in Christ Jesus through the gospel.
(Ephesians 3:3, 5–6)

6. Discerning of spirits

Paul, filled with the Holy Spirit, fixed his gaze on him, and said, "You who are full of all deceit and fraud."
(Acts 13:9–10)

But Paul was greatly annoyed, and turned and said to the spirit, "I command you in the name of Jesus Christ to come out of her!" And it came out at that very moment.
(Acts 16:17–18)

7. Faith

But about midnight Paul and Silas were praying and singing hymns of praise to God, and the prisoners were listening to them; and suddenly there came a great earthquake, so that the foundations of the prison house were shaken; and immediately all the doors were opened and everyone's chains were unfastened.   (Acts 16:25–26)

8. Healing

After this had happened, the rest of the people on the island who had diseases were coming to him and getting cured.
(Acts 28:9)

9. Miracles

The Lord, who was testifying to the word of His grace, [was] granting that signs and wonders be done by their hands.
(Acts 14:3)

AN APPARENT CONTRADICTION IN SCRIPTURE

First, Paul indicates we don't all have all the gifts:

And God has appointed in the church, first apostles, second prophets, third teachers, then miracles, then gifts of healings, helps, administrations, various kinds of tongues. All are not apostles, are they? All are not prophets, are they? All are not teachers, are they? All are not workers of miracles, are they? All do not have gifts of healings, do they? All do not speak with tongues, do they? All do not interpret, do they?
(1 Corinthians 12:28–30)

Paul then indicates we do have at least nine things to offer:

What is the outcome then, brethren? When you assemble, each one has a psalm, has a teaching, has a revelation [which would include a word of wisdom, a word of knowledge, discerning of spirits, and a prophecy], has a tongue, has an interpretation. **Let all things be done for edification.**
(1 Corinthians 14:26)

So which is it, Paul? Do we all have a tongue or don't we? Do we all have a teaching or are not all of us teachers? The solution, "a still more excellent way," is to be motivated by love to edify. (See 1 Corinthians 12:31–13:13.)

In the Great Commission, Jesus tells us we can all release healing and speak in tongues. (See Mark 16:17–18.) Therefore, to suggest that Paul is saying otherwise would create a huge contradiction, especially since Paul himself manifested these gifts.

Paul's stated desire was that we all speak in tongues and prophesy, with the goal that it edify the church. (See 1 Corinthians 14:5.) That is the key: if I am in the *gathered church community*, any gift I manifest *must* be for the *edification* of the church! That is why Paul put the "great love chapter" right in the center of his discussion on manifesting the Spirit. The more excellent way is to let *love* and a *passion to edify* rule as we operate in the manifestation of the Spirit. So even though each of us *can* manifest them all, when we are in the assembly of the gifted, out of love, we prefer one another and allow the Spirit to manifest Himself through the entire body.

I know a person who is a wife, a mother, a nurse, a gourmet chef, a musician, a gardener, a carpenter, a nurturer, a person of faith, a missionary, a leader, and a teacher.

This lady *offers all of who she is* to meet the needs of people she encounters. However, if a group is present with skilled carpenters, doctors, and gardeners, she would not need to provide all of those services herself, but could defer to others, only doing herself whatever would be *edifying* to the group she is with.

> A SPIRIT-FILLED CHRISTIAN CAN EXPRESS THE NINEFOLD MANIFESTATION AS THE NEED ARISES, BUT WHEN IN THE GATHERED CHURCH COMMUNITY, THIS WILL COME THROUGH VARIOUS MEMBERS.

My personal conclusion is that a Spirit-filled Christian can express the whole ninefold manifestation of the Spirit as the need arises, but when in the gathered church community, we will expect that this manifestation will come through the *various members* of the community and not from just one person.

WHAT IS PAUL'S REAL FOCUS HERE?

In 1 Corinthians 12, the words *"same"* and *"one"* are used *eight* times in reference to God. The emphasis is on the fact it is the *same* Spirit doing all these things, not different spirits, as the Corinthian believers would assume, having just come out of paganism. Pagans had a different god for each different thing. Paul says the Corinthians were led astray by *"idols"* in verse 12:2. They worshipped many false gods. Our *one* true God can manifest Himself in many ways. Paul says:

> Now there are varieties of gifts, but the **same** Spirit. And there are varieties of ministries, and the **same** Lord. There are varieties of effects, but the **same** God who works all things in all persons....For to one is given the word of wisdom through the Spirit, and to another the word of knowledge according to the **same** Spirit; to another faith by the **same** Spirit, and to another gifts of healing by the **one** Spirit.... But **one** and the **same** Spirit works all these things, distributing to each one individually just as He wills.
>
> (1 Corinthians 12:4–6, 8–9, 11)

When I repeat the same thing eight times in a row, I am *insistent:* *"Please, get this point!"* The focus of this passage to Paul and to the Corinthians was not on the specific gifts, ministries, or effects, but on the fact that no matter what the manifestation was, they were all revealing the same God. There is only one God who manifests Himself through His people in many different ways. There is not a god of prophecy, a god of tongues, and a god of miracles. There is *one* God who works all things in all people.

> THERE IS ONLY ONE GOD WHO MANIFESTS HIMSELF THROUGH HIS PEOPLE IN MANY DIFFERENT WAYS.

HAVE I FALLEN INTO AN ERROR SIMILAR TO THE CORINTHIANS?

It seems to me that we have been inclined to fall into an error that is not terribly far from the Corinthians. While the contemporary church accepts that there is only one Spirit, we have tended to cut up His manifestation into separate and distinct entities. *You* have the Spirit, but He only expresses Himself through you in one way, with prophecy. *You* have the Spirit who expresses Himself through you with healing.

It seems that Paul's point was that you have the Spirit and He will express Himself through you *just as He wills*—*however He wants to meet the need of the moment.* There is no need to limit how the Spirit will show Himself through you.

SPIRIT FRUIT AND SPIRIT MANIFESTATION

I believe we can all grow in a knowledge and skill in manifesting the Holy Spirit in all the ways mentioned in 1 Corinthians 12:7–11, including tongues, interpretation of tongues, prophecy, discerning of spirits, word of wisdom, word of knowledge, faith, gifts of healings, and miracles. If we accept this vision and press into it, this ninefold manifestation becomes available to us. The roadmap is to believe, earnestly desire, ask, love, and yield.

I also believe I am to express *all nine fruit* of the Spirit. The nine fruit are love, joy, peace, patience, kindness, goodness, faithfulness, gentleness, and temperance. (See Galatians 5:22–23.)

According to the verses that follow this list of fruit, we see that the nine fruit are released in the *same way* the nine gifts are released, which is by yielding from flesh control to Spirit control.

Both fruit and manifestation of the Spirit are released as I rely on the anointing of the Spirit to accomplish rather than the strength of my flesh.

Paul says:

*I have **been crucified** with Christ; and it is no longer I who live, but **Christ lives in me;** and the life which I now live in the flesh I live by faith in the Son of God.*   (Galatians 2:20)

If we live by the Spirit, let us also walk by the Spirit.
                                            (Galatians 5:25)

Crucifying the flesh releases both Spirit fruit and Spirit manifestation.

+ **Spirit *fruit* is released this way**: If I want *God's love*, I don't rely on my ability and try hard to love a difficult person. Instead I say, "God, I know the ability of my flesh is insufficient to love this person, so I turn from my ability to love and I ask that Your love flow through me toward them." I smile and tune to the flow, so I can sense His love flowing within. Then I say, "Thank You, Lord, that You are within me, expressing Your love and overflowing through me. I receive and release Your love toward this person right now."

+ **Spirit *manifestation* is released this way**: If I need *a word of wisdom*, I don't rely on my own ability and try to be clever. Instead I say, "God, I know the ability of my flesh is insufficient to figure this out, so I turn from my mind's ability to reason and I ask that Your wisdom flow through me to handle this situation." I smile and tune to the flow, so I can sense His flowing thoughts within. Then I say, "Thank You, Lord, that

You are within me, and that You have given me the mind of Christ. I receive and release Your wisdom now."

> **BY CRUCIFYING MY SELF-EFFORT AND FIXING MY EYES ON JESUS WHILE ASKING FOR THE SPIRIT TO PROVIDE, THEN TUNING TO THE FLOW, CHRIST IS RELEASED AND I STEP INTO SUPERNATURAL CHRISTIANITY.**

By crucifying my self-effort, a dead work (see Hebrews 6:1), and fixing my eyes on Jesus while asking for the Spirit to provide, then tuning to the flow (see John 7:37–39), *Christ is released* and I step into supernatural Christianity. (See Galatians 2:20.)

To position myself to receive and release the Spirit:

- **I honor the Holy Spirit** (see 1 Thessalonians 5:19) by asking for and acknowledging His presence within and upon me. (See Acts 2:4.)

- **I see Jesus present with me at my right hand.** (See Acts 2:4; Psalm 16:8; Hebrews 12:1–2.) I use my godly imagination and pray that the eyes of my heart be enlightened (Ephesians 1:17–18), tune to the flow, and step into a vision. Living present tense with Jesus is known as "abiding in Christ." (See John 15:1–11.)

- **I tune to flow as I speak and act.** (See John 7:37–39.) Spirit flow can be experienced as flowing thoughts, flowing images, flowing emotions, or flowing physical sensations.

A Personal Example

As a teacher, I begin by asking the Lord to allow me to sense the hearts of those in the room, so I can minister directly to their core needs. I picture Jesus teaching them. What is He saying and doing? What is He addressing? How is He addressing it? I begin teachings and sermons with a corporate prayer to honor the Holy Spirit's presence and invite Him to anoint our hearts to hear what the Spirit is saying, and to anoint all words spoken.

As I preach and teach, I honor Jesus at my right hand by envisioning Him there. I stay tuned to the flow that releases the Holy Spirit within. Ideas light upon my mind. As I speak these, they become words of wisdom and words of knowledge to the listeners, resolving the blocks and questions arising in their hearts. The end result for the listener is enlarged faith and a transformed life.

I call this entire process revelation-based learning and view my main ministry in the body of Christ as that of a prophetic teacher who releases living truth or revelation truth.

WHAT ABOUT AN IMPRESSION?

Some people call God's leading *an impression.* The progression of events could be as follows:

- I receive the stimulus of a spontaneous or flowing idea, image, emotion, or physical sensation, which leaves an impression or effect upon me.
- I could say, "I feel this impression from the Lord," or I could say, "The Lord spoke to me."

Of course, when Jesus spoke, He didn't say, "I have an impression from the Lord," nor did He say, "God said...." Instead, *He just spoke* and the people who heard were amazed at the authority of His teaching. (See Luke 4:32.) I prefer using Jesus's method. Rather than me telling people that what I am speaking is from the Lord, let them tell me that what I just said ministered deeply to them and they feel it was a word from God to them.

MANIFESTATION, GIFT, OR MINISTRY

There is a difference between me having a *manifestation* of the Holy Spirit, a *gift* of the Holy Spirit, and a *ministry* of the Holy Spirit. Note in the verses below the Bible calls *prophecy* a *manifestation*, a *gift*, and a *ministry*.

- *"To each one is given the manifestation of the Spirit ... to another* [is given] *prophecy"* (1 Corinthians 12:7, 10).

- *"We have gifts that differ...each of us is to exercise them accordingly: if prophecy..."* (Romans 12:6).

- *"He gave...some as prophets...for the equipping of the saints"* (Ephesians 4:11–12). This would be the ministry of a prophet as he is equipping or raising up other prophets.

MOVING FROM MANIFESTATION TO GIFT TO MINISTRY

Ministries generally begin as a manifestation, then grow into a gift and ultimately into a ministry.

A MANIFESTATION

Prophecy may be defined as hearing God's voice and speaking it forth. Jesus said, *"My sheep hear My voice"* (John 10:27). However, for the first ten years of my Christian life, I *did not identify* God's voice within me. Not that I didn't hear it, I just didn't identify when I heard it or know how to recognize it on any sort of a regular basis.

For example, late one Saturday night, we were on an expressway near Toronto, driving back to our home in Buffalo. One of the deacons from our church was in the back seat and had a thought come to him to pray for safety as we drove. He put his head down and prayed. At the same time, as I was driving, I had a thought come to me reminding me of an article I had read that drunk drivers are out late Saturday evenings so it is best to beware.

I glanced in my rearview mirror and, sure enough, a car was speeding toward us, swerving all over the road. I slowed down and pulled off to the side. He roared past and sideswiped the car in front of us, spinning around and coming to a stop facing us. Slowly my car approached him and I could see his eyes were red. He was dazed and I surmised he was either intoxicated or high on drugs. His car roared back to life and he made a U-turn, continuing on down the highway at breakneck speed.

Now we could call these just great ideas and an amazing coincidence that we were spared, or we could use the biblical words for what just happened. Our deacon received a word of wisdom that he acted on, I received a word of knowledge that I acted on, and through these, God supernaturally protected us from harm. God allowed us to avoid a calamity through the *manifestation* of the Spirit.

So even though I did not identify the fact that I was manifesting the Spirit in those first ten years, I actually was. I was unaware because I did not have sufficient definition and understanding concerning how one expresses the ninefold manifestation of the Spirit. The Bible says the manifestation is given to *every* person "*for the common good*" (1 Corinthians 12:7).

A GIFT

When I can *intentionally choose* to hear God's voice, I am then operating in a gift. It's not that I am demanding things from God, for He has already chosen to give me the Spirit. In the case of prophecy, I have simply learned how to posture myself so I can hear His voice as needed. Ten years into my Christian life, God revealed to me four keys to hearing His voice: quiet myself down, fix my eyes on Jesus, recognize His voice as flowing thoughts, and write them down. By doing this, I was able to identify His voice every day. Hearing God's voice has changed from a manifestation of the Spirit—an experience without me fully recognizing or understanding it—to a gift that I can operate as often as I choose.

A MINISTRY

At this point in my life, I can *equip others*. I can teach them how to hear God's voice daily and thus to prophesy. I know the four keys to hearing God's voice. I know the blocks that keep people from hearing His voice, and I know how to remove those blocks so they can hear daily. I equip them to walk in the gift of prophecy. This is now my ministry, and in surveyed results, 95 percent of those who have received this training have stated, "I can hear God's voice daily if I choose to."

So I have progressed from not being able to identify how to manifest God's voice to effectively training others to hear God's voice. I believe we all can go through a similar pattern of growth in the ninefold manifestation of the Spirit. (*Also see Appendix B, "Manifestation, Gift, and Ministry."*)

SUMMARY

+ **A Manifestation** (see 1 Corinthians 12:7): If I am a believer, the Holy Spirit is joined to my spirit and I manifest Him frequently, *whether I am aware of it or not.*

+ **A Gift** (see Romans 12:6): When functioning as a gift, I have learned how to quiet down so I can receive and *release the manifestation when necessary.*

+ **A Ministry** (see Ephesians 4:11–12): Now I can *equip others.* I know enough to train others how to operate in a specific gift.

This holds true for all the manifestation of the Spirit. As a believer, the Holy Spirit is one with your spirit and you manifest Him frequently, even if unknowingly. If you pursue the lifestyle of deep intimacy with the Lord and dependence on His initiative, you can learn to quiet yourself to receive any and all of the gifts whenever you need them for yourself or to minister to others. And as you learn and mature, the Lord will lead you to a ministry where you are able to nurture others in their growth in the gifts.

ACTION EXERCISE: TWO-WAY JOURNALING

Lord, how many of the ninefold manifestation have I experienced?

_____

_____

_____

Lord, what are the gifts currently present in my life?

_____

_____

_____

Lord, what is my *ministry?*

_____

_____

_____

Lord, what ideas from this chapter do You want to discuss with me?

_____

_____

_____

Read Ephesians 3:3–21 and 4:11–16. Ask God to give you a revelation of the truths that Paul is expressing concerning Christ in you, the hope of glory. Record what God reveals to you.

_____

_____

_____

Begin stepping out into the revelation gifts.

+ In your morning journaling time, prophesy over your day. Ask the Lord to show you who and what you will encounter and how He wants to respond to each through you.

+ If you know you will be connecting with someone during the day, ask the Lord for something to share with them to encourage, comfort, and build them up.

+ Before your next small group meeting, ask the Lord for a word for the group. Share it with the group leader before the meeting starts. With their confirmation and permission, share it with the group.

How I Received the Baptism in the Holy Spirit
by Anna Gibson

The first evening of the conference, my husband and I met Don and Kay. I heard they led groups in their home. That's what piqued my interest. Saturday morning, we arrived early. When Don and Kay walked in, I inquired about their meetings and how they did that. From that moment, Don gave us a prophetic word from the Lord and we were connected. We had lunch together, then from 4:30 until 11:30 p.m., we were with them. At 10:30, Don asked, "Are you filled with the Holy Spirit?" We said, "Well, yes...." He added, "With the gift of speaking in tongues?" Immediately, we said, "No!" "Oh goodness, no."

That moment opened up questions and I began to shake. I told them that for many years, I felt something in my stomach rise up and flow to my head whenever I prayed, but it was becoming so much more frequent that I was beginning to think I had a disease that would come on if I bowed my head. Don asked me if it made me feel like it just wanted to come out and I said, "Yes! I feel like my brain is going to explode!" He led us to his hotel room and there we yielded to the Holy Spirit and within moments, spiritual beautiful language was flowing from our mouths! The Holy Spirit was finally flowing! What a relief! I felt ten pounds lighter within minutes! How could this be and how can you explain this feeling?

My sweet Jesus brought this illustration to my mind: the Potter and the clay. When you find natural clay to work with, it is suggested to bring it in and dry it so you can smash it and grind it into a smooth powder. At this point, you pour a little water at a time to mix it in. Once you can make ribbons of clay through your fingers when you squeeze it, it is ready to be formed.

Before receiving this gift, I felt like a clay pot that had been formed but set aside and dried. I was thirsty. I was not a good vessel. I could not hold what was being poured into me. The occasional moisture was nice, but I was not where I knew I could be. When we met with Don and Kay, they took us to the Potter's house. My opinions, my analytical self, and my weariness were crushed and refined to powder. Yielding to the Holy Spirit, I felt Him adding water and mixing together my spirit and His. He threw me to the wheel and began spinning! I am refreshed! I am redeemed! I am whole! I have been made into a beautiful vessel! Already the demons are fighting; this is where the fire comes in. Just enough fire, just enough heat, will *bake* me. I will mature the longer I am in the fire/the kiln. I want to be completed in His time!

Had someone taught me earlier, there is no doubt I would have been speaking in tongues way back, at least ten years ago. I thank God for being patient with me. His mercy endures forever! I am His creation! I am proud of it!

8

EVERY GIFT OF THE SPIRIT IN EVERYDAY LIFE

by Charity Kayembe

*A man's gift makes room for him and brings
him before great men.*
—Proverbs 18:16

The gifts of the Spirit are great in the Bible, but what do they actually look like in our lives? When we *do* think of miracles or discerning of spirits happening today, we often tend to relegate them to the extraordinary, happening in *special* church services with *special* Christians.

However, it is not just the prophet and preacher who are anointed by God to demonstrate supernatural gifts. The Holy Spirit is for *everyone*, and all His gifts are available to all His children. Living by the Spirit is every believer's inheritance and it is not as difficult as we may have imagined.

But how do these mystical gifts work outside the four walls of the church, in our normal at-home and on-the-job routines? What does prophecy look like in a business meeting? What does a word of wisdom look like at school? We want to explore what partnering with the Holy Spirit in our everyday world looks like, and, most importantly, how you can do it.

CELLS OF GOD

What is most important for us to understand is that we have a 24/7 connection and communion with the Holy Spirit. We must live out our sacred union moment by moment because that is scriptural truth. (See 1 Corinthians 6:17.)

Imagine asking yourself, "How far away is my hand from me?" or "How distant and separate am I from my leg?" That seems silly because, of course, these are members of your own body. So too are we members of the body of Christ. (See 1 Corinthians 12:27.) *"Your life is hidden with Christ in God"* (Colossians 3:3) and *"in Him we live and move and exist"* (Acts 17:28).

WHEN WE LIVE IN UNION WITH GOD, HIS GIFTS EFFORTLESSLY FLOW.

So we are not seeking some power or gift that is separate from God or from us. We are simply living into our union with the Giver. We live from our oneness with the Holy Spirit and then these *gifts* effortlessly flow. This supernatural manifestation is simply expressions of the Giver Himself, living in and through us, His body. (See Galatians 2:20.)

Like a grown man wearing child's clothes, He overflows us. He's in us *fully* but far exceeds and surpasses us. In fact, He enlarges and expands us. Ephesians 3:19 talks about being *"filled up to all the fullness of God."* He spills out and overflows us as we wear Him, as we *"put on the Lord Jesus Christ"* (Romans 13:14).

God's fullness in us is like a cell of His body. We are partakers of His holy nature. (See 2 Peter 1:4.) We have His identity, the DNA of divinity. (See 1 Peter 1:23.) The fullness of His DNA is in each cell, yet obviously we know that the cell itself is not the fullness of God.

Scripture says we are *members* of Christ's body, so we can easily picture ourselves as *cells* of God. This is why we represent Him best when we come together in unity, joined as one as His body. We are growing up into Him, who is the head; together, we are the most complete representation of God to the world. (See Ephesians 4:13, 15.)

SUPERNATURAL INTIMACY

That is what the gifts of the Spirit are: a manifestation of the Holy Spirit's life through us. When we release His perspective and thoughts, we call it a word of knowledge or prophecy. When we release His heart, we call it a gift of faith or wisdom. When we release His power, we call it the gift of healing or miracles.

As a husband and wife give themselves fully to each other, the miracle of a baby is born. So too, when we give ourselves fully in intimacy to our Heavenly Husband, the Lord, miracles are born. We call these miracles *gifts of the Spirit*. We can almost think of them as the *children* of our union with God, the effortless fruit resulting from our oneness with Him.

It is helpful to picture them in this way because then we readily understand how they are a natural result of our love relationship with Jesus, the easy overflow of His unforced rhythms of grace resonating in our hearts. To release His gifts, we simply live out of our sacred union with the Giver Himself.

We see then how this is all about relationship with the Holy Spirit, which makes it less about *doing* something such as releasing gifts and more about being one with Someone. It's about experiencing God's life within, and sharing the overflow of that supernatural intimacy with those around us.

WORD OF KNOWLEDGE

So what would a day in the life of someone overflowing in the Spirit look like? It would look a lot like the life of a friend of ours, Brian McLaughlin, a high school teacher in a public school system near Knoxville, Tennessee.

My husband and I first met Brian in person when his church hosted our Hearing God Through Your Dreams workshop. We previously had emailed each other a few times regarding some of Brian's amazing visions of the night. Brian had listened through my training CDs several times and was very proficient at decoding his dreams already, but we had fun working together to more fully mine the symbolic revelation hidden within.

> MOST OF THE TIME, DREAMS ARE SYMBOLIC AND METAPHORICAL, BUT GOD CAN ALSO SPEAK TO US IN DREAMS LITERALLY, LOUD AND CLEAR.

Now, I teach that for *most* people, *most* of the time, dreams are symbolic and metaphorical. However, we know God can certainly speak literally, loud and clear, as well. Here is a great example where God downloaded accurate, literal information—a word of knowledge through a dream—about one of his students so Brian could intervene in a critical time of need.

Brian's Word of Knowledge in a Dream

I had a student (let's call him Frankie) who would come by after school every day to visit before he went home. Frankie was always smiling, easygoing, and kind to everyone. One day, he came into my classroom with a different demeanor. He was quiet and withdrawn. When I asked him what was going on, he wouldn't open up to me. All of this was very unusual, and *I had a feeling* this wasn't a simple matter of a breakup with a girlfriend or the stresses of school. He was like this again the next day, and once again, I could not get him to tell me what was wrong.

When I was getting ready for bed that night, *I asked God for a dream* that would help me minister to Frankie. I had a very simple dream that was very easy to interpret because it wasn't symbolic—it was a word of knowledge!

In the dream, I was standing in front of Frankie. He walked over to me and looked directly into my eyes. He said, "I secretly hate myself. I have a hard time believing that there's anything good about me. And sometimes I even wonder if I'm really evil." With that, I woke up. I didn't have to wonder what that dream meant! I thanked God and *typed up the dream on my phone* before I went back to sleep. I was deeply touched that God honored my request to help my student so quickly.

Frankie came into my classroom that day and we started talking. He was a little more open. *I didn't say I had a "word from God"* or share my dream. Instead, I asked him if he had a hard time finding good things about himself. "Yes," he said. I then asked him if he secretly hated himself. "Yes." Finally, I asked him if he sometimes wondered if he were really evil. "Yes."

I couldn't believe it! This boy was always so happy and smiling on the outside that I assumed all was well on the inside. That was just a veneer, hiding his inner struggle. That started a great conversation between us that was open and freeing. He talked about some things he hadn't shared with me before and we bonded closer together. *It started a series of conversations* about his mental health and the way he saw himself that I believe were very important in his life.

Without God sharing this word of knowledge, I would have never known how to help this young man I cared so much about.

A MODEL TO FOLLOW

The gifts of the Spirit, such as a word of knowledge, healing, or prophecy, are always to demonstrate the fruit of God's Spirit—His extravagant love. Brian felt God's heart of compassion and so he easily flowed in God's power of supernatural knowledge.

> THE GIFTS OF THE SPIRIT, SUCH AS A WORD OF KNOWLEDGE, HEALING, OR PROPHECY, ARE ALWAYS TO DEMONSTRATE THE FRUIT OF GOD'S SPIRIT—HIS EXTRAVAGANT LOVE.

This reminds me of Joseph in the gospel of Matthew. Over and over, we see that because Joseph received prophetic words of wisdom and knowledge through his dreams, he was able to protect and save baby Jesus's life. (See Matthew 1:20–25; 2:13–15, 19–21, 22–23.) Makes you wonder what kind of revelation God is downloading to *you* while you sleep!

I also appreciate Brian's approach in that he didn't come right out and tell Frankie he'd had a dream about him. We never want to make anyone feel uncomfortable so we don't present what God reveals as if we have inside knowledge or God told us their secrets. The goal is to make them feel *known* without making them feel *exposed*. This is a model for us.

FOUR KEY WAYS TO RECEIVE FROM HEAVEN

There are four key ways Brian purposefully positioned himself to receive from heaven:

1. He *felt* God's heart of concern and compassion for his student.

2. He was intentional and specifically *asked* God to give him a dream.

3. He was quick to honor the revelation he received and *recorded it* immediately in the middle of the night.

4. Finally, he *acted* on that information, ministering the Father's heart of encouragement and comfort in a thoughtful way, letting Frankie know that he wasn't alone.

And that is only the beginning! Brian regularly experiences the ninefold manifestation of the Spirit, which naturally overflows into his workplace. We've looked at one already and I have asked him to share an example of each different spiritual gift to give us a vision for how they can look in *regular, daily life.* As we quickly discover, however, Holy Spirit anointing transforms the ordinary into extraordinary and makes normal everyday living a supernatural adventure with God.

> HOLY SPIRIT ANOINTING TRANSFORMS THE ORDINARY INTO EXTRAORDINARY AND MAKES NORMAL EVERYDAY LIVING A SUPERNATURAL ADVENTURE WITH GOD.

Enjoy these powerful stories! Most of all, remember that the testimony of Jesus is the spirit of prophecy and the same kinds of miracles God is doing through Brian's ministry as a public school teacher He absolutely wants to do through you, too!

Brian's Word of Wisdom

As I have gone through my career as an educator in Tennessee, I have found myself working with government leaders on both a local and state level. After studying the life of Daniel in Scripture, I saw that he won over Nebuchadnezzar though his *"extraordinary spirit, knowledge and insight, interpretation of dreams, explanation of enigmas and solving of difficult problems*" (Daniel 5:12). Besides honoring my leaders, as David and Paul demonstrated in their testimonies, I needed to also be ready to solve problems that my leaders found difficult to overcome. By doing this, I believed that I would be able to share God's plans for our state's children, teachers, and school systems with decision-makers, thereby helping to transform our educational system to look more like God's kingdom.

I heard that the educational leaders in my local school system wanted to work on the school building in which I taught. They were preparing to ask our community leaders for millions of dollars and asked me to speak at a meeting with the city government. I spent some time soaking in God's presence on the rug beside my bed, where I go to spend quiet time with God. I will confess that I didn't ask God to show me anything specific, just something that would help me influence our government leaders in a way that would make Him happy. After a few minutes, God showed me a picture of my students and me running to the cafeteria in our school, racing each other to lunch. When we got there, I saw that the building had been transformed. Not only did I see cosmetic, aesthetic details, but also practical things as well. I saw how the lunch lines were conducted with improved efficiency. I also noticed the improvements on security and safety, including one-way reflective windows to keep outsiders from seeing into the cafeteria. I noted the color palette and materials used in the building and wrote all of this information down in my journal when the vision was over.

When I spoke at the community meeting, I was nervous, but I knew that God was supporting the construction project. We were granted several hundreds of thousands of dollars to hire engineers and architects to draw up plans for our new building, including a new cafeteria! When I later got together with my school leaders, I was able to give feedback on their plans, based on what God had shown me. I learned that things like efficiency and safety are very important to them, and it helped me learn how to counsel them better in the future.

Brian's Faith Made Manifest

After teaching for ten years, I was in dire need of white-boards in the front of my classroom. The old ones were so heavily worn down that no one could erase anything written on them. They needed to be replaced, but getting new ones shipped to my classroom would cost hundreds of dollars. I am a math teacher and the calculators I was given at the beginning of my career were dying. I needed at least ten calculators and each one cost roughly $100 apiece! This was going to be a huge expense and my school was not prepared to pay the bill.

My earthly father has always been an excellent provider for me and my family and we never experienced any financial hardships. Due to this, I have enjoyed a big boost to my faith in trusting my heavenly Father for finances and resources. On the last day of the school year, after packing up my classroom, I spent a little time talking to God. It was pretty short and simple. I prayed something like this: "Father God, I need some new whiteboards in my classroom and I'd really like to get some that will last me the rest of my career and even support the next teacher in my room. I'd also like enough calculators for every child to have access to one. I'd like some that are top-of-the-line and able to keep up with where technology is going in the future so we won't need different ones later. My kids really need these things. They deserve the best, You've put me in charge of them, and I love them and want to give them the best. Thank You!" I did a prophetic action, reaching up with my arms to bring down these resources for my kids and I pictured these items in my classroom and my kids using them. The prayer probably lasted no more than two minutes.

The very next morning, I met up with some friends of mine from church for breakfast. I shared with them what I had asked God for the day before. As I was talking, a woman who was sitting near us turned to me and said, "I have been teaching math for years and just retired. I own a set of calculators. Would you like them? I've been wanting to give them to a teacher who will take good care of them, and when I heard you talking, I believe God prompted me to give them to you." I was blown away! I wasn't surprised that God answered my prayer, but I was amazed at how quickly the problem was resolved. In addition to this, I decided to write a few grants and work with another teacher to raise some funds for my school. Every grant we applied for was accepted and we ended up raising so much money that we were able to get new whiteboards for not just my own classroom, but seven other classrooms, too! We even had a business send a check for $1,000 for any-thing we desired—and we hadn't even contacted them! Besides all that, an organization gave me an *additional* class set of brand new, top-of-the-line calculators! My cup truly ran over. Whenever we hit an apparent dead end, such as someone withdrawing funding, I would just tell God that I could see His fingerprints all over this story and I knew He was taking care of it. I say that just to make it clear that I wasn't without obstacles. I just tried to use my *shield of faith* to counter that opposition.

Brian's Gifts of Healing

As a public school teacher, ministering to students overtly is not something I do without God's prompting. Still, I have found that God makes *creative* ways for me to minister to children without directly praying over them. One such case happened just this year. I had a young man in class who I will call Nathaniel. He was clearly intelligent and very adept at math. I assigned him a seat in the back of the classroom, which meant that sometimes, I didn't have a great view of him. One day, I assigned some group work for the class to do. As I was walking around the classroom, I came close to Nathaniel's seat and saw that he was hunched over, trying to hide his face. He was crying. I tapped him on the shoulder and asked him if he would like to step out into the hallway. He nodded his head and I went out to talk to him privately a few minutes later.

In the hall, I asked him why he had been crying. "I had a seizure while you were teaching today," he said. "I started having them earlier this year and the doctors can't figure out why I'm having them. I'm really scared and I noticed over the past few weeks that I haven't been able to keep up in math as well as I used to. I'm worried that the seizures are affecting my mind."

As he said this to me, I was shocked. Five days earlier, God had given me a dream in which I saw Nathaniel wearing a straitjacket. His eyes had been crossed and he muttered nonsense to himself. In the dream, I tried speaking to him and bringing him back to his senses, but he only muttered louder when I did that. The dream finished with me marching down to the principal's office, demanding that something change. The principal said that he would fix it.

Once Nathaniel told me about the seizures, everything clicked into place. What I had assumed had been a symbolic dream about me was actually a prophetic dream for Nathaniel! Nathaniel was *bound*, represented by the straitjacket, and afraid of losing his mind. The symbols in the dream perfectly illustrated this. The dream also showed me that I had a responsibility to take this issue to God and intercede on behalf of my student whom I love. After the school day was over, I sat down at Nathaniel's desk and began to partner with the promise that God had given me in the dream. If I brought this issue to Him, He would handle it! I felt prompted by the Holy Spirit to agree with God's picture of Nathaniel: an intelligent young man who is free to learn in the peace of knowing he is sane and safe. After three months went by, I followed up with Nathaniel and asked him how his health was doing. He happily shared that he hadn't had any more seizures since that day in my classroom! God had indeed taken care of the problem! I did mention to him that he was important to me and I had spent some time praying for him that day. While I can't overtly evangelize in the secular school setting, that doesn't keep me from planting seeds that God can germinate later. I trust that God will use that memory to bring Nathaniel into a relationship with Him.

Brian's Miracles

In 2017, I began to feel a compulsion to minister to people with sickness and started pressing in for healing. I had to fight disappointment for nearly a year, as everyone

I prayed for either saw no improvement, got worse, or died! I knew I needed some guidance, so I studied miracles from people who lived miracle-saturated lives. Paul says to *"pursue love, yet desire earnestly spiritual gifts"* (1 Corinthians 14:1) and that is what I set out to do.

I studied the writings and sermons of Heidi Baker, Bill Johnson, Art Thomas, Randy Clark, and other Christian leaders who saw healings and miracles on a regular basis. One thing I took away from their testimonies was that these men and women often had to pray for people for months before a healing or miracle would take place. They had to make a conscious decision to believe God wanted people healed more than they did, regardless of the outcome of their prayer. After roughly nine months of meditating on God's Word and praying for others, I still had not seen a single healing. At this point, I was very disappointed. I got to a point where the last thing I wanted to do was pray for a sick person!

I went to a Wednesday night prayer service at my church on a cold October evening. Our worship leader, Fred, ended the worship music and said that a woman in our group had gotten some "bad news from her doctor" concerning the baby she was expecting. He pulled a chair up to the front of the church and asked her to sit there while we laid hands on her and prayed. I gave a heavy sigh and joined the others for prayer—no more than ten of us in all. I placed my hand on her shoulder and did my best to set my disappointment aside, but it was difficult. Suddenly, I had a strange feeling wash over me. I had an overwhelming sense of love for this woman I barely knew. It was like my own sister had come to me with this need and helping her was the most important thing in the world to me. I was baffled at the illogical flood of love I had for her and her child.

The next thing I knew, God showed me an image of an unborn baby in a womb. Written over the baby was the word "ella." God was showing me through a word of knowledge that this baby was a little girl and He used a Spanish feminine pronoun because both of her parents spoke Spanish. I had a phrase go through my head: "Too many fingers and too many toes." I assumed God was telling me one of the symptoms to deal with, so I prayed through that out loud. The next thing I knew, I felt that God gave me three things that we were to do as a group. I shared this with my friends and we followed the instructions. The mother stood up, thanked us, and returned to her seat in the church.

On the following Sunday, the woman we had prayed for shared with us that she had gone to the doctor and that all of the issues the doctor had warned her about were nowhere to be found on the ultrasound! We hadn't known it on Wednesday, but the doctor had expressed concern that the baby had Trisomy 13, a condition with a broad spectrum of problems, including too many fingers and toes! God had given us what we needed to pray in such a way that this little girl's genetic code was rewritten and we didn't even know what we were praying for! This wasn't just a healing—it was a miracle, as God broke all the rules of nature to change the chemical makeup of this precious little girl. I also think it is so neat to see how many different gifts the Holy Spirit used to make this happen.

Brian's Prophecy

While I'm not technically *supposed* to have favorite students, there are certainly some whom I bond with more deeply than others. Luke was one of those students. He would come by my classroom nearly every day just to hang out and visit. On one of those days, we were talking about what he thought he might do for a future career. "I don't know," he said. "What do you think I could do?" I thought for a minute. "Well, you are very thoughtful and care a lot about others. You are also a good leader and people feel comfortable around you. I guess I can see you doing…" and then I stopped. I realized that God was laying a prophetic word on my heart for this young man! In loving him and imagining his future, God jumped in with His own thoughts!

I knew this boy was a Christian and that his grandfather pastored a church. I felt from God that it was okay in this instance to tell Luke that I felt that what I was about to share *might* be a "word from God," but he would have to be the judge of that. If it built him up and affirmed some things he already thought God was saying to him, then great! And if not, then he could just set them aside and consider them later on down the road. He said he understood, so I began to tell him what I felt God was saying about his future. I told him that he was an engineer and very bright. I also told him that I felt that there were a lot of girls who would look at him as the protective, loving big brother they needed in their lives and he was destined to have a very important ministry to women. There were other things that I said, but those were the major points. I will never forget this big football player bending down to the shoulder on my five-foot-seven frame to rest his head and cry. Those words meant so much to him.

A couple of years later, after he graduated, Luke surprised me with a visit at school. He had joined the Army and was dressed in his military uniform. We hugged and cried and talked for a long time. He introduced me to his fiancée and we had a great talk. Before he left, he asked me, "Mr. McLaughlin, do you remember that one day you prayed for me and shared that word with me you felt God was telling you? Well, I'm working on helicopters for the Army now and taking classes to be an engineer. On top of that, I'm working with the Army to go visit soldiers who are sexually harassed or assaulted. I go in and talk to them and help them right after they report the offense. Remember how you told me I would have a ministry with women? I do that every day and it's my favorite part of my job."

I'm so glad to serve a God who has a plan for each one of the young people I love. I've learned that the more I love a person, the more likely I am to be a conduit of God's supernatural giftings to minister to them. It's no coincidence that Paul talks about love before he talks about prophecy in 1 Corinthians 13. Without love, prophecy can easily turn into words of condemnation or judgment instead of edification. If we want to do what God does, we need to start with the heart!

Brian's Distinguishing of Spirits

I received my baptism in the Holy Spirit just a couple of weeks before starting to teach. Talk about perfect timing! I soon found out just how the Holy Spirit wanted to help me minister to my students. There was a girl, who I will call Jennifer, in one of my classes. She was a great student, always raising her hand and eager to help out. I looked forward to seeing her each day. One day, however, the bell rang to start class and Jennifer hadn't shown up yet. Right as I was about to shut the door to my classroom, I looked down the fifty-yard-long hallway and saw Jennifer come around the corner. She was so far away that my eyes could just barely tell it was her. Suddenly, I had my very first Holy-Spirit-led supernatural experience. My vision was suddenly flooded with a fleeting image of Jennifer's eyes. This picture interrupted my natural vision in a way that caught me totally off guard. Her eyes didn't look cheerful as they usually did—they looked dark, insane, and mischievous. I had a thought come into my mind: "She has a spirit of rebellion."

I want to remind you that I was new to this charismatic, Spirit-led life I had found myself in. I had no idea what to do! I would love to have seen the expression on my face at that moment, trying to process what was happening. It felt like I was a little kid and someone had pushed me into the deep end of a pool, popped my arm floats, and threw in a demon too. I had a thought go through my mind, *Pray and tell it to be silent! You have authority!* Standing in my doorway, I muttered a prayer under my breath, telling the evil spirit that God had put me in charge of these kids and had made me their teacher. As long as I was there, I forbade the evil spirit from speaking or expressing itself in any way.

Jennifer was reticent in class from that point forward, but I could see in her eyes that day that there was something different about her. This was not the same sweet girl I had known. From that day on, she began to create chaos in her other classes and her teachers began to swap stories and share concern over her. She stayed silent in my class, though, and didn't cause any disruptions. That all changed, however, when I had to miss school to attend a meeting. My students said that on the day I was gone, when she realized I was missing, she jumped in the air, shouted, "I'm free!" and began to throw herself down on the floor and hurl herself against the wall. It stopped when I returned.

I'm so grateful God stepped in and told me what I needed to know about my student so that my classroom environment could stay safe and learning could still take place.

Brian's Speaking in Tongues

When I was baptized in the Spirit, I began speaking in tongues. This confused me and felt completely different than anything I had ever experienced. Because I was not using my logical, rational thoughts to say these words, I wondered for a long time if what I was doing was *legitimate*. Was the Holy Spirit really giving me words to say, or was I just babbling?

Years went by and I began to really wonder about speaking in tongues. After a long period of prayer and pondering, I found myself deep in prayer about a different matter one day. Alone in the car, I was praying to God and very moved in my spirit. Suddenly, without warning, I shouted "Eliyahu!" at the top of my lungs. I was startled and thought to myself, *That sounds like Hebrew.*

I pulled over and grabbed my phone. I found out that Eliyahu is the Hebrew version of the name Elijah, meaning, "My God is Yahweh." What is funny about this is that "My God is Yahweh" fit seamlessly with the prayer I was praying in English. My spirit cried out with words given by the Holy Spirit, and my brain was not part of the equation. This began a series of events in which God would show me that when I was speaking in tongues, I was really saying something significant, whether I understood the meaning or not. I even had a dream where everyone was speaking Hebrew and there were subtitles under their faces. When I woke up, I grabbed my concordance and looked up the last three words I could remember—and they were really Hebrew! I'm sure God had a good time watching me process that experience.

Brian's Interpretation of Tongues

This is the gift I have the least experience with, but I do have enough to know that it is available to me and I can grow in it. We all have spiritual senses and my spiritual sense of sight is probably my strongest. God engages with me that way the most often and I seek to utilize it the most frequently. While attending a Randy Clark conference in Kentucky a couple of years ago, I had an experience where I saw the name *Katie* written in front of me. I found out that it was the name of the young woman standing next to me, whom I did not know. It started a beautiful ministry opportunity I won't soon forget.

Randy talked a lot about impartation and how he believed that our gifts and spiritual senses were being awakened by our gathering together as the body of Christ, hungry for God's presence. I noticed that from that point on, sometimes as I was praying with my eyes closed, God would show me a word typed out in the darkness of my eyelids. One by one, I would say these foreign words in my prayer time. I finally tried translating these words into Google one day and found out that I was worshipping God in other languages, including Hebrew, Greek, and Spanish. It was amazing!

I didn't want Google to be my translator forever, though, and wanted to know what God was saying directly from Him. One day, as I was praying in my prayer language, I felt like I needed to lay my hands over my heart. I had a sense that what I was praying was for me. As I did this, I began to repeat the word, "Shanti, shanti, shanti…" While I didn't know what I was saying exactly, I knew the *general* meaning. It was for me, for my benefit. I felt that I was ministering to myself.

Reaching for my phone once again, I went to Google and searched for the meaning of "shanti." I found out that it is an old Sanskrit word for "peace." I was literally speaking peace over myself in a foreign tongue! This period of my life was also a very difficult one for me and I took great comfort in the way that I now saw how God desired peace for my heart.

ALL OF LIFE IS MINISTRY

I know you are as inspired by Brian's testimony as I am. Another significant fact is that Brian is not in church leadership. He is actively involved in his local fellowship, but not on staff or in any official role there. I appreciate that because we usually associate the kinds of miracles Brian walks in with church leaders. We know pastors in a pulpit can flow in the anointing and missionaries overseas can release spiritual gifts, but most of us aren't in those narrowly defined positions traditionally identified as *ministry*.

> WHEN WE LIVE AND WORK HEARTILY FOR THE LORD, IN EVERY AREA OF OUR LIVES, WE ARE ACTIVELY INVOLVED IN SPIRITUAL MINISTRY.

The truth is, *everything* is ministry! Whatever we do, we do our work heartily as for the Lord rather than men. Because it is Him we are serving, we are all, every day, in every area of our lives, actively involved in spiritual ministry.

Brian is just as anointed in his classroom on Monday morning as his pastor is at church on Sunday morning. God's gifts and power flow just as mightily in and through our Spirit-filled school teachers, scriptwriters, and sales managers working outside the four walls of the church. In fact, they can flow even more easily!

Sometimes, when a gifted communicator shows up in church, we think, "They would make such a great preacher!" Or when a talented musician joins our church, we immediately want to make them part of the worship team. Usually when we recognize the Holy Spirit's anointing on someone, we tend to promote them and want to keep them on staff and inside the church.

The problem with that is that then the most anointed and gifted leaders are not out there being light in the world, influencing their cities and nations. (See Matthew 5:14–16.) We know we are to be the salt of the earth (see Matthew 5:13), but all too often, we are huddled together in the salt shakers of our local churches. Obviously, it is much easier to make an impact on every mountain and flavor our culture when we are out in the world.

If you are gifted in organization or leadership, stay at your place of business and bring the anointing of God to your job. Continue being the administrative assistant or CEO of your company and let the Holy Spirit flow through you, releasing His divine creativity, wisdom, and power into the marketplace.

> LET THE HOLY SPIRIT FLOW THROUGH YOU, RELEASING HIS DIVINE CREATIVITY, WISDOM, AND POWER INTO THE MARKETPLACE.

Let your light shine brightly, knowing that if God has called you to your job, then your job is your ministry and the fullness of His glory will invade that place because you show up there. You are the gateway of heaven and release the presence of God and all His gifts there. Your gifts will make room for you and bring you favor before great men (see Proverbs 18:16), just like it did for Brian.

THE REST OF THE STORY

So what do Brian's colleagues and leaders think of his performance on the job? I'll let Brian share more of his Spirit-led backstory, the honor that flowing with God has already afforded him, and the incredible places it is taking him in the near future:

> About three years ago, God began to prompt me to pray for my community and my state's education system. I felt convicted that He had a plan He wanted to put into place in both areas. About nine months later, He had me apply for a fellowship that trained teachers on how to be advocates for students in governmental settings. I began meeting with state senators and representatives, as well as other government leaders and influencers.
>
> The next thing I knew, God was telling me that I was going to be the next *Teacher of the Year* for Tennessee and that I would have a chance to meet with the president and pray over him. Sure enough, I was selected to be the 2020 Teacher of the Year for Tennessee and I will be meeting the president this spring at the White House! It's pretty wild! I have been a high school teacher in a public school setting for almost twelve years now and I've learned just how much impact a "regular guy" can have on his spheres of influence. It's a big responsibility, but God does all the heavy lifting.

Brian is an awesome example of a modern-day Joseph or Daniel, influencing the highest authorities with the wisdom of God he receives through his visions by day and by night. The Holy Spirit's anointing has made him *"a man skilled in his work,"* and truly, *"he will stand before kings"* (Proverbs 22:29).

Now we have an idea of how spiritual gifts can work in our normal routine at home, in school, or on the job. God loves variety and creativity and will certainly enjoy surprising us! But we know we are given the manifestation of the Spirit for the common good and now we have a vision for what that can actually look like in our everyday life.

> GOD LOVES VARIETY AND CREATIVITY AND WILL
> CERTAINLY ENJOY SURPRISING US!

Purpose in your heart to pray into these powerful potentials. Observe these supernatural possibilities and prophetic prom- ises into your world. Collapse heaven's gifts and glory into your family, business, and nation. All of creation waits for the revealing of mature sons and daughters. Allow His Spirit to reign in life through you!

ACTION EXERCISE

Have you believed in a sacred/secular split, thinking that pulpit ministry is more spiritual than any other work? If so, repent and ask God to give you His vision of the workplace and how all of life is a mission field ripe for the harvest.

Are you in the job God wants you to be? If so, do you realize you are an anointed administrator of grace, truly a minister of the Gospel in that realm and sphere of influence? If that's not how you see yourself, ask the Lord to show you His version of your job situ- ation and the reason He has called you to it for such a time as this.

Have you flowed in spiritual gifts outside the church? When were some times you shared a word of wisdom, knowledge, or healing with someone in your neighborhood or on the job? What was your experience and how did that feel? Ask the Holy Spirit to remind you of the steps you took to connect with His river within

during those supernatural moments so you can proactively position yourself to do it again and again.

_____

_____

_____

_____

_____

How I Received the Baptism in the Holy Spirit
by Roma Flood

I had only been saved for about six weeks and desired more than anything to be filled with His Spirit and speak in tongues. I awoke in the middle of the night and went into another room of the house and a few syllables came to me. I practiced them over and over so that I would remember them in the morning. But that seemed to be that and nothing else happened.

Then I went to a ladies' weekend camp with a wonderful prophet who gave me an amazing word, but I still couldn't speak in tongues. I returned home after camp and all the family were out. Despondently, I unpacked my suitcase in my bedroom, telling God that I really thought He'd fill me with His Spirit over the course of the weekend. Then, as I was talking to Him, my lips started to tingle and strange words flowed out of my mouth.

I walked into the lounge room and the presence and the glory of God was so thick it seemed to fill the whole room. I couldn't stand under the weight of His glory and went down on my knees, grabbing hold of the piano so I didn't fall. My whole mouth, tongue, and nose were tingling. Amazingly, the Lord still blesses me with this gift of tingling as I call it, which I love because He reminds me of His glorious presence and His everlasting love for me.

9

DREAM GIFTS: HOW TO RECEIVE FROM THE HOLY SPIRIT WHILE YOU SLEEP

by Charity Kayembe

He gives to His beloved even in his sleep.
—Psalm 127:2

We have learned that releasing spiritual gifts is as easy as connecting with the Giver of those gifts, the Holy Spirit Himself. That is why we want to get out of our heads and into our hearts because God doesn't live in our heads. Ephesians 3:17 tells us that Jesus lives in our hearts, and John 7:37–39 tells us that the *"rivers of living water,"* the Holy Spirit, flow from our *"innermost being."*

We also know that as believers, our spirit is joined with the Holy Spirit, down deep in our innermost being. (See 1 Corinthians 6:17.) Therefore we want to live from our spirit and our sacred union with God there. When we experience this zone of heart-based living, science calls it being in the *alpha brain wave state.*

SCIENCE OF SPIRITUALITY

Any activity that dials us down from faster beta brain waves into slower alpha and theta brain waves will help us connect to

God's river within, as it slows us down into our hearts, where He lives. Science has shown us there are many simple and effective ways to shift gears and slow our brain waves, including closing our eyes, listening to soaking or instrumental worship music, visionary meditation, breathing deeply, dancing and other physical expressions of worship, emotional freedom technique (EFT) tapping, and praying in the Spirit.

> GOD ACTIVELY DESIRES TO EXTRAVAGANTLY LAVISH HIS GIFTS AND LOVE UPON US, SO MUCH SO THAT HE DOESN'T LIMIT HIMSELF TO DAYTIME-ONLY REVELATION.

God actively desires to extravagantly lavish His gifts and love upon us, so much so that He doesn't limit Himself to daytime-only revelation. He has designed us to easily and effortlessly move into the alpha and theta state naturally. In fact, we all experience these meditative brain waves every single night!

Right now, as you are wide awake reading this book and engaging your mind, you are experiencing faster, analytical beta brain waves. However, just as you fall asleep at night and just as you wake up in the morning, you are in the alpha brain wave state. The slower frequencies of alpha and theta are more prayerful and reflective. When we're not quite sure if we are awake or asleep and the veil between the physical world and spiritual world is thin, that's alpha. We also experience these more relaxed brain wave frequencies when we are asleep and dreaming.

While science calls this alpha and theta, Scripture calls it being *"in spirit."* Jesus told us to *"worship in spirit"* (John 4:24). John said, *"I was in the Spirit on the Lord's day"* (Revelation 1:10) and met the Lord. (See Revelation 1:12–18.) Later, he said, *"I was in the Spirit"* (Revelation 4:2) and proceeded to see the throne of God and all manner of heavenly visions. He was not in his head; he was in his heart. He was in the alpha state and his spiritual senses were opened wide to see and hear the mysteries of the kingdom.

> WHEN WE RECEIVE DREAMS, OUR ANALYTICAL MIND IS OUT OF THE WAY AND WE ARE ABLE TO RECEIVE A PURE FLOW OF REVELATION STRAIGHT FROM FATHER'S HEART TO OURS.

We can see then how important dreams are as an effective communicative medium with heaven. When we receive dreams, our analytical mind is out of the way and we are able to receive a pure flow of revelation straight from Father's heart to ours. Indeed, Scripture reveals that when we are asleep, our heart is awake to commune with our Beloved. (See Song of Solomon 5:2.)

Dreams are God's contingency plan ensuring He would always have a way to connect with us. Our Father knows that one of the best times to get our attention is when we're asleep, and He promised He would reveal Himself in visions and speak to us in dreams. (See Numbers 12:6.) Throughout Scripture, God used dreams to deliver words of wisdom, words of knowledge, and prophecy. Let's not miss out on this powerful way to receive an overflow of the Spirit into our lives!

THE GIFT OF WISDOM THROUGH A DREAM

Most of us recognize King Solomon for his legendary wisdom, which we know that God gave to him as a gift. What is often overlooked, however, is *when* God imparted that supernatural gift. In 1 Kings 3:5–15, we discover it actually happened in a dream.

We naturally expect God would have orchestrated this epic encounter during the day and we assume God would have wanted Solomon awake for such a significant event. Instead, we find that the entire conversation and impartation took place in a dream.

What is most exciting to realize is that the wisdom Solomon received through his dream is the same wisdom we can receive every night through our dreams too. The Hebrew word for what Solomon asked for and received is *shama*, which is a "hearing" heart. (See 1 Kings 3:9, 11.) He asked for a listening heart, one that could clearly hear the Lord's direction and guidance.

In effect, Solomon wanted what Adam and Eve had in the garden of Eden. They initially lived from their hearts and spiritual communion with God. They knew only good because God was with them. They were dependent on His voice and lived out of relationship with Him. Their sin was to choose independence, to use their own minds to discern good *and evil.* (See Genesis 3:5.)

Solomon wanted to go back to God's original intent for mankind and chose the opposite of Adam and Eve. Solomon did not want to rely on his own mind's best guess. He wanted to return to the lifestyle of Eden, not making decisions by what his physical eyes saw or his natural ears heard, but instead ruling with righteous judgment. (See Isaiah 11:3–4.)

> SOLOMON DID NOT WANT TO RELY ON HIS OWN MIND'S BEST GUESS. HE WANTED TO RETURN TO THE LIFESTYLE OF EDEN.

Upon awakening from his dream, this anointing was demonstrated immediately as two women came before Solomon, both claiming the same baby as their own. He resolved the dispute with a word of wisdom. (See 1 Kings 3:16–27.)

When all Israel heard of the judgment which the king had handed down, they feared the king, for they saw that the wisdom of God was in him to administer justice.

(1 Kings 3:28)

Solomon employed spiritual gifts in his governmental office and his fame as a wise king spread throughout the land.

THE SPIRIT OF WISDOM HIMSELF

It was the Spirit of wisdom, the Holy Spirit, with whom Solomon connected, just as Adam and Eve had done long before him. Through his dream, the spiritual portal was opened and he had the chance to access anything he wanted. Rather than asking for long life, riches, or the deaths of his enemies, Solomon chose to hear God's voice. He asked that his heart be reconnected to God's heart so he could live out of fellowship with Him.

Solomon did not just receive a pile of detached information in his brain. That could have made him knowledgeable, but it would never make him wise. Instead, he was given the gift of being able to listen in to the spirit realm and hear the counsel of heaven. He was given the gift of restored communion and intimate relationship with the Spirit of wisdom Himself. (See Isaiah 11:2.)

And just as God promised, Solomon *was wiser than all men"* (1 Kings 4:31) and no one could rival his wisdom until the King of Kings came to earth.

Jesus was baptized with the Holy Spirit, the Spirit of wisdom, and He, too, lived out of the supernatural. He did nothing on His own initiative based on what He saw in this natural world. (See John 5:19, 30.) He did only what He saw His Father do and spoke only what He heard His Father say. (See John 8:26, 38.)

Solomon and Jesus both relied on the spirit realm to reign in life, accessing the wisdom of heaven through their dreams and visions. We can do that, too.

A GIFT OF PROPHECY FROM A WEIRD DREAM

You might be thinking, *Great—good for Solomon.* His dream was pretty straightforward, after all. It was obvious and easy to see how God blessed him with the gift of wisdom while he slept. But perhaps your dreams aren't that literal. Perhaps you think your dreams are crazy, not biblical.

First of all, no dreams are crazy. What might seem to be ridiculous is often revelation. What seems to be silly can be sacred and symbolic.[12] God spoke through all kinds of *crazy* dreams in the Bible too!

> NO DREAMS ARE CRAZY. WHAT MIGHT SEEM TO BE RIDICULOUS
> IS OFTEN REVELATION, AND WHAT SEEMS TO BE SILLY
> CAN BE SACRED AND SYMBOLIC.

How about some sheaves of wheat bowing down to you? Or the sun, the moon, and the stars bowing down to you? I don't know about you, but while I can picture some wheat bent over and *bowing*, I have no idea what a bowing star would look like. And yet these are the dreams that Joseph had. (See Genesis 37:5–7, 9.) The wheat and stars were symbolic, representing his family. And his family literally did end up bowing down to Joseph in waking life years later. (See Genesis 42:6.)

We see God gave Joseph a predictive word about the future, a gift of prophecy, in his dreams. While his dreams appeared to be strange on the surface, they were merely symbolic. Once the symbols were decoded and the main action of *bowing* matched up with waking life, it was easy for everyone in his family to immediately translate God's message through the picture language of the dream.

The message of the dream revealed heaven's perspective; it was God's prophetic word to Joseph. (See Psalm 105:19.) During the many years of waiting for the word to be fulfilled, Joseph certainly had the opportunity to doubt. Scripture for the most part is silent, but we can assume it would have been very easy for Joseph to fall into fear, anxiety, and depression when he was thrown into the pit and left for dead, or wrongly accused and thrown into prison.

---

12. To discover how God speaks through your visions of the night, every single night, see: Mark Virkler and Charity Virkler Kayembe, *Hearing God Through Your Dreams* (Shippensburg, PA: Destiny Image, 2016).

In those moments, Joseph had a choice. He could look at the things that are seen—the terrifying predicaments he found himself in—or he could look at the unseen, the eternal realm of the Spirit. Because he honored his dreams, he could pull out those *snapshots of the Spirit* and remind himself of what God had to say about him. He could meditate on God's promised potentials as revealed through the dreams; he could observe to collapse those prophetic possibilities into his world.

By seeing what God saw, Joseph could feel what God felt. Supernatural faith in a future he had only glimpsed through his dreams sustained him on his long journey from the pit to the palace. Because Joseph was found faithful and honored God's message through the dreams, God honored Joseph and the dreams' prophetic word of knowledge did come true.

A GIFT OF FAITH FROM A CRAZY DREAM

Similarly, God gave a Midianite soldier a prophetic word of knowledge in his dream, which Gideon overheard and his faith was strengthened as a result. (See Judges 7:13–15.) The Midianite dreamt that a loaf of bread invaded their camp and destroyed their army. Now that is a crazy dream! His friend interpreted it for him:

This is nothing less than the sword of Gideon… God has given Midian and all the camp into his hand.   (Judges 7:14)

While a loaf of bread attacking an army seems silly, we realize it's simply symbolic. And the message is, in fact, sacred. Even through the strangeness, God is speaking!

Most of the time, dreams are not literal. For example, Gideon didn't have to meditate on a loaf of barley bread; that was just a symbol. The bread represented his army; so instead, he was to meditate on the meaning of the symbol. By matching up the main action in the dream with waking life, the message was clear:

Gideon's army was going to defeat the Midianites. Gideon received a gift of faith through this dream word from heaven.

By meditating on God's version of the situation—that victory was imminent—Gideon was encouraged. By seeing what God saw, he was able to feel God's peace, faith, and fearlessness. By observing the message of the dream and receiving the prophetic revelation hidden in the symbols, he was able to collapse that message. He manifested and made real in his waking world what heretofore remained a potential possibility in the spiritual realm. Gideon observed the victory God revealed through the dream, and then acted on the dream's message. *He made the dream come true.*

> GOD DOWNLOADS WORDS OF WISDOM AND KNOWLEDGE,
> GIFTS OF FAITH AND PROPHECY, AND ALL MANNER OF REVELATION TO
> OUR HEARTS WHILE WE SLEEP.

Literal or metaphorical, straightforward or symbolic, God speaks to us in dreams. He is downloading words of wisdom and knowledge, gifts of faith and prophecy, and all manner of revelation to our hearts while we sleep. In our dreams, in our visions of the night, when we fall into deep sleep and slumber in our beds, God opens our ears and instructs us. He enlightens us with the light of life. (See Job 33:14–18, 29, 30.)

To *unwrap* the Holy Spirit's dream gifts, first we must decode the symbols and translate the imagery to discover the interpretation. It is that interpreted message from God to which we pay attention. It is that gift of wisdom, faith, word of knowledge, or revelation given through the dream upon which we meditate. We set our hearts to observe the prophetic meaning of the dream in order to collapse its promised potential into manifested reality in our waking world.

MARKETPLACE "MIRACLES" RECEIVED THROUGH DREAMS

We have already looked at the incredible story of Jacob's quantum sheep, which observed striped sticks, and then produced striped offspring. *(See chapter five, "Back to Eden: Restoring God's Super to Our Natural.")* Jacob lived in an agrarian society in which livestock was his livelihood. God taught Jacob how to cultivate wealth through a dream. Jacob obeyed the angel's seemingly bizarre request, resulting in abundant financial provision for his family.

Jacob reminds me of a contemporary dreamer who also achieved great prosperity by honoring his visions of the night. Larry Page, founder of Google, had a dream when he was a twenty-two-year-old graduate student at Stanford University. In the dream, he somehow managed to download the entire Internet onto his computer. Once downloaded, he carefully examined the links between sites.

> GOOGLE'S FOUNDER DREAMT HE SOMEHOW MANAGED TO DOWNLOAD THE ENTIRE INTERNET ONTO HIS COMPUTER. WHEN HE AWOKE, HE WROTE DOWN THE CONNECTIONS HE SAW IN HIS DREAM.

He awoke, spent a couple of hours writing down the connections he saw in his dream, and then spent the next year working it out and perfecting it. This was the algorithm for the original Google search engine. By honoring his dreams and acting on them, Page became one of the wealthiest people in the world.

The stories of Jacob and Larry Page are strikingly similar. God gave Jacob a lucrative business strategy through a *crazy* dream; he acted on its prophetic message and became *"exceedingly prosperous"* (Genesis 30:43). Obviously, that is an apt description of Larry Page's financial portfolio as well! Both of these men acted on the revelation they received at night while they slept, and upon awakening, they made their dreams come true.

DREAMING WITH GOD

I had the privilege of meeting one of these business-oriented dreamers in person at a training workshop. Carol Robinson attended our conference in Kingston, Jamaica, and shared with me how God has been speaking to her through dreams for years. The process she described resembles Larry Page's Google revelation. There is a flash of insight in her night visions that she then works out upon awakening.

For example, the Lord will give her the name of an herb or a description of its benefits in a dream, which she will then research when she awakens. Carol says it's a two-way conversation with God after she receives the dream, as He continues to teach her. Carol has made God her business partner, and He made her dreams come true.

WORDS OF KNOWLEDGE THROUGH ANGELIC DREAMS

Every good thing given and every perfect gift is from above, coming down from the Father of lights. (James 1:17)

This Scripture means that every blessing in our lives is from God. Regardless of the medium through which He chooses to provide that blessing, we always honor Him and give Jesus the glory and gratitude for those gifts.

THE HOLY SPIRIT GAVE WEIGHTY WORDS OF WISDOM AND KNOWLEDGE—PROPHETIC REVELATION THAT KEPT JESUS ALIVE— ALL WHILE JOSEPH SLEPT.

The beginning of the gospel of Matthew is fascinating. Passages abound with supernatural involvements and divine interventions that were written as examples for us. (See Matthew 1–2.) We read these sacred stories and our hearts glory in expectation as we understand the promise and precedent being set: the Father's clear intention is for heaven to intersect our very own everyday lives!

One incredible pattern we quickly discover is that four times in two chapters, God tells us that He communicated with Joseph through dreams. The Holy Spirit gave weighty words of wisdom and knowledge—prophetic revelation that kept Jesus alive—all while Joseph slept. It is also significant that God delivered these spiritual gifts through the ministry of an angel.

1. Joseph was encouraged by an angel in a dream to take Mary as his wife. (See Matthew 1:20–24.)

2. Joseph was instructed by an angel in a dream to move to Egypt. (See Matthew 2:13–15.)

3. Joseph was directed by an angel in a dream to return to Israel. (See Matthew 2:19–21.)

4. Joseph was warned by God in a dream to avoid Judea. (See Matthew 2:22–23.)

We see that God is giving Joseph direction about marrying the mother of Jesus and how to protect baby Jesus from the evil men out to kill Him. Remember that at this point in our historical timeline, Jesus is a tiny infant on a rescue mission from heaven to save humanity from their sin. Obviously, if Jesus dies as a baby, He will never grow up and be able to die on the cross, He will never be raised from the dead, and the Holy Spirit will never be poured out. Everything hinges on Jesus's safety as a baby.

Knowing this, you would think God might want Joseph awake when He provides these critical strategies for avoiding Herod and his murderers. At the very least, you would think God might want to speak to Joseph personally, since the stakes were so high.

Instead, God chose to use the medium of dreams and the ministry of His angels. The word *angel* means *messenger*, and according to Scripture, they are God's messengers. This is why we should listen to angels. They are bringing us supernatural revelation from heaven: gifts of prophecy, wisdom, and knowledge.

Throughout the Bible, God explains that He considers the messages He speaks through angels to be messages from Himself. A clear example of this is the story of the centurion Cornelius in Acts 10. An angel came to Cornelius, instructing him to find Peter, telling him specifically where Peter was staying and with whom. (See Acts 10:3–7.) Later, when God instructs Peter to go with Cornelius, there is no mention of the angel. Look at God's perspective of that angelic encounter in Acts 10:19–20:

> *While Peter was reflecting on the vision, **the Spirit said** to him, "Behold, three men are looking for you. But get up, go downstairs and accompany them without misgivings, for **I have sent them Myself**."*

The Holy Spirit clarified that the supernatural knowledge the angel delivered to Cornelius was actually a divine word personally from Himself.

We see this same principle in the familiar Christmas story of the shepherds keeping watch over their flocks by night. Upon hearing the extraordinary angelic announcement of their Savior's birth, what was the shepherds' immediate response?

> *When the angels had gone away from them into heaven, the shepherds began saying to one another, "Let us go straight to Bethlehem then, and see this thing that has happened which **the Lord has made known to us**."*   (Luke 2:15)

Again, the shepherds considered a message from angels to be a message from God Himself. And because they honored that supernatural knowledge delivered through the angel to be a word from the Lord, they were among the first to worship Jesus. Listening to angels did not distract the shepherds or take them away from the Lord; instead, it brought them closer to Him.

In chapter eleven, we will consider more of the varied and biblical ways God intends for heaven to break into our world as He blesses us with His gifts and revelation. What we have confidently established from our examination of Scripture thus far is that the Holy Spirit often downloads words of wisdom and knowledge to dreamers while they sleep. These gifts are often delivered on behalf of the Holy Spirit by His ministering spirits, the angels. (See Hebrews 1:14.)

We know *"Jesus Christ is the same yesterday and today and forever"* (Hebrews 13:8). What He did in the Bible, He wants to do in our lives as well. All day and all night, whether we are awake or asleep, we can receive everything God has for us. We purpose in our hearts to be open to accepting heavenly revelation however the Holy Spirit sends it, whomever He chooses to send it through.[13]

ALL DAY AND ALL NIGHT, WHETHER WE ARE AWAKE OR ASLEEP, WE CAN RECEIVE EVERYTHING GOD HAS FOR US.

GPS: GOD'S POSITIONING SYSTEM

Joseph certainly wasn't the only one who received words of wisdom and knowledge while he slept. Another biblical hero who was blessed with these spiritual gifts through his dreams is Paul. In Acts 16, we find him wondering where to go on the next step of his missions outreach. First, he had been forbidden by the Holy Spirit to go to Asia, and then the Spirit of Jesus did not permit him to go to Bithynia. (See Acts 16:6–7.) So where was Paul supposed to go?

---

13. To learn more about how to safely and biblically engage angels in everyday life, see: Charity Virkler Kayembe and Joe Brock, *Everyday Angels* (Shippensburg, PA: Destiny Image, 2018).

In answer to his heart's question, Paul had a night vision of a man beckoning for him, saying:

> *"Come over to Macedonia and help us." When he had seen the vision, immediately we sought to go into Macedonia, concluding that God had called us to preach the gospel to them.*
> (Acts 16:9–10)

God will often speak to us in our dreams about whatever is going on in our waking world. Just like Paul trying to determine where to go on his mission trip, whatever we are thinking about during the day and praying about as we fall asleep is usually what our dream revelation will speak to in the night.

Another example is American abolitionist Harriet Tubman who received direction and divine instruction from God while she slept. She said God showed her maps and helped her find safe houses to guide slaves to freedom on the Underground Railroad.

SACRED SLEEP

As we have seen, God blesses us with an overflow of His Spirit and extraordinary gifts through our dreams. It is truly amazing to see all the significant events that take place in Scripture while people are sleeping! While we have already looked at several instances, we would be remiss if we didn't consider two more incredible examples to discover what principles can be applied to our own lives.

The establishment of the Abrahamic covenant was God's supernatural contract with the Jews, pledging His faithfulness as they were called and chosen by Him. God's covenant with Abraham was the promise that Jesus would come one day, and in Him, all the world would be blessed. (See Genesis 18:18.) The foundation of thousands of years of faith began with this spiritual agreement between our heavenly Father and Abraham, our father of faith.

Again, you would think, for such an epic event, God might want Abraham to be awake. Instead, He establishes the covenant at night, in the dark, while Abraham is asleep. (See Genesis 15:1–21.) Years later, God reaffirms the covenant to Abraham's grandson Jacob *in the same manner*. (See Genesis 28:11–17.) God chooses to meet Jacob at night, while he's sleeping, in his dreams.

Why is this relevant? What does this have to do with us? So much! The weighty revelation for us to wrap our hearts around is that in the Bible, God never once said, "It's *just* a dream." God never once said, "You were asleep, so it didn't count."

Instead, we see the opposite. Scripture is our example for how God communicates with us. The Father fully expects His children to receive the gifts, covenants, impartations, and blessings He has for us through our visions of the night. Abraham and Jacob both received prophetic words that inspired faith in their hearts through their dreams. May we receive all the spiritual gifts God is releasing through our hearts while we sleep!

> ABRAHAM AND JACOB BOTH RECEIVED PROPHETIC WORDS THAT INSPIRED FAITH IN THEIR HEARTS THROUGH THEIR DREAMS.

THE GIFT OF HEALING IN A DREAM

When I was teaching a "Hearing God Through Your Dreams" workshop in New Zealand, one of our host pastors shared an awesome testimony with me from one of the women in his church. Because it demonstrates receiving the gift of healing through a dream at night, I want to share it with you as well, to build your faith for how the Holy Spirit can release His gifts to you even while you sleep.

This woman had been very sick. In her dream, a doctor came to her and gave her a pill, which she swallowed. In the dream, she sensed this was *Doctor Jesus*, the Great Physician. When she awoke the next morning, she was completely healed! No more symptoms, no more pain. Just divine restoration and health. Praise God!

Just like King Solomon received the impartation of the spiritual gift of wisdom through his dream, so too, this daughter of the King received the impartation of the spiritual gift of healing through her dream. They both awoke and the dream came true.

DISTINGUISHING OF SPIRITS IN A FUN DREAM

In case you haven't guessed, one of my favorite ways the Holy Spirit overflows our lives is through dreams! In order to find the sacred meaning hidden in dreams that we might think are silly, we can simply ask a few questions and match up the key action and emotion of our dream with what is going on in our waking life. Add in a couple of symbols to decode, a few fun wordplays, and some thinly veiled biblical references, and we've got ourselves a revelation from heaven, handed to us on a soft pillow every night of our lives.

Let me give you an example of receiving a prophetic word of wisdom that also released the gift of faith through my dream, my vision of the night. In the Old Testament, Jacob wrestled with God. (See Genesis 32:24–32.) The other night in my dream, I wrestled with Him, too.

Dream: We were on an exciting 007 type of mission. My husband Leo was on Expedia.com, planning a trip. I playfully wrestled and tried to pin down a mysterious guy whose attention I earnestly desired, and he gave me a rose. In the last scene, we saw a family recording and editing a film they were producing. We also poured several glasses of water, but someone said they spiked the drinks, so the dream ended with us trying to determine if our drinks were alcoholic or not.

Action: Wrestling and pinning down, receiving, producing, trying to distinguish

Emotion: Holy jealousy, desire

Setting: In waking life, Dad and I are writing this book, *Overflow of the Spirit*

Interpretation: In order to determine what area of my life the dream is speaking to, I ask, "Where in my life am I experiencing these things? Where am I feeling holy desire and trying to wrestle and pin something down? Where am I receiving something? Where am I producing something?"

> ONCE WE MATCH THE EMOTIONS AND ACTIONS FROM THE DREAM TO WAKING LIFE, WE KNOW WHAT AREA GOD IS SPEAKING TO US ABOUT.

Once we match the emotions and actions from the dream to waking life, we know what area God is speaking to us about and the symbolism becomes easy to decode. I'll share the interpreted message and ultimate meaning of the dream first, then go back through the symbols to unpack it piece by piece to show you how I got there.

My heavenly husband is Jesus (see Isaiah 54:5), and He said it was *"expedient"* (John 16:7 KJV) for Him to go away because then He could send another to us, the Holy Spirit. In the dream, this was symbolized by my husband Leo planning a trip on Expedia.

We are to *earnestly desire spiritual gifts* (see 1 Corinthians 14:1) and our family is recording, editing, and producing a book about that; the family film in the dream represented our book in waking life. The emotion of holy desire and the action of recording and editing a project as a family were identical to my waking world.

This book is about the Holy Spirit and His gifts. We are *wrestling* with principles in Scripture, attempting to *pin down* spiritual gifts and how to practically experience and release them. The ninefold manifestation of the Spirit is summed up and symbolized by the gift of *discerning of spirits* in the dream, depicted metaphorically when we were trying to discern if there were *spirits* in our drinks!

DECODING THE DREAM

Through the dream, God was encouraging me that I am successfully receiving His spiritual gifts, represented by the gift of the rose. I am practically walking by His Spirit, as in the dream, I was actively discerning and *distinguishing spirits*. Above all, God is pleased that our family is seeking to equip and empower His bride, the church, to live more fully from her union with Him and the overflow of His Spirit and gifts. This is our assignment, the exciting 007 kingdom mission.

In my dream, I was trying to pin down the Holy Spirit, and He did allow me to do this. Obviously, He was stronger, but He let me do it anyway. The main emotion in my dream was desire, a holy jealousy, for this mysterious, unfamiliar guy, who represented the Holy Spirit. Yes, the Holy Spirit *is* mysterious and unfamiliar. (See 1 Corinthians 2:7.) It's true that sometimes, God does download clear revelation and we are grateful for that understanding and clarity. But just as we embrace His revelation, we also need to embrace His mystery.

It was easy to match that key emotion from my dream with the Scripture on how we are to *"desire earnestly spiritual gifts"* (1 Corinthians 14:1). This helped to pinpoint what area God was focusing on in my waking life: His spiritual gifts.

I realized all over again that it is all about intimacy with God and relationship. The gifts all flow from that place of fellowship and friendship with Him. We never want to divorce the gift from the Giver. We never want to look at the prophecy in and of itself as a *commodity* separate from God. Prophecy is not a self-contained gift that we unwrap, but our best Friend's voice. A word of wisdom or a word of knowledge are not *things* to use or operate in mechanically; they are our Father's perceptions and His heavenly perspective on situations and circumstances.

> MIRACLES AND HEALING ARE NOT INDIVIDUALLY WRAPPED
> PACKAGES OF GOODNESS THAT ARE DISASSOCIATED FROM GOD.
> THEY ARE SIMPLY AN EXPRESSION OF HIM.

Miracles and healing are wonderful, but they are not individually wrapped packages of goodness that are dispensed in any way disassociated from the Healer. They are simply an expression of *Him*. Where the Spirit of the Lord is, there is freedom. Where the Healer is, there is healing. Where the Spirit of wisdom and understanding is, there are words of wisdom and knowledge. Where the God of hope is, there is faith. Where the Spirit of might is, there are miracles. The gifts are simply an expression of His fullness, an overflow of His thoughts, feelings, and strength.

So it's less about working His gifts and more about working *with Him* and allowing the fullness of His life to flow through us. His thoughts flow through our minds as knowledge and interpretative understanding. His words flow through our mouths as prophecy and praying in the Spirit. His feelings flow through our hearts as discernment, wisdom, and faith. His power flows through our hands in healing and miracles.

HEARING GOD'S HEART

These were the spontaneous thoughts that bubbled up from my heart upon awakening and pondering my dream. After we get an initial interpretation and understanding of any dream, however, we still need to check in with God through two-way journaling to ask Him if there is any other revelation He wants to share. This is what He had to say:

Char, it's awesome you are writing this book and I love that you love Me and even want to try and pin Me down! I just don't want you to feel like it's always necessary though. That is, it's not imperative that you understand and can predict everything about Me, what I'm going to do and how I'm going to do it. That would be boring! Remember, mystery is My calling card. It's way more fun all the way around when life isn't 100 percent routine and predictable. You want to *not know* some things; it's better that way!

Like Christmas. You don't want to know about those gifts under the tree, do you? It's better for them to remain a mystery for a time, especially for a child. The excitement builds, you anticipate and wonder. Being in a state of wonder is a good thing for you. It's one of the many things I appreciate so much about kids and one of the reasons I said you should be more like little children to enter My kingdom. Live in awe and wonder and mystery and let that be okay. Let it be *awe*some and *wonder*ful!

Yes, embrace and receive all the revelation I share. And be equally grateful to remain in a state of mystery and awe at what you don't yet understand. It's an unfolding journey. I don't want to just hand you a roadmap so you can go off on your own and simply follow the directions. I want to be your personal Guide, accompanying you along the way, giving you the tour of life Myself.

And with regard to the gifts of My Spirit, they are simply a natural overflow of intimacy with Me. They are the natural overflow of conversation and fellowship with Me. As you live to your union with Me—you in Me, Me in you, our spirits joined as one—the natural fruit of that supernatural unity is My Spirit flowing out through you. Not just in you, but flooding and overflowing you.

The overflow of My thoughts as you live to the mind of Christ—those are words of knowledge and wisdom. The overflow of My feelings as you live from your Father's heart—that is faith and discernment. The overflow of My strength as you live out of My divine nature—that is the working of miracles and healing and power.

So the closer you live to Me and with Me and in Me, the easier all of this naturally overflows. It's not something you work up or manufacture. You know the river within flows without you pushing it. Instead, you just learn to position yourself to connect with the flow of My river in your heart.

In the dream you were trying to discern and distinguish and differentiate. This is encouraging confirmation to you, that you are discerning spirits, that you are effectively flowing in My gifts. Discerning My Spirit from other spirits, distinguishing my thoughts from yours, differentiating my holy emotions from your own feelings.

Distinguishing and discerning—those actions came up in the dream symbol of trying to ascertain if the drinks were spiked with alcohol, and also the act of *pinning down* means essentially the same thing too. Pin down the truth about who's who and what's what. So twice your dream showed that as the key action. And that is the revelation.

The revelation that is most helpful to understand about the gifts of the Spirit is that you're not going after something *out there*. You don't have to go far off to heaven and carry them all the way back to earth. You know heaven is within you. You know I'm in you, too. Which means, all those gifts, those natural overflows of My divine thoughts, kingdom emotions, and supernatural power, it's all inside you. Already.

It's not far off and away. It's not something distant. It's just like the kingdom. It's inside you. It's just like eternity. I've placed it in your heart. It's just like My nature and fullness and Spirit, it's all within you *already*. And wherever I am, My gifts are, because they are not commodities separate from Me, they are expressions *of* Me.

Which makes all of this really easy. It's back to simply living to your union with Me, out of your union with Me. Understanding that separateness is an illusion, you are a new creation in Me, and our spirits are one.

SPIRIT-LED QUIET TIMES

Through these examples we understand how God initiates a conversation with us through the visions He gives us in the night. By honoring our dreams, we allow Him to set the tone for our morning devotional time together, focusing on whatever the Holy Spirit highlighted while we slept. We decode the symbols and translate the imagery to understand the dream's meaning, and journal with the Lord to fully hear His heart.

> BY HONORING OUR DREAMS, WE ALLOW GOD TO SET THE TONE FOR OUR MORNING DEVOTIONAL TIME TOGETHER.

Knowing we can meet with God in our dreams makes sleep sacred. It's exciting to drift off into dreams because heaven only knows what kind of supernatural gift, miracle, or revelation we might experience in the night!

As we have seen from these personal and diverse examples, God cares about what we care about. Whether you are a software engineer, homeschool mom, political representative, or kingdom entrepreneur, He wants to help you with whatever you've got going on in your life. Your heavenly Father knows all the answers and He already has the solution you're looking for.

When you go to bed, ask Him for His perspective on your problem or project and expect to receive His supernatural insight. He is the giver of every good gift and He can't wait to share His understanding and counsel with you, often through a word of wisdom, knowledge, or prophecy while you sleep.

Meditate on that revelation; ponder God's perspective as revealed through the dream, observing His vision and version of the situation. Remember to pray in the Spirit as you contemplate His message as this energizes your times of godly imagination and infuses them with supernatural power, further accelerating their manifestation and *collapse* into our world.

Invite heavenly creativity and spiritual gifts into your life by receiving an overflow of the Holy Spirit's revelation while you sleep. Dream your way to wisdom, faith, healing, and miracles tonight!

ACTION EXERCISE

Did you know you could receive an overflow of the Holy Spirit's life and gifts while you sleep? Has this ever happened to you? Describe the experience.

_____

_____

_____

_____

_____

Have you tended to ignore your dreams or have you valued them as revelation from heaven? Has this chapter adjusted your perspective at all? If you have not honored dreams the way Scripture honors dreams, repent and ask the Holy Spirit to give you His perspective on them.

When you go to sleep tonight, place a notebook and pen beside your bed or keep your cell phone handy for voice recording. Ask the Lord to speak to you through your dreams and expect to receive His creativity and counsel in the night. Upon awakening, immediately record your dream and interpret it with God.[14] Thank the Holy Spirit for His gift of wisdom and revelation and act on the message He's given you. Make your dreams come true!

14. If you need help, learn simple keys for dream decoding in the free crash course at glorywaves.org/dreams.

How I Received the Baptism in the Holy Spirit
by Tim Lindsay

I was really afraid of being deceived, and God led me to a crazy, *hanging from the rafters* kind of church where all sorts of manifestations were happening. God did give me a dream to tell me He wouldn't let me be deceived. I had wanted to speak in tongues for ages and had tried and had been prayed for by the movement's chief prophets a number of times but couldn't seem to get anything.

One day, I was jogging and talking to God when the words "God is good" appeared inside my chest and a phrase came out of my mouth. I could literally see the words inside my chest. So I just repeated that phrase for a while.

I didn't get anything more for some time, but eventually, I got some other words and then finally a free flow now. I don't usually know what I'm saying, but sometimes, I get a feeling for what it is about. I've noticed different tongues for different purposes.

10

"HEAL THE SICK..."

*As you go, preach, saying, "The kingdom of heaven
is at hand." Heal the sick, raise the dead,
cleanse the lepers, cast out demons.*
—Matthew 10:7–8

YOU ARE HEALED AND THE SYMPTOMS ARE DISAPPEARING

After open heart surgery, my heart was in atrial fibrillation (AFib) fairly continuously. I realized my heart had been traumatized by the operation and picked up a spirit of fear. So each morning, I was praying for healing as I laid my hands on my heart, using our ministries' "Inner Healing for an Organ Prayer Worksheet." After about five days, the Lord began to say repeatedly, "Mark, I have healed the AFib."

The following day, I asked Him why I still had the symptoms of AFib. His reply was, "You are to confess that AFib is healed and the symptoms are disappearing." Wow! That was a confession that was different for me. I grabbed hold of it and began speaking that over myself every day. It reminded me of Abraham speaking his name, "I am Abraham," by which he would be declaring, "I am the father of a multitude of nations." (See Genesis 17:5.) At that point, his wife was not even pregnant with their first child and he was ninety-nine years old. Well, three months later she became pregnant and the promise was manifest.

The Lord said, "Mark, I spoke the worlds into existence. You too must speak your healing into existence." So for about two months now, I have been speaking that the AFib is gone, the symptoms are disappearing, and my heart beats in perfect rhythm. Today, the portable electrocardiogram unit that hooks up to my iPhone reported no AFib. We are moving in the right direction! It doesn't say that every day, but my confession remains constant: "My heart is healed and beats in perfect rhythm and the symptoms of AFib are disappearing."

KINGDOM POWER PROMOTES KINGDOM PURPOSES

The kingdom of God is manifest when we do the works of the Father. (See John 3:21.) When we destroy the works of the devil (see 1 John 3:8), the kingdom comes (see Luke 11:20). When we heal the sick, *"the kingdom of God has come near"* (Luke 10:9). As the church, we are *"the light of the world"* (Matthew 5:14). Every place our foot treads, we bring light, kingdom power, and kingdom wisdom into the situation. Like Jesus, we set captives free. (See Luke 4:18.) What a glorious calling we have!

The various manifestation of the Holy Spirit that deal with healing include gifts of healings, effecting of miracles, faith, discerning of spirits, words of wisdom, and words of knowledge. God's voice is central as we minister healing. We quiet our own thoughts and ideas by focusing the eyes of our heart on the truth that Jesus is right here with us to meet the need.

> WE FOCUS THE EYES OF OUR HEART ON THE TRUTH THAT JESUS IS RIGHT HERE WITH US TO MEET THE NEED.

By tuning to flow, we look to see what He is doing, then we do the same. We listen to hear what He is saying, then we speak it forth. Our faith that Jesus wants to heal is based solidly on the revelation of the Scriptures. However, without real-time revelation, we don't know *how* He wants to perform the healing. As we follow the initiatives of heaven, we see the Holy Spirit manifest Himself and the kingdom comes on earth.

DELIVERANCE AND HEALING

Jesus would often discern that demons were an active agent in an infirmity, so casting them out was an integral part of the healing process for Him and His apostles.

> *When evening came, they brought to Him many who were demon-possessed; and He* **cast out the spirits** *with a word,* **and healed** *all who were ill.*   (Matthew 8:16)

> *A great throng of people…had come to hear Him and to be* **healed of their diseases**; *and those who were troubled with* **unclean spirits were being cured.**   (Luke 6:17–18)

> *The twelve were with Him, and also some women who had been* **healed of evil spirits and sicknesses**: *Mary who was called Magdalene, from whom* **seven demons had gone out**.   (Luke 8:1–2)

> *The people from the cities in the vicinity of Jerusalem were coming together, bringing people who* **were sick or afflicted with unclean spirits, and they were all being healed.**   (Acts 5:16)

> *In the case of many who had* **unclean spirits, they were coming out** *of them shouting with a loud voice; and many who had been* **paralyzed and lame were healed.** (Acts 8:7)

As we imitate Christ and follow His flow, we will also cast out demons and heal the sick. And, like Jesus, most of this ministry will be done on the streets. I believe that is the next revival Jesus is bringing to the church—ministry outside the church walls where the dying need our touch. If we are willing to believe for this and step out in faith, we will see it happen. Come on; be a believer!

Normally, when I think of the ninefold manifestation of the Spirit, I think of them operating in a church service; we go to church to receive a healing, prophecy, tongues or their interpretation, word of wisdom, word of knowledge, or discerning of spirits. However God has challenged me to expand my vision. There really isn't an *outside* of church, since we *are* the church, and wherever we are, we as the body of Christ manifest Jesus. Brian's testimony in chapter eight certainly demonstrates that.

> THE NINEFOLD MANIFESTATION OF THE SPIRIT DOES NOT HAVE TO HAPPEN INSIDE A CHURCH BUILDING. WE ARE THE CHURCH; WE AS THE BODY OF CHRIST MANIFEST JESUS.

KINGDOM POWER RIDES ON THE CARRIER WAVE OF KINGDOM EMOTIONS

[Jesus] *felt compassion for them and healed* their sick.
(Matthew 14:14)

Faith that activates miracles is empowered by the energy of the Holy Spirit, which is switched on when love, joy, compassion, gratitude, or thankfulness are present.

When I deeply love the person I am ministering to, and I follow the flow of the Spirit within me, I see results. Some keys to ministering healing effectively may include laying on of hands to impart God's energy, casting out demons, and speaking healing to the body. (See Mark 16:17–18.) Expect the Spirit to direct your prayers and your ministry. Do nothing of your own initiative, but only what you hear the Father saying and see the Father doing. Be open to creative new ways of ministering—like spitting and making mud as Jesus did (see John 9:6)—while not discarding established practices, such as the simple command, "Be healed!" Expect to receive words of wisdom and words of knowledge. Expect your faith to rise. Expect healing and miracles through your hands.

HEALING SOAKING PRAYER

One of my favorite and most effective ways to pray for healing is with a *soaking prayer* session. I encourage three to five people to sit comfortably around the person being prayed for and to appropriately lay their hands on the individual. They tune to the flow and pray as led by the Spirit. As they see the healing power of God flowing through their hands as energy and light, they soak the person in compassion, prayer, and healing power for fifteen minutes. There can be times of silence and times of spoken prayer. There is nearly always improvement in the person being prayed for as well in those who are praying. This can be repeated as necessary.

> IN A SOAKING PRAYER SESSION, THE HEALING POWER OF GOD FLOWS THROUGH THE HANDS OF THOSE PRAYING AS ENERGY AND LIGHT.

The advantage of having a few people tuned to the Spirit and praying as they are led is that there will be a greater array of the manifestation of the Spirit released, bringing forth a greater work of the Spirit. I always recommend a team of at least two to minister together (see Luke 10:1), with the ministry of a prophet and a teacher blending especially effectively. (See Acts 13:1–2.)

Jesus healed all who came to Him. He relied on His Father's initiative and displayed the manifestation of the Spirit in the process. The ministry approaches that follow illustrate the Spirit's ninefold manifestation in healing and miracles.

MIRACLES ARE RELEASED AS I FILL ALL FIVE SENSES OF MY HEART WITH GOD'S INTENTION

1. *The ears of my heart hear God's spoken word for the situation.* I honor spontaneous thoughts as coming from the spirit world. (See John 5:30.) I listen to hear what the Spirit is saying right here, right now.

2. *The eyes of my heart see God's vision of the miracle completed.* I see spontaneous images from the spirit world. (See John 5:19; Revelation 4:1.) I watch to see how Jesus ministers to the person, and I do the same. I look not at what is seen (the infirmity) but what is unseen (complete healing).

3. *With the mind of my heart, I ponder, meditate, and muse* on both biblical truths (*logos*) and what the Spirit is saying to me right now (*rhema*). (See Luke 2:19.) I don't allow thoughts of doubt or unbelief to have a place in me, but I only see God's word accomplished.

4. *With the will of my heart, I make decisions that I speak* and live out. (See Acts 19:21.) As my heart is filled with the *logos* and *rhema*, I purpose in my spirit to agree with God and I confess truth, saying the same thing as the Lord is saying.

5. *The emotions of my heart begin to affect my behavior.* (See Galatians 5:22–23.) As I see the good plans the Lord has for me and the one I am ministering to, I am filled with joy and gratitude. As the spiritual reality becomes my reality and the excitement and thanksgiving overflow, I cannot keep them in but must release them in acts of faith, worship, and obedience.

"*Heart faith*" is born by a *rhema* word and a vision from God. Both are held in the heart through pondering, speaking, and acting until a miracle is released. (See Mark 11:23.) All five senses of my heart are filled by God.

ABRAHAM MODELS THE BIRTHING OF A MIRACLE

Abraham, our father of faith, modeled faith that brings forth miracles by:

+ **Receiving a spoken word** from God concerning His promised destiny. (See Genesis 12:1–3.)

+ **Receiving a vision** of the promise already fulfilled and as he gazed upon it, his faith grew. (See Genesis 15:5–6.)

+ **Believing** what God had revealed. (See Romans 4:20–21.)

+ **Speaking** the promise before it was physically evident. (See Genesis 17:5.)

+ **Receiving** the miracle birth of Isaac at the age of one hundred. (See Genesis 21:1–5.)

> EVERY MOMENT OF EVERY DAY, YOU ARE FILLING THE FIVE SENSES OF YOUR HEART WITH EITHER LIFE OR DEATH.

Every moment of every day, you are filling the five senses of your heart with either life or death. I have chosen to be aware of the thoughts and images I am incubating to ensure they all are coming from God so I birth only His kingdom reality. I journal and ask God for His thoughts and images concerning my marriage, my children, my work, my ministry, and my health, and that is what I meditate on until they are manifest in the physical world. If you follow this model provided by Abraham, you will find God performing miracles in your life.

DIFFERENT GIFTS OF HEALINGS

In addition to miracles, we have gifts of healings. I believe there are many ways to be healed, such as forgiving those who have hurt us (see Mark 11:24–25), fasting (see Isaiah 58:5–8), use of herbs (see Ezekiel 47:12), exercise (see 1 Corinthians 9:26–27), and great nutrition (see Daniel 1:15), to name a few. (*See more in Appendix C, "Dig Deeper with These Links."*)

I want to share a story from one of our friends. As you read it, ask the Spirit to speak to you, teach you, and give you *rhema* for today. This is Malachi Talabi's journaling while meditating on the verse, "*They will lay hands on the sick, and they will recover*" (Mark 16:18).

Did You Lay Hands on the Sick as Commanded?
by Malachi Talabi

Question: *Lord, what is going on with my family health-wise? Do You have anything to say?*

Jesus: I am a healer. The enemy will try to make you think that I am passive, but I am present. I see and hear and feel your distress for I am touched with the feeling of your infirmity. There are many examples of people or situations where saved people had sickness. James wrote, "*Is anyone sick among you?*" and Timothy needed wine for his stomach's sake.

"[You shall] *lay hands on the sick, and they will recover*" (Mark 16:18). There is a genuine gift of miracles but *recovery* is just as miraculous! Your children shall recover, and that is the vocabulary I want you to use—recovery. It's your job to pray and it's My job to help them recover.

Question: *Lord, why do they get sick in the first place? Why do they have eczema? You died for this stuff. The Word says, "No plague shall come near my dwelling." This is something I don't understand.*

Jesus: Just because I've given you an inheritance doesn't mean that you don't have to stand. The enemy will try and wrestle you in these areas!

Reflection: *It seems that God was differentiating healing and miracles and making recovery the thing to focus on. I went to meditate on Mark 16:17–18.*

Jesus: You are asking Me to do what I instructed you to do, which is to walk in authority. I've seated you above these things. *You* shall lay hands on the sick and they shall recover. I stopped laying hands on people after My resurrection! After My resurrection, you don't see Me lay hands on anybody. That is for you to do; it's for you to walk in. How are you ever going to walk in your authority if I don't give you opportunities to exercise your authority? People pray that I would touch their child but it's for *them* to touch their child, for I said, "You shall lay hands..." There are so many things you are asking Me to do that I instructed you to do. *You* are to deal with the devil and *you deal with this sickness.* It's time to walk in your authority.

Action: *I started laying hands, declaring, commanding and praying, and telling them they were recovering. It was phenomenal the rate at which my children's skin and hands began recovering! This has truly increased my faith.*

A HEALING MODEL

I would like to share with you a seven-step model that I have seen work very effectively in ministering healing.

1. COMPASSION

Smile, ask their name, tune to your heart, and express love to them, telling them, "Of course, Jesus wants to heal you. ... Jesus includes everyone. ... You absolutely are included."

2. ASK, "WHAT'S WRONG?"

Ask, "Where does it hurt?" and "What does God want to heal *now?*" Focus intently on one item at a time. Ask the individual, "How long have you had this and what event occurred at the time this problem began?" Ask, "May I pray for you for healing? May I lay my hand on you? Now, simply receive as I pray. Sense and share what you are feeling, and any thoughts or images that come to you, as these are important messages from your heart."

3. LISTEN TO GOD

Relax, smile, and ask, "Lord, grant me words of knowledge concerning how to pray for this person." Then receive any information the Lord may want to reveal by tuning to spontaneous emotions, spontaneous bodily pains, emotional pains, images, and words. Lovingly share these. Specifically confess sins, especially *unforgiveness and accusative thoughts or words toward self and others*, and follow any other specific directions God gives. Command all spiritual forces connected with these sins leave now. If you don't discern any special revelation bubbling up, then minister healing based on the general promises in the Bible and Jesus's example of healing *all* who came to Him.

4. INVITE GOD'S PRESENCE AND POWER TO HEAL

"Lord, pour Your love and healing power on this person according to Isaiah 61:1–3. Holy Spirit, we welcome Your presence. Glorify the Son by revealing your wonderful healing power. God, send angels with healing on their wings." With your eyes open, watch the person for signs of the Holy Spirit moving upon them, such as fluttering eyelids, becoming flushed, gentle trembling, and peace. Now the love and power of the Lord are present to heal! (See Luke 5:17.)

5. COMMAND THE HEALING IN JESUS'S NAME

Lay your hand on the infirm spot, being sensitive when praying for the opposite gender. Command the affliction or pain to leave. Use short prayers. Both the individual and the prayer counselor are to stay relaxed and smiling so you do not block the flow of the Holy Spirit. Maintain this attitude: *"Healing is easy* because Jesus has already done the work; by His scourging we *are* healed. He has already obtained this healing for us." (See Isaiah 53:4–5; Psalm 103:3; Psalm 147:3.) Rebuke demons and command them to leave. Cancel every assignment of the powers of darkness against the person's mind, body, and spirit, command pain to go and trauma to leave all cellular tissue. Speak restoration and normal function of all cells and body parts. Be detailed and specific. "Function normally in Jesus's name!" See God's light penetrating the area. You focus God's healing light on the infirm spot just as you would focus a magnifying glass on a piece of paper so that the sun's rays are intensified and set it on fire. God's focused healing power releases miracles. (See Luke 11:34–36; Habakkuk 3:4.) You are simply declaring, believing, and seeing His divine energy penetrate the area. Speak the faith, trust, peace, and protection of Psalm 91.

6. TEST IT OUT

Ask for and receive God's vision of the body functioning normally, letting gratitude and thanksgiving flood your heart as you ask the person to do something they could not easily do before. Miracles manifest *as you step out in faith*, believing and *receiving* in childlike joy. (See Mark 11:22–24.) As the lepers *went*, they were healed. (See Luke 17:14.) *"Get up...and walk!"* (John 5:8).

7. REPEAT IF NECESSARY

If you pray and see no visible change in the natural, or you see a partial healing, then pray again immediately until you have prayed three or four times and either they are completely healed or you note no further improvement. Repetition weakens and defeats the enemy. (See Luke 18:1–8; Mark 8:23–25; James 5:17; 1 Kings 18:41–45.) With each prayer, express a little more love, belief, and gratitude, staying open to using various prayer approaches as the Spirit guides you. Close by praying a blessing. Be sure to determine if they have ever invited Christ into their lives. If not, lead them in a salvation prayer.

ACTION EXERCISE

Lord, what do You want to say to me from this chapter? What are the practices that I need to focus on and internalize and live out of?

_____

_____

_____

_____

_____

Journal and ask God for His thoughts and images concerning your marriage, children, work, ministry, and health. Perhaps do this over five days. Then meditate on *only* what He has revealed in each of these areas. Birth His kingdom reality in each area of your life.

When you meet someone who is in pain, tune to the overflowing Spirit within, looking to see what Jesus is doing. With His guidance, ask the hurting person if you can pray for them. With their permission, pray for their healing, release from pain, and recovery.

Practice: Healing prayer, laying on of hands, listening to God to discern root causes of the infirmity, and casting out of demons.

Let this become normal and natural. It is true that every new activity is awkward for the first dozen or so times, but then it becomes comfortable and ultimately you become skilled if you continue on.

Make it your decision: I will manifest kingdom compassion, power, and authority.

How I Received the Baptism in the Holy Spirit
by Rev. Davidson Okoko

I had been reading *Releasing the Supernatural* when something special happened on Sunday at Salem Center. The presiding minister prayed for us all and handed out handkerchiefs to everyone who attended. I went home with that handkerchief and slept. The next morning, as I was about to wake up from bed, I discovered that I had mumbled some words that did not make any sense.

I was encouraged by a Christian brother to continue to pray and develop the language. That was what I did. I can confidently say that the gift of speaking in other tongues that I received came from the anointed handkerchief. Rev. Kenneth E. Hagin called it "the tangibility of the anointing." The anointing in that handkerchief transferred to me. This is confirmed in the Bible: "*God was performing extraordinary miracles by the hands of Paul, so that handkerchiefs or aprons were even carried from his body to the sick, and the diseases left them and the evil spirits went out*" (Acts 19:11–12).

11

REVELATION BRINGS LIFE

REVELATION COMES IN MANY WAYS

Revelation from the *"Wonderful Counselor"* (Isaiah 9:6) comes in many ways. Let's review. The ninefold manifestation of the Spirit listed in 1 Corinthians 12 is usually divided into three categories:

1. **Speaking gifts:** tongues, interpretation of tongues, prophecy

2. **Power gifts:** faith, gifts of healings, miracles

3. **Revelation gifts:** discerning of spirits, word of wisdom, word of knowledge

Of course, the Bible is clear that the overflow of His Spirit through these nine gifts is not the only way in which God's revelation and power break into our world. For example, He gives revelation through angels, dreams, visions, inspiration, illumination, and *"our hearts burning within us"* (Luke 24:32). Scripture records God's voice coming through a donkey (see Numbers 22:28), guidance coming from a book being read to combat insomnia (see Esther 6:1–3), and wisdom through the counsel of a friend (see Esther 4:13–14).

Healing can come by looking at a bronze snake (see Numbers 21:9), stepping into troubled waters (see John 5:4), and dipping into a muddy river (see 2 Kings 5:1–14). God's voice can sound like a gentle blowing, still and small (see 1 Kings 19:12), or like the roar of many waters (see Revelation 1:13–15). Need I go on? I suspect the possibilities are endless. We can expect God to break into our life with His wisdom and power in a host of different ways.

WE CAN EXPECT GOD TO BREAK INTO OUR LIFE WITH HIS WISDOM AND POWER IN A HOST OF DIFFERENT WAYS.

In addition, there is no indication in Scripture that the Spirit is limited to manifesting or revealing Himself in only the nine ways listed in 1 Corinthians 12. I believe that this list is representative, not exhaustive. It gives a *few* examples of the ways the Spirit may manifest Himself through His people; *it does not list the only ways* He may do so. Whenever we speak or act out of the initiatives of heaven, when we say or do anything from the flow of the river within us, we become expressions of Christ on earth and manifest a revelation of the Holy Spirit's life in our world.

I expect the same idea applies when it comes to the nine fruit of the Spirit. There may be more than those listed in Galatians 5: love, joy, peace, longsuffering, gentleness, goodness, faith, meekness, and temperance. For example, what about things like gratitude (see Colossians 2:7), thankfulness (see Colossians 3:16), mercy (see Matthew 5:7), honesty (see John 16:13), and wisdom (see Ephesians 1:17)? Whenever we express the character of God, not as a work of our flesh but as an overflow of the river within, it is a fruit of the Spirit.

In this chapter, I want to share some examples of God's revelation gifts in action. I believe we manifest them all the time, but we are often unaware that the spontaneous thought, image, or emotion is a revelation from God. Look for the words of wisdom, words of knowledge, and prophecy as you read. Notice how naturally and easily they are received. By seeing them in the stories of others, you will begin to recognize them in your own life.

A Word of Knowledge by Helen Milne

It seems that God directs me to speak in tongues day and night when my mouth is not otherwise engaged. I particularly do it when driving as it doesn't in any way affect my concentration on the road.

I was actually driving along a busy road thinking I should open a new bank account for a business venture. I had already decided to use a different bank and was considering whether it should be bank A or bank B. I didn't have any preference or knowledge of how each bank operated. I thought, "Oh, I think I'll go along to bank A," so I continued driving and looking where it might be found. Then it was as if I heard a correction in my spirit that felt like, "Turn around and go to bank B." It was perhaps like receiving a word of knowledge; it was compelling, insistent. So I thought, "Okay, Father, if that's your instruction, here I go," and turned the car right around to go to the second bank whose location I already knew. It surprised me that my Heavenly Father would intervene this way, but I am always very excited to have an instruction from the Most High and do it immediately. He thinks of us all the time and I am amazed and just love it. He always knows what is ahead (sometimes far ahead) of us and prepares us for that.

Another time I needed a change and asked the Lord where I should go. I awoke one morning to see clearly the name of the town where I now live written in large white letters before my face. Immediately I went there to buy property and joined the church there, where I married.

I am always excited when I find myself speaking tongues as I understand that God is eliciting the prayers He needs to hear from His saints. I also feel that it is keeping my spirit very close to Him, washing me constantly, and developing the strength of His spirit in me. This excites me.

PROPHETIC DECREES

The next few examples include prophetic decrees. Prophecy includes announcing what God is speaking. This is part of creating our future reality. God spoke the worlds into existence. The Israelites were supposed to declare what God said, "I have given you the promised land" (see Exodus 12:25), but instead they decreed, "We are going to die in the wilderness" (see Exodus 14:11). They would not change their faith or their decree and bring it into line with what God had planned for them. Sadly, they received what they declared. (See Numbers 14:28–32.)

Let us learn from their mistakes. Let us believe and speak *only* what God speaks.

A Prophecy from Flavien Williams

The vision: *I see the image of a large evergreen tree and I can hear the Lord saying...*

Speak to the roots, speak to the roots, speak to the roots. The strongest part of a tree is the roots. The nation of America is as an evergreen tree to Me. My child, speak to the roots. Do not look at the leaves or the branches. Do not look at what is happening around you. Do not look at the distractions of the enemy. I want you to speak to the roots. Remind Me of My prophetic promises over this nation. Remind Me of the prayers that were prayed for this nation. Remind Me of the obedience of the founding fathers. Remind Me of the many evangelical seeds that were sown into this world from this nation. Remind Me of the love this nation has for Israel. Remind Me of the many prayer warriors who warred in prayer for this nation. As you do this, you will see a light, a light, a light of My love, My grace, My mercy, My faithfulness erupt from the very foundation of this great nation. My promises are yes and amen. I will cause the roots of this nation to become alive with My presence. I will bring about transformation from the very foundation of this nation. Speak to the roots, speak to the roots, speak to the roots. Bring Me into remembrance of My promises. I will burn up the works of the enemy in the fire of My revival. Speak to the roots.

Having seen a great wave coming towards me in the spirit, this is what I hear the Lord saying...

A wave of My glory. A wave of My glory. A wave of My glory is going to sweep through My church. I will wash out everything that is not Me. I will cause a cleansing in My people that will bring about a purity in My people. I am going to wash My people white as snow. I will cause honesty and integrity, kindness and love, grace and peace, love and joy, compassion and wisdom to erupt in My church. I will cause a cleansing that when My people go out in the world, they will radiate with My love, My grace, and My compassion. I am causing a shaking of My glory because My church has come alive with the fullness of My grace. A wave of My glory. A wave of My glory is sweeping over My people. A mighty outpouring of My grace, a hunger like My people have never seen before. A wave of My glory. A wave of My glory. A wave of My glory.

While meditating on the image of a door I keep seeing, I hear the Lord saying...

Behold I am opening up a door in the heavens. Yes, I am opening up a door in the heavens. As you rise up higher and seek Me with all of your heart, I am causing My revelation knowledge to suddenly be accessible to you. Come up higher, come up higher. Do not be distracted by the news. Do not be distracted by the warring in the streets. Do not be distracted by what is going on in society. Come up higher, come up higher. Remember, My child, light is brightest in the darkest of hour. Come up higher and see Me pour My glory down on your land like it has never occurred before. Breakthroughs, miracles, salvations, deliverances, healings, inventions, innovations, strategies, insights, wisdom, knowledge, and understanding like you have never seen before. I am birthing something new in My people as they seek Me with all of their hearts. Doors, doors, doors of revival are opening. Come up higher. I am going to pour My glory down on this nation and the world as My people seek Me with all of their heart. I will give My people eyes to see, eyes to see, eyes to see into the spiritual realm so that they can grab a hold of the victory I have already secured for them at Calvary. Come up higher, come up higher, come up higher.

A Prophetic Decree from Jacqueline McKool

Recently, as I thought about the Islamic influence that has quickly and resolutely infiltrated our nation, I asked the Lord specifically how to pray about it.

The Lord spoke and said that five times a day, the Islamic prayers and declarations released into the atmosphere are in agreement with the enemy, giving him legal ground to advance his evil plan on this nation. The consistent, unified Islamic prayers and the declarations of special interest groups, whose agenda is contrary to God's Word, currently outweigh the voices of the people of the kingdom of God. The Lord also said that if His remnant would declare aloud that He is the one true God even just once a day, then an acknowledgment of His sovereignty would be released into the airways *every minute of the day!*

Example of a Declaration

Yahweh God, the great I Am, He alone is God, and there is none beside Him. Jesus, His only begotten Son, is our Savior, the Lord of Lords, and King of Kings, the One who was, who is, and is to come. All glory, praise, honor, majesty, splendor, and dominion are His forever and ever. Amen.

It is time that we, the remnant, the called out ones of the body of Jesus Christ, release our voice, the breath of our Creator, by the power of the Holy Spirit, and declare who the one true God is over this nation. Our collective voice has more power than any other and will supersede the voices aligned with the enemy.

Father God has spoken; we can take back the airways over this nation that belong to us by the victory of the cross of Christ Jesus, airways that are permeated with ungodly chants, statements, decrees, invocations, and threats. We must mobilize and use our most powerful weapon, the Word of God, and by our spoken word, nullify the decrees of darkness and take back our nation in the name of our redeemer Jesus, the King and Lord of America!

I call you, brothers and sisters, to take the Lord God at His word; declare Him as the one true God and fill the atmosphere with His praise at least once a day. Ask the Holy Spirit to remind you or set a reminder on your smart phone.

Together, the gates of hell will not prevail against us! (See Matthew 16:18.)

Sing the glory of His name; make His praise glorious. Say to God, "How awesome are Your works!" Because of the greatness of Your power Your enemies will give feigned obedience to You. (Psalm 66:2–3)

WORDS OF WISDOM

I define inner healing as *allowing God to replace the pictures in the art gallery of your mind, removing pictures that do not have Jesus in them and replacing them with pictures that do.* I find inner healing occurs often as the Wonderful Counselor counsels me during my journaling times.

> **FOR INNER HEALING, ALLOW GOD TO REMOVE PICTURES IN YOUR MIND THAT DO NOT HAVE JESUS IN THEM AND REPLACE THEM WITH PICTURES THAT DO.**

One morning, I looked in my mind's eye at Washington, D.C., and all I could see was corruption, lack of integrity, and ineptness. It made me both angry and fearful: angry because no one would stand up and do the right thing, and fearful because their terrible spending habits could destroy the entire economy.

I realized that anger and fear were not the Spirit's fruit (see Galatians 5:22), so I decided to journal about this. I asked Jesus to show Himself in my mind's image of Washington. What I was viewing did not have Jesus in it, so it obviously was a lie since Jesus is everywhere. Because it was a lie, it was producing some pretty ugly emotions.

I put a smile on my face, relaxed, and asked Jesus to show me where He was in the scene. Into my mind flowed an image of Jesus seated on a throne above the United States Capitol and the White House. His long robes flowed over the buildings and His glory streamed over them and those who lived and worked there.

Jesus spoke: "I rule in Washington, D.C."

I reflected, "Well, of course He does. He is King of Kings and Lord of Lords. And yes, I sure don't know why He puts certain people over us, but the Roman government was far worse than our government, and yet Jesus was clear that they had no power other than what God granted them."

> *Pilate said to Him, "You do not speak to me? Do You know that I have authority to release You, and I have authority to crucify You?" Jesus answered, "You would have no authority over Me, unless it had been given you from above."*
>
> (John 19:10–11)

I said, "Yes, but God, they are removing You from all institutions in America!"

God reminded me of a similar situation in the Bible and His reaction to it:

> *Why are the nations in an uproar and the peoples devising a vain thing? The kings of the earth take their stand and the rulers take counsel together against the LORD and against His Anointed, saying, "Let us tear their fetters apart and cast away their cords from us!"* (Psalm 2:1–3)

The nations in David's day were also attempting to remove God from their lives, to throw off His moral restraints so they would have no cords to bind them and they could do anything they pleased.

God wasn't too concerned about their puny efforts.

> *He who sits in the heavens **laughs**; the Lord scoffs at them. Then He will speak to them in His anger, and terrify them in His fury.* (Psalm 2:4–5)

If God can laugh, then I can, too. Laughter is so much better than getting all down in the dumps, fearful, angry, and depressed.

So I have decided to laugh and I highly recommend that you do the same. It is healing to your whole body and a testimony to your belief that the Lord is still on His throne. We can also ask for the nations to become the Lord's.

Ask of Me, and I will surely give the nations as Your inheritance, and the very ends of the earth as Your possession.

(Psalm 2:8)

We are the church; let's rise up with a victory shout and declare the truth: *"The earth is the LORD's, and all it contains"* (Psalm 24:1), and *"the Most High is ruler over the realm of mankind"* (Daniel 4:17)! *"There will be no end to the increase of His government or of peace"* (Isaiah 9:7).

> WE ARE THE CHURCH; LET'S RISE UP WITH A VICTORY SHOUT
> AND DECLARE THE TRUTH:
> "THE EARTH IS THE LORD'S, AND ALL IT CONTAINS."

I now hold a new picture in my mind concerning Washington. I now see Jesus ruling. This journaling time that included a word of knowledge—Jesus saying, "I rule in Washington, D.C." —was a life-changing experience. With this statement, the Lord was reminding me of a truth I had forgotten or not applied to the situation. A reminder of the right truth to fit the situation I am in could also be considered a prophecy.

Revelation and Encouragement from a Friend's Journaling

Lord, what is the good that You are bringing forth in my life through my failure?

I always take everything and turn it for your good. That is what I do. That is what I specialize in. I am the only One that can do this. The enemy of your soul cannot, and you or anyone else does not have that divine capability to take what seems dark and disastrous and turn into a beautiful work of art. In My divine perspective and My eternal power, I see the much bigger picture as I did before I formed and spoke the vastly enormous universe.

The good that I am bringing forth in your life is that you will walk more deeply and move more wisely in Me. You will come out of this with a much keener sense of the snares of the enemy and also, and more importantly, one that will lean more heavily on your Beloved. You are weak and I am strong. You are clay and I am eternal and the One that strength and power flows from.

One main lesson I want you to learn is to be much more aware of Me in you. Christ in you. *In* you, son. Not outside, not one day will be in you, but in you *now*. You often walk through life feeling alone, abandoned, and somehow feeling left empty-handed. You ask Me, "Where are you, Lord?" I am here, son. I am *so* here. Yet, often you are unaware of the life-giving power that I have placed within you. Christ in you, the hope of ever seeing My glory. The same power that raised Me up out of the bowels of death and hades resides *in* you. I would like you to go through Scripture and look up all verses on *Me in you*. Glory in flesh. Power residing in weakness. Glory dwelling in human form. Your eyes have been on *you* the last few days, on how horrible you are, on how weak you are, on how insufficient you are.

Did I call you to make yourself your dwelling place? Did I ask you to come forth in power and strength and be the mighty man who is able to conquer anything? No. I have repeatedly laid out in My word the secret to an over-coming and victorious lifestyle. It is only by looking at Me, being caught up in who I am in you, in what I have already accomplished for you in My death and resurrection. Fix your eyes on Jesus. Look *full* in His wonderful face.

Wisdom Concerning Marriage (Anonymous)

I see the day you both stood at the altar before Me. I see it and I blessed it and I was in it and I am still in it. You have doubted My hand and My provision because your eyes were on the wrong things. They were not on the strengths but on the weaknesses. They were on the *what ifs* and the lacks instead of on the promise before you and the beauty of My gift to you. I specifically chose you two to walk together.

Your wife is a jewel, a rare gem prepared for you, son. I saw the weaknesses and strengths in both of you and saw a perfect match where one would complement the other. Let go of all the *what ifs* and other possibilities. Let them go for good. Dwell on My gift to you.

WORDS OF KNOWLEDGE

It would appear that Jesus had a vision ahead of time concerning Nathanael, a man He was going to meet that day. This is an example of a word of knowledge.

Jesus saw Nathanael coming to Him, and said of him, "Behold, an Israelite indeed, in whom there is no deceit!" Nathanael said to Him, "How do You know me?" Jesus answered and said to him, "Before Philip called you, when you were under the fig tree, I saw you." (John 1:47–48)

When Jesus met the Samaritan woman at the well, He again spoke a word of knowledge:

> *The woman answered and said, "I have no husband." Jesus said to her, "You have correctly said, 'I have no husband'; for you have had five husbands, and the one whom you now have is not your husband; this you have said truly." The woman said to Him, "Sir, I perceive that You are a **prophet**."*
>
> (John 4:17–19)

These are the kinds of stories we tend to think of when talking about spiritual gifts and they are truly amazing. There are those who receive similar revelations today, those who have the ministry of a prophet and have honed their prophetic skills through practice, such as Shawn Bolz and the late Bob Jones. Their accurate knowledge of the details of strangers' lives excites and inspires us, maybe even inciting a bit of holy jealousy in us! Watching their ministry, we may feel discouraged that we are not used in the same way and conclude that we are *ungifted* and unanointed. One of our goals for this book is to make it clear to you that if you are living in a close relationship with Jesus and living out of the Spirit's flow, *you* are also expressing the gifts of the Spirit. It's time to recognize and honor them.

> IF YOU ARE LIVING IN A CLOSE RELATIONSHIP WITH JESUS AND LIVING OUT OF THE SPIRIT'S FLOW, YOU ARE EXPRESSING THE GIFTS OF THE SPIRIT.

GOD'S REVELATION WORKS EVERYWHERE

You have a specific unique gifting and anointing. I believe God anoints, calls, and commissions each of us to minister His grace to His world *through the gifts He has given to us*. Since the earth is the Lord's and the fullness thereof, there is no sacred/secular split. God's revelation works in the church, your home, and in the marketplace. It works everywhere!

DESIGN OF THE TEMPLE

Then David gave to his son Solomon the plan of the porch of the temple, its buildings, its storehouses, its upper rooms, its inner rooms and the room for the mercy seat; and the plan of all that he had in mind, for the courts of the house of the LORD, *and for all the surrounding rooms, for the storehouses of the house of God and for the storehouses of the dedicated things.... "All this," said David, "the* LORD *made me understand **in writing by His hand upon me**, all the details of this pattern."*   (1 Chronicles 28:11–12, 19)

TABERNACLE CRAFTSMEN

Now the LORD *spoke to Moses, saying, "See, I have called by name Bezalel.... **I have filled him with the Spirit of God in wisdom, in understanding, in knowledge, and in all kinds of craftsmanship**, to make artistic designs for work in gold, in silver, and in bronze, and in the cutting of stones for settings, and in the carving of wood, that he may work in all kinds of craftsmanship....In the hearts of all who are skillful I have put skill, that they may make all that I have commanded you."*
                (Exodus 31:1–6)

Let every skillful man among you come, and make all that the LORD *has commanded.*   (Exodus 35:10)

A BUSINESS PLAN

Our friend Bill Dupley shared a similar gift the Lord gave him. He relates:

When I was a chief technologist, I regularly asked God for wisdom. I once had to write a business plan for a company. A business plan has several components; one part has to do with identifying the inhibitors to the company's growth. The Lord spoke to me and told me explicitly what was restraining the company's growth and how to fix the problem. The president of the firm implemented my suggestions and has increased his delivery capacity by thirty times as a result.

HANDEL'S MESSIAH

George Frideric Handel wrote his renowned sacred oratorio *Messiah*, containing the well-known "Hallelujah Chorus," in 1741. Handel said he heard the music of heaven as a flow within him. He later told a servant, "I did think I did see all heaven before me and the great God Himself seated on His throne, with His company of Angels!" He spent twenty-four days feverishly writing the 259-page musical score, which he concluded with this note, "To God alone the glory."

Handel experienced throne room worship, and put into musical score what he saw and heard, releasing the worship of heaven on earth. His *Messiah* still inspires us centuries later.

INVENTIONS

George Washington Carver was a prominent American scientist and inventor in the early 1900s who developed hundreds of products using peanuts, sweet potatoes, and soybeans. He also taught farmers about crop rotation and increasing yields.

Carver said he heard from God while sleeping. If he went to bed thinking of "an apparently insoluble problem, when I woke the answer was there."

He once asked God to tell him the mystery of the universe. "But God answered, 'That knowledge is for me alone.' So I said, 'God, tell me the mystery of the peanut.' Then God said, 'Well George, that's more nearly your size.' And he told me."

DISCOVERY OF INSULIN

Canadian physician Frederick Banting had a dream that led to a breakthrough in diabetes research. Awakening from a dream one night, he wrote down the following words: "Tie up the duct of the pancreas of a dog. Wait for a few weeks until the glands shrivel up. Then cut it out, wash it out and filter precipitation." This procedure led him to discover insulin.

MY MINISTRY

For months, God had led me to focus intensely on seeking to discover how to hear His voice. Then, one morning, I was awakened by a loud voice, as God said, "Get up. I am going to teach you to hear My voice." Over the next several hours, God showed me four keys to hearing His voice from Habakkuk 2:1–2. These transformed my life and the lives of millions we have shared them with.

A few years later, I had spent months searching out every verse on being in Christ and having Christ in me. Finally the revelation was ready to spring forth. For three days, I closed my eyes and typed from the flow. The result was the book *Naturally Supernatural*,[15] which has set thousands free from the strivings of the flesh.

Each morning when I awaken, I tune to the flow and receive not only words of love and encouragement from my heavenly Father, but revelation in the area of my current passionate pursuit. You can do this also!

CREATIVITY IN YOUR AREA OF SPECIALTY

Honor the flow of the Spirit through you to release wisdom, knowledge, and excellence in everything you put your hand to. An artist will receive revelation in their artwork, a musician in

---

15. Mark and Patti Virkler, *Naturally Supernatural: Letting Jesus Live Through You* (Shippensburg, PA: Destiny Image, 1994).

revelatory music, a craftsman in creativity with his hands, and a mom in raising her children. Don't despise your gifting or be jealous of those whose gift is different than yours. Honor what you receive and you will receive more. Be faithful with what you are given and you will be given more.

> DON'T DESPISE YOUR GIFTING OR BE JEALOUS OF THOSE
> WHOSE GIFT IS DIFFERENT THAN YOURS. HONOR WHAT YOU RECEIVE
> AND YOU WILL RECEIVE MORE.

HOW TO RELEASE DIVINE CREATIVITY

Passion: God's anointing rides on the waves of His love and compassion. (See Matthew 14:14.) No love, no anointing! Have a love and passion for the area that is before you to master. Choose to receive and release God's love concerning the area. Be passionate to master this area by the grace of God. Defeat is not an option! You will not quit until He has shown you the keys.

Immersion: Immerse yourself thoroughly in the topic, filling your heart and mind with researched information. Read, ponder, meditate, and ask questions, knowing that when you seek Him with all your heart, you will find Him. (See Deuteronomy 4:29; John 16:24, James 1:5.)

Revelation: Continually ask God for revelation and insight. Posture your heart for revelation as you drift off to sleep by asking God the question you are seeking to resolve. Make sure your heart is clear and ready to receive by processing any negative emotions before going to sleep. In that way, your heart can spend dream time releasing new creative revelations for you rather than guiding you out of an emotional pit.

Creativity: When you awaken, tune to the flow and release, downloading from your spirit the insights it has gleaned during the night. Sometimes, I have soft soaking music on. Don't check your emails or do busy work first thing; instead use this sacred time of day to release divine creativity. I often revise several times, always staying tuned to the flow, until my heart with a deep inner knowing says, "We've got it!"

God will grant you revelatory gifts that bless you and, through you, bless humanity. Release His revelation, prophecy, words of wisdom and knowledge, and divine creativity! You may want to review again what the voice of God releases into your life. (See Deuteronomy 28:1–14.) God's revelation produces anointed results in every area we touch.

ACTION EXERCISE: TWO-WAY JOURNALING

Lord, what are the key gifts and skills You have anointed me with?

_____

_____

_____

Lord, what is the current passion of my heart that You want this anointing applied to?

_____

_____

_____

Lord, what steps do You want me to take to fully carry forth this commission and anointing?

_____

_____

_____

Lord, who have You given to work alongside me to support and extend this anointing and commission?

_____

_____

_____

How do You want me to draw upon the gifts of those You have given to me?

_____

_____

_____

How I Received the Baptism in the Holy Spirit
(Name Withheld)

I was baptized in the Holy Spirit and received tongues about a year apart. I had been a Christian about six months in a traditional church when my sister took me to have prayer ministry. After the ministry, I was on the way home and began to have spiritual experiences. I did not realize it at the time, but I had been filled with the Holy Spirit. The traditional church I was attending did not teach about the Holy Spirit. Meanwhile, my prayer life and reading of the Bible had become accelerated since becoming filled with the Holy Spirit, and I also began seeing visions and having God dreams.

About a year later, I attended a crusade that came to my city and responded to an altar call. As I was already a Christian, we prayed for the baptism of the Holy Spirit and tongues. I was asked to worship God and told to simply start saying, "Holy, holy, holy…" and just let the tongues flow as the minister laid her hands on me.

The first time we prayed, I didn't speak in tongues, and so the lady went to move on to someone else, but I said I'd like to try again. I strongly desired in my heart to speak in tongues. I did receive tongues the second time we prayed. This time, the tongues came gushing out, much to our surprise.

12

KEEPING THE MAIN THING THE MAIN THING

Then the Lord God called to the man, and said to him,
"Where are you?"
—Genesis 3:9

GOD'S ORIGINAL INTENT

God called out as He wanted to spend time with Adam and Eve in their garden. God had created man and woman with free will so He could have someone to commune with, share love with, share ideas with, and fellowship with. Even though this plan was temporarily derailed because Adam and Eve chose sin, God restored mankind back to His original intent by sending His Son Jesus, whose death on the cross restored the possibility of fellowship.

Jesus lived as God intended, listening to the voice of His Father, seeing His visions (see John 5:19–20), and releasing His compassion through the gifts of healings and miracles (see Matthew 14:14). God's original intent was now reestablished and modeled by His Son Jesus.

Jesus declared, *"My sheep hear My voice"* (John 10:27), restoring the opportunity for two-way communication between God and man. The goal was for us to become intimate friends with Him (see John 15:15), abide in one another's presence (see John

15:1–11), and release God's healing touch to the world (see Luke 9:1–2).

It took me ten years to learn how to hear His voice. (*We shared that story and the four keys God taught me in chapter two.*) Once I heard God's voice and *touched God directly*, not indirectly through my theology, I found out that He was much more loving than I had ever dreamed. He repeatedly tells me how much He loves me, and lets me see others through His eyes of love.

A pastor once told me he quit journaling because God just kept saying the same thing every day, that He loved him. Really? Is this a reason to tune God out? My wife and I tell each other, "I love you" every morning and evening, and often during the day. I am sure glad we haven't tuned each other out or stopped listening because we find these words repetitious.

Because isn't that what life is all about? Isn't that what Christianity is all about—loving God, being loved by Him, and loving others? Any desire for the gifts or manifestation of the Spirit must flow out of our love for God and love for people. Any other foundation is but sand. When our ministry of gifts is birthed in our intimate fellowship with the Lord, they will truly be manifestations not only of His power but also of His love.

> WHEN OUR MINISTRY OF GIFTS IS BIRTHED IN OUR INTIMATE FELLOWSHIP WITH THE LORD, THEY WILL BE MANIFESTATIONS NOT ONLY OF HIS POWER BUT ALSO OF HIS LOVE.

In this chapter, I share journaling examples from various people of what the Bible would call *the greatest thing*. Let's never allow this message to become so repetitious that we no longer want to hear it. The gifts, ministries, and effects are wonderful, and we are exhorted to earnestly pursue them, but we must never forget that they are a manifestation of a Person whose essence is Love. The more time we spend talking and sharing life with the Lord, the more like Him we will become and the more we will manifest Him in all of His wonderful ways. Our relationship with Him must always be our chief focus.

Because *He is Love*, as we become like Him, we will become more loving to those around us. It is no coincidence that the love chapter of 1 Corinthians 13 is in the middle of Paul's teaching on how the Spirit manifests Himself through us. If our desire to move in the gifts of the Spirit is not solely motivated by our love for others, if every word and work does not flow from a heart of compassion for the lost and hurting around us, they become nothing but noisy gongs and clanging cymbals. (See 1 Corinthians 13:1.)

GOD SHARES HIS HEART IN JOURNALING

Listen to the Father's heart for all His children in these bits of journaling from around the world. Respond to His call of love.

The Conveyer Belt

I saw gift boxes on a conveyor belt. As the boxes of gifts came by, I was excited to receive them. The vision stopped and I was confused! What was this? What did it mean? I looked again, asking God what it meant and the vision continued. I saw more boxes on the conveyor belt, and then I felt Jesus say, "Out of the many things I can give you, the best thing I can give you is Me!" I watched as He then jumped on to the conveyor belt and came towards me. He stepped off and held my hand.

Thoughts from the Lord started to flow: Many people get carried away with the gifts! They are so focused on the gifts they don't realize that *I am* the greatest gift. This can become an obsession. I am the main thing; I am the main gift; I am the greatest thing that you can receive. Tongues shall cease, prophecy shall fail. When all is said and done,

I am the main thing and I want you to keep the main thing the main thing!

Gifts are coming and you will begin to operate in the gifts, a variety of gifts, and they will excite you. You will enjoy them. But I want you to remember that I am the greatest gift: My presence, fellowship with Me, talking with Me, walking with Me, spending time with Me. As the gifts begin to flow and operate in you, keep the main thing the main thing. Keep your eyes on Me; focus on Me. No gift is greater than the Giver and as tempting as it may be operating in the gifts, shouldn't your focus be fellowship?

My Ministry or My Identity

Lord, do You want me to aspire to the office of a prophet? And what do You want me to do to prepare for whatever Your call is?

Yes, son. I have called you to be a seer, a prophet, one who will speak whatever I ask you to speak. Why do you think I have taken you through the deep waters of affliction and have allowed you to walk through deep valleys of rejection, misunderstanding, and loneliness? I have been preparing you for such a time as this.

You need to know, son, that this is My calling. You did not think this up. You did not wake up one day and say, "I am going to be a prophet." I spoke to you the first time concerning this calling in 1979 when you did not even know what a prophet was. Did I not say to you that I would give you the mouth of a prophet and the heart of a martyr? I did. I said it and put that into your heart. I have had to allow over forty years to go by to bring you closer and closer to that call and where you would be one to speak My words to both the church and the world. There are many who are not willing to speak My words because of the fear of man and the fear of the reactions of man. I have been giving you wisdom over the years, causing this skill to come to maturity so that you will stand before the men and women of the earth and proclaim only what I am saying. This office' can only come out of a heart that has been broken and seasoned, one that has allowed Me to take you through the seasons of bitterness and death. There is tremendous responsibility in being one who carries the deep secrets of My heart and one who will speak them at the right time and will speak My heart and out of My heart. This is not an easy walk. At times it will cause seasons of darkness and uncertainty. I have placed key people in your life who will be able to come alongside you and help you to walk through and to continue in the purpose and plan for your life. You have wrestled many times with My call on your life and I am reassuring to your heart that this is My way, My calling, and My desire for your life.

Lord, it really scares me and yet excites me. One part of me is terrified of the thought of this call and the responsibility and weight of it. What others will say: "Who, you? Why you?"

Son, I walked that exact way and experienced Myself the same dealings of man. I simply stayed connected to Father and walked day by day in the assurance of being His Son. He was well pleased with Me as a Son first. Out of that, I was able to walk in all the other plans and purposes Father had for Me. You are learning to find your identity in Me as a son. Not as a pastor, not as an evangelist or missionary, nor as a prophet, but as a son. You are My son. That is where I want you to find your complete identity and purpose. It is never My intention for any of My children to find their purpose and identity in what I have called you to do, but *only* in what I have called you to be. A son. Walk as a child, a son of God. A prince amongst men. One who is wrapped in the robe of My righteousness and one who will refuse to stand on anything else. Know, son, you are not to find your identity as a prophet, but only as a son.

Do not promote yourself as a prophet; I will do that in due time. Yet, do not be afraid to accept when others will declare and agree with My calling you as a prophet. Agree and accept this calling from Me, son. It is My mantle that I place on you and I will bring others to confirm and acknowledge and encourage you to move forward in this calling. Recognize it, accept it, embrace it, and live it. It is My will, son.

I See the Beauty in the Beast

In stillness this morning, I saw this inner vision. I saw a wild beast running towards Jesus. The beast was trying to bite Him. Jesus put His scepter into its mouth, between its teeth, and then started stroking the beast. The beast transformed into a sheep; then as Jesus continued to stroke the sheep, the sheep transformed into Jesus! Then Jesus spoke to me:

You are the beast, you are the sheep, you are being transformed into My image as you are touched by Me. Run to Me in any state that you are, with any issue that you have. Come to My throne of grace with boldness, for what I have shown you is beauty and the beast.

The truth is I see the beauty *in* the beast! There are so many things that My people see that are beastly about themselves but I see the beauty *in* the beast! I transform you as I touch you.

The woman with the issue of blood touched Me! Just by being in touch with Me, you are led into transformation. Transformation comes from touching; touch Me and allow Me to touch you and this contact will transform your very DNA.

This is what the woman with the issue of blood received, a touch at DNA level. The issues in her blood were not just period pains; they represent her nature! Her DNA, the fabric of her being. You see, she touched my fabric (garment) and it changed her fabric (what she was made of). The fabric of her being. The issue also represents generational curses she had, issues *in* her blood, things that were handed down in her blood line. Touching Me dealt with these issues. Are you enjoying this? I can tell! As you spend time with Me you'll understand great mysteries!

You are transformed by what you touch and what touches you. Anything you have constant contact with will eventually transform you! You can see that this is a picture of laying on of hands. I touched many people and if they stayed in touch with Me then they would move from healing of their body to a transformation of their being.

Now you see why it's important to stay in touch with Me because you are transformed by what you touch and what touches you. People are afraid because they think I see the beast so they won't come to Me. They try to deal with the beast themselves. But I don't see the beast; I see the beauty in the beast. And if you can harness your prophetic eyes, not only will you be transformed but you'll also start to see the beauty in the beasts inside of you and the beauty in the beasts around you.

Come boldly to His throne, and let Him touch you. (See Hebrews 4:16.)

My Date with the Lord

I am a Korean by blood but was born and grew up in Soviet Russia, so Russian is my native language. Now I am a citizen of South Korea but not perfect in speaking Korean. I was born again with the help of a Bible in English and information on Christianity which I found on the Internet in English. Below is my first two-way journaling with Jesus, as I went on my first date with Him.

I want to ask, "Lord, do you love me? How do you love me? How do you see me?" I imagine myself as a girl seven or eight years old, with a short hairstyle that I always hated (like a square pot). I'm wearing a very simple sleeveless cocoa color cotton dress. I look very dull in my vision. Then I'm trying to imagine myself in pretty, colorful dresses but cannot recall any from my childhood. I try to put on my daughter's flowery silk dress, which I made for her long time ago, but it looks too fancy on me and doesn't match with my square-pot hairstyle. So I decide to meet Jesus in my dull cocoa dress.

Jesus is sitting on the grass on a green hill and watching the Sea of Galilee. It is bright late morning and everything looks so fresh and peaceful. I am approaching Him... I pick some poppies for Him... I come to Jesus and give flowers. I feel shy. I don't look up... I just see His snow-white robe. He takes the flowers and I feel that He smiles. He says nothing; He is waiting. I ask, "L-l-lord, d-d-do you l-l-love m-me?"

He gently takes my hand and suggests sitting by Him on the grass. I feel that He is happy. I'm waiting for Him to say, "Of course, I love you!" But instead, He says:

Look around. Isn't it beautiful? Our Father God created all these beauties! And *you* are also His beauty. He created this world with great love. He put into this world love immeasurably. I know that you worry that you look so dull. You think that people don't like you and hate to be with you because you are very boring. Forget it! I see you like a gentle pretty field flower that makes happy any passerby. I love you as you are. Remember, God created you with great amount of love. *It is in you.* Be yourself. Don't torture yourself trying to change yourself according to these world standards. Relax and enjoy what you are! Don't worry about fancy lives of others. I love you, God our Father Almighty loves you! Smile now. How do you feel?

A Heavenly Encounter

While walking along the Sea of Galilee with Jesus, we were suddenly transported to heaven, where we stood in a meadow with very green grass. I saw a young version of my dad there along with a beautiful young woman. Her face was flawless. I recognized her from pictures I had seen. It was my mom.

My dad picked me up (in this vision I was probably about three years old). I don't remember my dad ever picking me up. My mom leaned over and touched my face and said, "My sweet Becky, I always have loved you and I always wanted to be your mom." My dad just kept smiling.

Then, just as suddenly as the vision began, I was back on the hillside with Jesus and He started to laugh and said, "I love all My kids."

As a result of this heavenly vision, I no longer live in fear of what people think. I do not assume that people will reject me and I am very sure that Jesus loves me and that I am okay just the way He made me. God is so good. He blows me away!

Shine on Everyone

I see You, Jesus, completely radiant with perfect white light with Your arms open wide, calling me to Yourself. As I run to Your embrace, I am swallowed up and saturated with that Light, that holy radiance. I see that beautiful Light starting at the crown of my head and filling me entirely; as it does, it reveals anything You haven't planted in me and completely eradicates it—wrong thoughts, inaccurate beliefs, doubts, fears, negative memories, offenses, and any physical abnormalities.

My child, I am illuminating the eyes of your understanding, cleansing you physically and spiritually, washing away the world and infusing you with real life, *zoe*, My life.

As you absorb My radiance, it fills you and leaves no room in you for the negative.

You will walk through this day radiant with My love and My life.

Shine on everyone you come in contact with. As the light in Me fills and saturates your entire being, it restores your mind, will, emotions, and physical body. Your youth is renewed as the eagle's; you will walk and not faint, you will run and not be weary! You have My confidence and boldness flowing through you. Let the outraying of My light in you be seen by all! I love you, Ann.

Your Beauty Is As...

Narnie, you are a picture of great beauty and your beauty is as the radiance of a sunrise. It is as the beauty of a sunset. It is as a flower fully open. It is as the mountain streams. Narnie, this is Me radiating out through you. I give you a beauty that is alive and real, bursting with life from Me. When you look at Me, I want you to see great beauty that has great power and majesty. A power that radiates life and holiness.

But Narnie, I also want you to see the tenderness of a shepherd caring for the heavy ewe as she births her wee lamb. As the lamb takes its first wobbly steps to seek its mother's nourishing milk, Narnie, I want you to see Me in action as I am full of life-giving love. My love is full of richness and life, strength and power. I want you to see this in Me, Narnie. I love you. You are worth everything it has taken for Me to win you.

Oh, Jesus, thank You! I love You so much! Holy Spirit, please open the eyes of my heart so that I may see Jesus like this and worship Him and follow Him in love and truth.

I Am Not a Theory. I Am Not a Process. I Am Not a Rule of Thumb

I am a Person and in My Person is all that pertains to and feeds life and love and thriving.

Knowing the Scriptures without knowing Me is like watching life from behind a thick pane of glass, a sealed up window, an enclosed, tasteless, scent-free, sterile box from which you see all of the colors, watch all of the movement, excitement, and expression, yet it cannot touch you for you are separated, shielded from it by the glass.

I am not the author of the window for I made you to swim in and be fully submerged and immersed in flowing and fluid life in all its capacities with fully alive sensations, emotions, and experiences in depth.

What immense sadness, what sorrow to see, to watch as a spectator and not be able to touch, to taste, to fully experience what I created and designed for you to enjoy. I have prepared in extravagance for you, life and love in fullness beyond your comprehension.

This window-gazing life has never been My heart for you, not now, not ever.

I am not out of reach. Life—real, pulsating, burning, thriving passionate life—is available and fully accessible. It was prepared for you; I did so with you in mind.

Come. Come and eat. Taste, taste and see. Touch and feel and *live*.

Which Law Is Most Important?

I'm walking my dog and talking to Jesus. "I am too critical of people, Lord."

Jesus: It's those laws.

Yes, it's those laws in my head that I hold everyone to, including myself. That standard.

Jesus: It's not that there are no laws; it's that the laws should never supersede the love. The love is what governs life, not the laws. You think that I hold you to the laws, but I hold you to the law of *love*. Laws are external, but love is internal. When you hold people to only what they should *do*, you are not allowing them to *be*. It is who they are that should matter to you, not what they do.

The next morning while I was walking my dog, I came upon a woman who was cutting the roses at the entrance to our clubhouse. My mind immediately judged her by the law of "she should not be cutting our roses." Then, it was like a switch was turned on in my brain by the Holy Spirit to show me who she is, not what she does.

Jesus: She is a woman who loves flowers and the beauty of them and who wants to treasure that. Perhaps she is alone and is never given cut flowers. You can relate to that, Pamela. She just longs to have some of their beauty in her home. Can you feel her longing? Can you sense her guilt over having been caught doing something that should bring her joy?

Wow! That was such an immediate answer to my prayer! I was overwhelmed not only by the love of God for me to show me how to be free from judging, but I was overwhelmed by His love for her! This is utterly awesome! My heart is profoundly touched by this! I am moved to tears.

Our Transparency Toward One Another Will Increase. Are You Ready For That?

Thank You, Father, for Your mercy on my loved one. Yesterday was a long, fearful, prayerful day. And now life continues, by Your grace. What would you have me hear from You this day, Lord?

Spirit to spirit is the true union of love. Friends and lovers cherish one another, allow mistakes, listen quietly, share and bear one another's joys and sorrows, allow great freedom, weep together, dance together, walk together life's jumbled path. Within each unique heart there is the ability to interface with many other hearts. As you continue to turn to Me, listen for Me, perceive My voice, I will share more and more of My heart with you. Not just words on a page, concepts in your mind, knowledge of My ways, but experientially, you will feel what I am feeling. Yet, only as you are able to bear.

As you share with Me your innermost thoughts and emotions, unafraid, without fear of judgment or punishment, freely and without restraint, our transparency toward one another will increase. Are you ready for that?

Are you prepared to share and receive at that level and dimension? I am not far away. I am as close as your next breath, your next heartbeat. Our relationship is to be a divine miracle of Life to life, Love to love, Spirit to spirit. Look for Me 24/7. Be attentive to My voice, My thoughts, My touch. I will show and share with you not only the daily doing, but also the daily being, for you are My dearly beloved, and I am yours.

Your Friend and Lover, Jeshua

Am I Enough?

After hearing that same question ring in my own head and heart for many years, I finally did it! I asked God Himself, "Am I enough?" That I was so hesitant to do so was a huge indicator of my core belief regarding my own value. The words below are from the nine pages of free-flowing and uninterrupted journaled response that bubbled up from the still small voice of the One who created and loves me beyond my wildest hopes and dreams. The healing that took place that day and in the days since has changed my thoughts, my heart, and my life forever. May it speak to you and heal you as well.

I made you. You did not make yourself. You were My plan, and I hold the patent. I alone am the Planner, Designer, and Creator of you. How then could you not be enough? I, the Divine Artist and Creator of all life, designed and built you to My own specifications, with My eternal and omniscient purposes and plans as well as My delight in mind. Don't I do *all* things well?

Who questions the Creator? Surely not those who are My most magnificent and highest creation? How inappropriate and inaccurate would the assessment of those which I create be? Since that which is created cannot see all, understand in fullness, are not all wise and knowing, and have not been since before time or space began, how then could such an assessment be fully just and true?

Am I alone not the all-knowing, all seeing, all wise, Was, Is and Is To Come? Am I not the One who fashioned your life and your frame even down to the most minute and intricate details of your being? Was it not I who painted your personality with its unique colors and textures unlike any other?

Do you know that I even established your posture? That's right; I even planned the way you stand, and the gait with which you walk. Do you realize that it was Me who calibrated your heart to leap at things that move you most deeply? I intentionally included all of these things in the mix when with My own hands, I knit you together in your momma's womb.

Don't you know that nothing in you was a standard ingredient? In you, there are no fillers. Do you also know that I never followed a recipe in My creation of you, for you, My love, are one of a kind? You are the only one who is uniquely and wonderfully you. In fact, I threw out the specs when I was finished. Do you realize how much I love that about you; that there will never be another one like you ever again?

Have you ever wondered why even in the case of identical twins, there are clearly perceivable differences in both appearance and attributes if you take the time to look closely? I never have and never will make two exactly the same. All, each one, has planned and purposed uniqueness imprinted upon and with them.

Was I remiss in My design of you? Did I scrimp on the recipe or withhold anything?

Who Told You That? Did I accidentally spill an over-abundance of anything into the mix so that you are somehow *too much* in any capacity? *Who Told You That?*

I will ask you again, beloved. Do you not know that I do *all things well?* Do you not know that when I made you, My design was *good, very good?* No mistakes, no deficiencies, and no excesses.

Am I Enough? Where does that kind of question evolve and grow? In what soil was it planted? From what spirit does it come? Surely you know that it cannot evolve in a place of belonging and acceptance and unconditional love? Such a question is not found *in Me* and is not *of Me.* Therefore, neither should it dwell, remain, or grow in you.

I ask you again, beloved, where did it come from? Of what nature is it? It has no place in you and is not befitting of a son or daughter of the King of Kings.

It was birthed on a lying, accusing tongue full of poison and bitter jealousy and rage and all manner of comparisons and dissensions, divisions, and rivalries. It is a thief and a robber intent on destruction and you, beloved, are its intended target.

Ahh, but fear not, little shepherded one, for who is your Father? Of what lineage are you? Whose voice do you hear and know? Who is Truth? You are safe and secure in Me.

"Am I enough?" is not a kingdom question for it savors of the unspoken yet implied possibility that there are deficiencies and flaws in My design.

I will tell you how I see you and how I designed you. I will tell of My plan and purpose in the beautiful and wondrous pattern and design that is you. I will also address your submission to a lying, accusing tongue that injects such a question.

From before time began, My plan with all the specs for your life were on My design table. I looked at them daily in eager anticipation of your beginning long before the day of your creation. From the beginning of time until the day you were born, I never once re-worked, reconsidered, scratched a plan, or single attribute. No, not even once!

You were designed to be sunshine and light bursting forth as well as ever unfolding love, deep and rich and wrapped in strength, wonder, and joy all in vast varieties and quantities.

With great joy, I liberally poured into your being gifts and abilities wrapped in passionately unique and wondrous expression and emotion. You are a regal and beautifully complex tapestry and a mystery.

SIMPLE ENOUGH FOR A CHILD

I hope these journaling examples have inspired you and given you food for thought. Hearing God's voice, catching the initiatives of heaven, is so simple! You don't need to be super spiritual to catch the flow of the Spirit within you, which is the first step to intentionally manifesting the gifts. Our friend Kathy offers a "Supernatural Boot Camp for Kids," teaching them the four keys to hearing and seeing in the Spirit. Here are some of their experiences:

+ L saw Jesus building castles in the sand, and He asked her to join Him. He told her she was His princess.

+ J said, "I heard God tell me to move the skateboard to the garage. I did. Daddy was backing up in the truck and he went off the curb. He would have ran over my board had I not obeyed God."

+ J and Jesus played hide-and-go-seek in the forest. They hid behind the trees and ran through the forest.

- Z slid down rainbows with Jesus. Jesus was laughing and didn't want to stop playing.

- L followed the steps of healing prayer and prayed for her sister's foot. The pain immediately left.

- Z and J prayed for a lady and the pain in her wrist went away.

These kids so enjoyed getting to know the Lord. Don't you want to know Him this way, too?

HIS PRESENCE IS THE GIFT

As we have seen from our glimpse into these love letters from heaven, Jesus is the true gift. Knowing the Holy Spirit personally is our heart's desire and living out of a revelation of the Father's lovingkindness toward us is what this book has really been about. Of course we seek the Giver; His gifts are simply the natural overflow of our intimate relationship with Him.

Charity's Dream About Spiritual Gifts

In waking life, my husband Leo and I had been asked to lead a couples' Bible study; we quickly discovered we were the only Charismatics in the group. Although sincere in their faith, no one else was interested in pursuing the gifts of the Spirit. This left me seriously questioning if we were the right people to be leading the group. I was feeling stressed after one of these meetings, wondering how I could authentically live out my supernatural relationship with God in a way that would be relevant and *salty*, showing the others how walking in the Spirit enhances the flavor of every part of life.

Dream: That evening, I had a dream that resembled one of those Tim Allen Christmas movies where the old Santa Claus is retiring and needs a new, younger replacement—*me!* I wasn't at all confident I could fulfill this role, but then I was bestowed with the magical Santa super-powers. With that special commissioning, I was ready and excited about my new position and calling.

Interpretation: The key action of the dream was that I was being given a new responsibility and the key emotion was that I was full of self-doubt. To zero in on which area of my waking life the dream is speaking to, I simply ask, *Where in my waking world do I have a new responsibility that I'm unsure about?* This helped me easily pinpoint God was speaking about leading the Bible study, the new *job* I felt unqualified for.

Through the dream, I was able to see His perspective of the situation. I wasn't with this group by chance; my steps were ordered by the Lord. I immediately understood that this was a picture of God equipping me with His supernatural grace and power for the new leadership position. I was very encouraged that He had clearly placed me there, and not only that, but His Spirit had also given me wisdom and anointing—special superpowers—to minister effectively in the job He called me to do.

That was exciting! And at once, I was peaceful and optimistic concerning the group and all the Lord wanted to do in and through us there. However, I did still have one small issue regarding the specific symbols used, and I did not hesitate to let God know about it. I mean, really, Santa Claus? I explained to Him that that was very unspiritual, not to mention entirely extra-biblical.

Jesus just laughed and said, "Aw, come on, Char. Don't you get it? You are a carrier of My presence and presents. You're bringing Me and My gifts to the group!"

Okay, God. I guess if You put it like that then You're right: Santa *is* the perfect symbol to communicate Your message!

And what was His message? What was the truth He was disclosing through the dream? The revelation was that as we are carriers of His *presence*, we are also inherently carriers of His *presents*. We are not able to represent Christ well without an overflow of His gifts through us. And as we live to our sacred union with Him, His life flows effortlessly through us to heal and serve and bless those around us.

Just as God explained, we are carriers of His presence, and where His presence is, His gifts are. We can simply focus on Jesus and cultivate our personal relationship with Him, knowing that the fruit of unity always manifests in time.

> WE ARE CARRIERS OF GOD'S PRESENCE,
> AND WHERE HIS PRESENCE IS, HIS GIFTS ARE.

The Father desires nothing more than to do life with us, sharing the unfolding journey together with His beloved children. So whether you are in school, at home, on the job, or in the gym, live to the glorious mystery of Christ in you. Live to your identity as a son or daughter of the King of Kings. Live to your sacred supernatural union with the Holy Spirit.

Through spending time together with God Himself, we are infused with His Spirit in ever new and deepening ways. This results in transformative life—the peace, power, and presence of heaven overflowing into our world every day, in our everyday lives. We gratefully revel in God's perfect design, original intention, and ultimate master plan as we live to this truth: we are naturally supernatural carriers of His presents because more than anything else, we are carriers of Him.

ACTION EXERCISE

Lord, what do You want to speak to me concerning our love relationship?

_____

_____

_____

Lord, have I given love its rightful place? Am I loving myself, You, and others in the way You would have me love?

_____

_____

_____

Spend some time thanking the Lord for the extravagant love He has lavished upon you. Allow yourself to receive His affirmation and affection. Experience a fresh revelation of how it feels to be a cherished son or daughter, favored and deeply loved by the Father.

ABOUT THE AUTHORS

Active in ministry since 1972, Mark Virkler has authored more than fifty-five books in the areas of hearing God's voice and Spirit-anointed living. His works include *4 Keys to Hearing God's Voice*, *Counseled by God*, *Your Extraordinary Life*, and *Prayers that Heal the Heart*. Altogether, his books have been translated into over fifty languages and have provided curriculum for the establishment of more than 250 church-centered Bible schools around the world.

Mark and his wife, Patti, are the founders of Communion with God Ministries, which provides online monthly video training to more than a hundred nations. Mark is also president of Christian Leadership University, an online school offering degrees from associate to doctorate. During the past twenty-five years, CLU has provided over a hundred courses to more than 15,000 students in 127 nations.

For more than thirty years, Mark has traveled extensively on six continents to conduct workshops on spiritual healing and developing intimacy with God. Over a million people have watched his interviews on *Sid Roth's It's Supernatural!*

Mark and Patti make their home in Orlando, Florida.

* * *

Charity Virkler Kayembe is passionate about the sacred supernatural and making the mystical practical in believers' everyday lives. She has worked with her family in ministry for twenty-five years and holds advanced degrees in biblical studies. Charity has been featured on *CBN*, *Sid Roth's It's Supernatural!*, *Charisma*, and *The Elijah List*.

Her books include *Hearing God Through Your Dreams*, *Everyday Angels*, and *Unleashing Healing Power Through Spirit-Born Emotions*. Charity conducts training workshops on dream interpretation and seer realm activation and writes about walking by the Spirit on her blog at GloryWaves.org.

She and her husband, Leo, have traveled to over seventy nations and live in upstate New York.

APPENDIX A:
PRECISE DEFINITIONS PROMOTE
CHRISTIAN SPIRITUALITY

When I can precisely define something, I can intentionally pursue it with understanding and know when I have arrived at my destination. Below are a number of precise definitions for various spiritual realities. The goal is to help you experience these realities.

For example, I sought God's voice for years, but never defined it as flowing thoughts, which are especially pure when my eyes are fixed on Jesus and I am asking Him for input. Lacking a precise definition, I was not aware that I had arrived at my goal. I was longing for something I already had. Now that I have precisely defined it, I can live out of God's voice intentionally and continuously.

LET THE SPIRIT UTILIZE YOUR MIND

*"Let us **reason together**," says the* LORD, *"Though your sins are as scarlet, they will be as white as snow; though they are red like crimson, they will be like wool."* (Isaiah 1:18)

+ The only command in the Bible to *reason* is to *reason together with God. This Spirit-led reasoning involves* picturing Jesus at our side (see Acts 2:25; Hebrews 12:1–2) and asking Him to anoint our reasoning (see Ephesians 1:17–18) as we tune in to the Holy Spirit (see John 7:37–39), letting the Spirit's *flow* guide our reasoning process. Divine creativity, wisdom, revelation, intimacy, and healing are realized this way.

+ Notice in Isaiah 1:18 that godly reasoning includes imagery: *"Though your sins are as scarlet, they will be as white as snow; though they are red like crimson, they will be like wool."* When God reasons, He uses pictures: "sins as scarlet" is an image of my need; "white as snow" is a picture of His provision to meet my need. When we meditate (see Joshua 1:8), we yield both our thoughts and imaginations to the Lord, and honor the flowing thoughts and images that appear. (See, for example, Revelation 4:1–2; Psalm 16:8.) Since emotions are byproducts of pictures, we will also be experiencing God's emotions. This is the way I choose to reason, preach, and teach.

+ Live in the pictures of those things God says are so. For example, see Him with you (see Acts 2:25; Psalm 16:8); see that He has provided *more than enough* (see Deuteronomy 28:1–14); see His Spirit joined to your spirit (see 1 Corinthians 6:17); see your new shining heart, your clean heart, your healed heart, your empowered heart (see Ezekiel 36:26; 2 Peter 1:4); see yourself wearing Christ's robe radiating with righteousness and reflecting His glory as you walk through your day (see Galatians 3:27). Living in these truths will empower you to be the overcomer you were meant to be.

DISCERN THREE SOURCES OF THOUGHTS

1. *The Holy Spirit's thoughts are spontaneous thoughts* that line up with the names and character of God. These include Wonderful Counselor, Prince of Peace, Comforter, Teacher, Creator, Healer, and Giver of Life.

2. *Evil spirits' thoughts are spontaneous thoughts* that line up with the names and character of Satan, which include accuser, adversary, liar, destroyer, condemner, thief, and murderer.

3. *My thoughts* come from my own reasoning process, and are sensed as cognitive, *connected* thoughts, which I build through reasoning.

Choose *only* God's thoughts; take every thought captive to Christ! (See 2 Corinthians 10:5.)

FIVE KINDS OF IMAGES

Every imagination of the thoughts of his heart was only evil continually.   (Genesis 6:5 KJV)

1. *Evil imagination*: picturing demonic things (see Jeremiah 16:12 KJV)

2. *Vain imagination*: picturing what I want (see Romans 1:21 KJV)

3. *Godly imagination*: picturing things God says are true (see 1 Chronicles 29:18 KJV)

4. *Divine visions*: a flow of images that are especially pure as my eyes are fixed on Jesus and I am praying for the eyes of my heart to be enlightened (see Ephesians 1:17–18)

5. *Dreams*: God's wisdom and counsel to us during the night (see Numbers 12:6)

Choose to *only* gaze upon God's pictures! Since emotions are byproducts of what we see in our minds and hearts, your emotions are automatically transformed whenever you are gazing upon God's images.

REASONS I ALWAYS NEED TO KNOW WHAT I AM PICTURING

*They…walked in the counsels and in the **imagination** of their evil heart, and **went backward**, and **not forward**.*
                                        (Jeremiah 7:24 KJV)

If we are holding the wrong images, we end up going backward!

+ *Images purify*: the intuitive/spontaneous flow comes from the vision being held before your eyes; therefore you purify your reception by having your spiritual eyes focused on Jesus.

+ *Images create or avoid idolatry*: seeing the thing you are praying for as a larger picture in your mind than the One you are coming to results in receiving a distorted answer back from God. (See Ezekiel 14:4; Numbers 22:15–35.) Proper prayer begins by lifting your eyes to the Lord. (See Matthew 6:9.)

+ *Images assist in spiritual transformation and establishing Christlikeness*: We are transformed by what we look upon. We are to fix our eyes upon Jesus and be transformed into His likeness. (See 2 Corinthians 3:18; 4:18; Hebrews 12:2.) It is called "coming to the light" or "abiding in Christ." (See John 15.) Whatever you focus on grows within you and whatever grows within you, you become. This is God's method of establishing righteous behavior in our lives.

+ *Wrong images weaken*: Looking at our sin and flaws and trying to battle them doesn't provide real victory.

+ *Proper images establish true Christian spirituality*: Seeing and radiating Jesus is the only true approach to spiritual growth. (See 1 Corinthians 12:7–11; 2 Corinthians 3:17–18, 4:17–18; Hebrews 12:1–2.)

+ *Proper images assist in throne room worship*: Throne room worship is defined as "joining the heavenly chorus in the throne room in praise, worship, and adoration before our king." Since we are seated with Christ in heavenly places, we are already present in the throne room. (See Ephesians 2:6.) As we look into the spirit, we can see the worship taking place before our Lord. As worshippers on earth, we are joining with this multitude in the heavens and together we are worshipping before our king. (*See cwgministries.org/throne for more.*)

⁜ *Proper images assist in soaking in God's presence*: To *soak* in God's presence is to rest in His love rather than to *strive* in prayer. Soaking is making a conscious decision to enter into God's presence to experience Him. It is two lovers sharing love together. He is the Divine Lover of the universe; we are His espoused bride. In soaking, we enjoy His love and share love back to Him. It is a divine encounter that utilizes the senses of our hearts and spirits. (*See cwgministries.org/soaking for more.*)

GREEK WORDS DEFINED

Logos: A Greek word translated "word," it means "the entire communication process." One example of *Logos* is the Bible, the Word of God. The Bible is to be meditated upon (see Joshua 1:8) and treasured in your heart (see Psalm 119:11).

Rhema: A Greek word translated "word" that means "when words leave one's lips." The Spirit's voice in our hearts is one example of *rhema*, while verses leaping off the pages of the Bible and into our hearts is another example. *God's voice* sounds like flowing, spontaneous thoughts that light upon our mind. (See John 7:37–39.) The Holy Spirit is sensed as a river that flows within. (*For more, see cwgministries.org/all-uses-rhema-bible.*)

Naba: A Hebrew word translated "prophecy," it means "bubbling up." When I want to prophesy, I see Jesus present in the situation and ask for His thoughts. (See Acts 2:25; Psalm 16:8.) I speak forth the thoughts and words that are bubbling up within me. "Seeing Jesus" can begin with a godly imagination that then transforms into a flowing vision. Again, keep everything simple and childlike.

Paga: A Hebrew word translated "intercession"—God's voice leading me in prayer. One literal definition is "to strike or light upon by chance," or "an accidental intersecting." Spirit-led intercession is sensed as spontaneous thoughts that light upon my mind while I am praying. I honor these thoughts as they have been sent by God, so I fix my eyes upon Jesus, and tune to the flow and pray, being guided by the flow. (See Hebrews 12:1–2; John 7:37–39.) Childlike faith allows you to live this way comfortably.

ACHIEVE SAFETY AND SUCCESS BY UTILIZING SPIRITUAL ADVISORS

Safety and success: God's paradigm/system for success is not the brilliance of my mind, but rather the multitude of counselors and confirmation by two or three others. (See Proverbs 11:14; 2 Corinthians 13:1.)

My spiritual counselors are people who are alongside or ahead of me in the area being discussed, to whom I turn for spiritual advice. They are willing to seek God with me and share with me, for my prayerful consideration, what they sense in their hearts. I do not ask them what they think. I ask them what God is speaking in their hearts concerning the issue.

HOW TO RECEIVE WELL-ROUNDED COUNSEL

I want to ask God who is on the team that He has placed around me, who have the various heart motivations listed below. Then I seek out their input, especially for all major decisions. I ask them what God is speaking to them in their hearts, not what they think about a situation being discussed.

1. *Apostle:* heart for the whole; sees the whole picture and where this idea fits

2. *Prophet:* heart for creativity; senses what is right for this moment

3. *Evangelist:* heart for sharing; is passionate to see that my idea gets proper promotion

4. *Pastor*: heart for loving; ensures that love is at the center of the project

5. *Teacher*: heart for truth; ensures that it is clearly communicated

A BALANCED DEFINITION OF SUBMISSION

"Openness to the Spirit-led counsel and correction of several others, while keeping a sense of personal responsibility for my own discernment of God's voice within."

+ *Spirit-led counsel* means I am not asking what they think, but what they sense in their hearts

+ *Several others*—I am going to three, not just to one

+ *Sense of personal responsibility*—I ask God in prayer to show me how to properly fit together the counsel my three advisors have provided

THE RELATIONSHIP OF MIND, HEART, AND SPIRIT

The language of the mind is man's unanointed, analytical reason, which is rebuked by Jesus three times in the Gospels. (See Matthew 16:5–12; Mark 2:5–12; 8:15–21.) The alternative to this is what Scripture commands, *reasoning together with God*. (See Isaiah 1:18.) This is defined as reasoning guided by the flow. It is the only command in the Bible to reason, so all reasoning is to be done together with God.

People who rely on their left brain must be instructed to ask God to guide their reasoning process and then to allow the flow to guide their reasoning, while their eyes are fixed on Jesus at their right hand. Sometimes more right-brain individuals, after hearing from God, will add to that word with their own analytical thoughts, believing they are still in the right brain and still hearing from God. Both left-brainers and right-brainers must learn to honor what is from the Spirit (flow) and not lean on their own *self-directed* analytical thinking.

If Jesus didn't reason on His own, then we are not to reason on our own. (See John 5:30.) Whenever I have the option of using one of my faculties myself, or tuning to the flow and allowing the Holy Spirit to utilize it, I always choose the Holy Spirit. I believe this provides me a huge edge for success.

The language of the heart is flowing thoughts (see John 7:38), flowing images (see Acts 2:17), flowing emotions (see Galatians 5:22–23), and meditation and pondering (see Psalm 77:6). Sensing God's movement in our hearts can be called illumination, revelation, revelation knowledge, perception, discernment, word of wisdom, word of knowledge, or prophecy.

The centrality of the heart: "*the springs of life*" flow from the heart (see Proverbs 4:23), so we are told, "*Trust in the* LORD *with all your heart and do not lean on your own understanding*" (Proverbs 3:5). Wisdom "*rests in the heart*" (Proverbs 14:33), it provides health to our entire body (see Proverbs 14:30), it "*ponders how to answer*" (Proverbs 15:28), and it can make our life a "*continual feast*" (Proverbs 15:15). Note God's emphasis in the Bible: the words *heart* and *spirit* show up *1,300 times* while *mind* and *think* are found less than 200 times. God wants us to live out of our hearts rather than our heads.

Man's spirit is sensed as underlying attitudes, motivations, and character traits. For example, we could tune to God with an attitude of reverence, awe, and respect, a motivation of seeking Him diligently, and a character trait of humility and dependence upon Him. The Bible indicates a 95 percent overlap between man's heart and spirit. Man's spirit is to be joined to the Holy Spirit. (See 1 Corinthians 6:17.) In the Old Testament especially, an individual is broken into only two parts, body and soul. (See Psalm 31:9.) The word "soul" in this case is used to describe the entire non-material parts of man, so it would include heart and spirit as parts of the soul.

Thus I consider there to be a 95 percent overlap between man's soul, heart, and spirit. *(For more, see cwgministries.org/spirit.)*

God's fuel for our hearts is faith, hope, and love. (See 1 Corinthians 13:13.) If you do two-way journaling daily, God will automatically fill you up on this fuel so you can run smoothly throughout the day. If you tank up on anger, fear, doubt, or bitterness, you will run rough all day.

MAKING WISE DECISIONS BY USING THE LEADERS' PARADIGM

We can view the six pillars below as providing a solid foundation upon which to make wise decisions and discern truth. I have chosen to honor and combine these six ways the Lord speaks to us. I call this the *leaders' paradigm* as I sense that leaders utilize this approach whether they have defined it or not. For all major decisions especially, I use this model.

PILLAR ONE: ILLUMINED SCRIPTURES

And they said to one another, "Did not our heart burn within us while He talked with us on the road, and while He opened the Scriptures to us?"   (Luke 24:32 NKJV)

This pillar is experienced as the Holy Spirit illuminating the Scriptures to you. You sense them leaping off the page or just coming to your attention spontaneously.

PILLAR TWO: ILLUMINED THOUGHTS IN ONE'S MIND

It seemed fitting for me as well, having investigated everything carefully from the beginning, to write it out for you in consecutive order.   (Luke 1:3)

This pillar is experienced as the Holy Spirit guiding your reasoning process through spontaneous impressions.

PILLAR THREE: ILLUMINED WITNESS IN ONE'S HEART

> *Immediately Jesus, aware in His spirit that they were reasoning that way within themselves, said to them, "Why are you reasoning about these things in your hearts?"*   (Mark 2:8)

This pillar is experienced as an impression perceived in your spirit. Deep inner peace or unrest is often part of this experience.

PILLAR FOUR: ILLUMINED COUNSEL OF OTHERS

> *Where no counsel is, the people fall: but in the multitude of counsellors there is safety.*   (Proverbs 11:14 KJV)

This pillar is experienced as you ask your spiritual advisors to seek God for confirmation, additions, or adjustments in the guidance you sense God has given you.

PILLAR FIVE: ILLUMINED UNDERSTANDING OF LIFE'S EXPERIENCES

> *You will know them by their fruits. Grapes are not gathered from thorn bushes nor figs from thistles.*   (Matthew 7:16)

This pillar is experienced as you ask God for insight and understanding concerning the fruit life is demonstrating. God gives you revelation about what has caused the fruit.

PILLAR SIX: ILLUMINED REVELATION FROM GOD THROUGH DREAMS, VISIONS, PROPHECY, AND JOURNALING

> *And it shall come to pass afterward that I will pour out My Spirit on all flesh; your sons and your daughters shall prophesy, your old men shall dream dreams, your young men shall see visions.*   (Joel 2:28 NKJV)

This pillar is experienced as you receive direct revelation from God through dreams, visions, and two-way journaling in which you write out your prayers and God's answers.

I want all six pillars to be flashing green lights. If one is flashing a red light, I will hold off and not move forward. Red is a warning that something is not right. Seek the Lord and adjust until there are no red lights.

I might have five green lights and one neutral, and that would be fine. I just don't want any lights flashing red, as I want to avoid danger and making mistakes. I don't want to die in the wilderness. I want to arrive at my promised land!

APPENDIX B:
MANIFESTATION, GIFT, AND MINISTRY

The ministry that God has given to you is built upon your spiritual DNA and the manifestation of the Holy Spirit flowing through these basic spiritual gifts God has graced you with. Using the chart below, you can identify your ministry (right column), your spiritual DNA (middle column), and the ways the Holy Spirit is manifesting Himself out through these (left column).

Discerning your ministry and gifts enables you to minister with boldness!

MANIFESTATION, GIFT, AND MINISTRY		
Manifestation Gifts: the Holy Spirit meeting individuals' specific needs. These are called *"varieties of effects"* (1 Corinthians 12:6) and listed in 1 Corinthians 12:8–10. All nine are available to you.	**Endowment Gifts:** a personal spiritual grace DNA package given to all. These are called *"varieties of gifts"* (1 Corinthians 12:4) and listed in Romans 12:6–8. Ask, "What do I *love* doing?"	**Equipping Gifts:** People serving the church with a ministry function. These are called *"varieties of ministries"* (1 Corinthians 12:5), and listed in Ephesians 4:11–12.

This chart was inspired by Peter Wollensack's excellent book *Discovering Your Spiritual DNA (Hamden, CT: Harvest Equippers International, 2014)*. Used with permission.

MANIFESTATION, GIFT, AND MINISTRY

Speaking Gifts:

1. Tongues – heart flow guides my vocal cords; strengthens my spirit

2. Interpretation of tongues – flowing thoughts interpret the message given in tongues

3. Prophecy – flowing thoughts which are God speaking His mind for the moment

Power Gifts:

1. Faith – an instantaneous welling up of faith within me

2. Gifts of healings – wisdom and anointing to provide a precise remedy to specific health needs

3. Miracles – an instantaneous release of divine energy producing immediate change

Revelation Gifts:

1. Discerning of Spirits – an immediate inner awareness of the presence of a spiritual force

2. Word of Wisdom – the wisdom of God which appears as flowing thoughts, pictures, or feelings

3. Word of Knowledge – the knowledge of God which appears as flowing thoughts, flowing pictures, or flowing feelings

1. Prophetic – loves creative flow, creating things

2. Server – loves helping in any capacity

3. Teacher – loves training and equipping

4. Exhorter – loves providing people steps they can take to move forward in their lives

5. Giver – loves freely providing time, money, abilities

6. Leader – loves organizing, guiding, inspiring

7. Mercy giver – loves expressing compassion, comfort and healing

You have blends of multiple gifts and ministries. One is your strongest.

Out of the heart flow the issues of life. (See Proverbs 4:23.)

These are not titles, but our function. Others confirm that we function in this way.

1. Apostle – can train and equip believers to launch and oversee new ministries

2. Prophet – can train and equip others to improve their spiritual "eyesight" and to put into words what is seen in the spirit realm

3. Evangelist – can train and equip believers to proclaim the gospel of the kingdom, especially to a non-believing world. Will evangelize utilizing their endowment gift

4. Pastor – can train and equip others to guide and care for God's people

5. Teacher – can train and equip others to hear God's voice and experience biblical realities.

Paul began as an evangelist, then pastor, teacher, prophet, and apostle. Cultivate and mature in in your giftedness and ministry throughout your lifetime!

This chart was inspired by Peter Wollensack's excellent book *Discovering Your Spiritual DNA* (Hamden, CT: Harvest Equippers International, 2014). Used with permission.

APPENDIX C:
DIG DEEPER WITH THESE LINKS

HOW FAR COULD YOU GO WITH A BIBLE SCHOOL IN YOUR POCKET?

Can I really experience a School of the Spirit in my home? Yes, you can!

+ You don't have to go away to Bible school or a school of ministry.

+ You can live in any city, in any country, attend any church, and still earn a Diploma in Applied Spirituality from Christian Leadership University's School of the Spirit! CLU provides *interactive* spirit life training modules that feature fully downloadable video training experiences and online quizzes, direct to your laptop, tablet, or smart phone.

TEAM UP WITH A COACH AT YOUR SIDE!

Don't you think it's time *you* team up and focus with a coach at your side so you speed forward and enter your promised land? There is no easier way to grow than to join a group of like-minded people and focus intently, under the direction of the Holy Spirit and a coach who is ahead of you in the area you are pursuing. A cord of three is not quickly broken. You support one another through the training process and by *focusing intently*, you become a doer of the Word and not a hearer only. (See James 1:25.) Make sure you are taking the proper steps that will allow you to experience your promised land!

DISCOVER 22+ INTERACTIVE E-LEARNING MODULES BY MARK VIRKLER AND CHARITY KAYEMBE

Learn more and try our *free* Course Sampler today: www.CLUSchooloftheSpirit.com

Each interactive Spirit-Life Training Module contains:

» Entire series of downloadable videos

» MP3 audio sessions

» Complete PDF ebook

» Step-by-step guidance from the Interactive Learning Management System

» Personal Assessment Tools

» Certificate of Completion awarding 5 CEUs

» Coaching

When you meditate on revelation truths in the context of a CLU School of the Spirit module, you are required to fully integrate the life-changing principles. Nothing is left to chance. You will learn what you are supposed to learn and your life will be transformed by the power of the Holy Spirit.

We guarantee you *will* master a new skill in each training module. We can teach you in just three months what it took us years to learn because we have gone ahead and prepared the way. And these exercises are so spiritual in nature, you can easily complete them as part of your daily devotional time.

Sign up here to receive free access to the streaming videos for a different one of our modules each month, and then be given the opportunity to own it at a special discount: CWGministries.org/ subscribe

A SAMPLING OF OUR TOP TRAINING MODULES

1. *Hearing God's Voice* – cluschoolofthespirit.com/hear

2. *Hearing God Through Your Dreams* – cluschoolofthespirit.com/dreams

3. *Prayers That Heal The Heart* – cluschoolofthespirit.com/prayers

4. *Everyday Angels* – cluschoolofthespirit.com/angels

5. *How to Walk By the Spirit* – cluschoolofthespirit.com/walk-spirit

6. *Unleashing Healing Power Through Spirit-Born Emotions* – cluschoolofthespirit.com/unleashing

7. *Overflow of the Spirit* – cluschoolofthespirit.com/overflow

For information on revelation truth, see: CLUOnline.com/ our-unique-approach

ADDITIONAL RESOURCES ON MIRACLES, HEALTH & HEALING

Vibrant Health! Miracles plus gifts of healings; hyperlinked index to 100+ articles: cwgministries.org/VibrantHealth

60+ ways to pray: www.cwgministries.org/devotionals. I have used all sixty effectively. Below are a few key prayer models to begin with:

+ Cleansing cellular memories promotes health: cwgministries.org/cellular

+ Prayers that heal the heart and cast out demons: cwgministries.org/7prayers

+ New creation celebration meditations: cwgministries.org/SpiritualTransformations

+ *Energeo*, the power of God, heals: cwgministries.org/ReleaseDivineEnergy

+ Healing for an organ prayer: cwgministries.org/healingorgan

+ Speaking in tongues health benefits: cwgministries.org/tongues

OTHER RESOURCES FROM MARK AND PATTI VIRKLER

Mark and Patti Virkler are co-authors of more than fifty books on Christian spirituality, as well as founders of Communion with God Ministries and Christian Leadership University.

+ *Books, audio, video, and personal spiritual trainers:* cwgministries.org

+ *Online college degrees through distance learning:* cluonline.com

+ *Diploma in Applied Spirituality through e-learning modules:* cluschoolofthespirit.com

+ *Salvation website:* www.bornofthespirit.today

+ *Health website:* www.takechargeofyourhealth.today

+ *Over 600 blogs* by Mark and Charity, topically indexed: cwgministries.org/allblogs

+ *Receiving Baptism in the Holy Spirit:* cwgministries.org/holy-spirit-baptism

+ *Personal Spiritual Trainers:* cwgministries.org/pst

Host Mark in your community to speak at your church or event. Details on available training and workshops at: cwgministries.org/events

Mark blogs regularly at: cwgministries.org/blogs/mark-virkler

Facebook: www.facebook.com/mark.virkler

Instagram.com/communionwithgod

Twitter.com/markvirkler

Podcast: cwgministries.org/podcast

RESOURCES FROM CHARITY KAYEMBE

Host Charity in your community to speak at your church or event. Details on available training and workshops at: GloryWaves.org/seminars

Charity has developed training resources on the sacred supernatural and how to make the mystical practical in believers' everyday lives: GloryWaves.org/products

Videos: Watch teaching sessions and interviews at: GloryWaves.org/free-media

Angels: Discover what Scripture reveals about angelic interaction and seeing in the spirit at: GloryWaves.org/angels

Dreams: Learn the basics of how to translate God's messages to you while you sleep in the free dreams crash course at: GloryWaves.org/dreams

Charity blogs regularly at GloryWaves.org/blog

Facebook.com/GloryWavesMinistries

Instagram.com/GloryWavesMinistries

Twitter.com/glory_waves

Welcome to Our House!
We Have a Special Gift for You

It is our privilege and pleasure to share in your love of Christian books. We are committed to bringing you authors and books that feed, challenge, and enrich your faith.

To show our appreciation, we invite you to sign up to receive a specially selected **Reader Appreciation Gift**, with our compliments. Just go to the Web address at the bottom of this page.

God bless you as you seek a deeper walk with Him!

WE HAVE A GIFT FOR YOU. VISIT:

whpub.me/nonfictionthx

WHITAKER
HOUSE